MW00461749

Exploring Christian Holiness

Volume 3
The Theological Formulation

Volume 1
THE BIBLICAL FOUNDATIONS
by W. T. Purkiser, Ph.D.

Volume 2
THE HISTORICAL DEVELOPMENT
by Paul M. Bassett, Ph.D., and
William M. Greathouse, M.A., D.D.

Volume 3
THE THEOLOGICAL FORMULATION
Richard S. Taylor, Th.D.

EXPLORING CHRISTIAN HOLINESS

Volume 3
The Theological Formulation

by
Richard S. Taylor, Th.D.

BEACON HILL PRESS OF KANSAS CITY
KANSAS CITY, MISSOURI

Copyright 1985
Beacon Hill Press of Kansas City

ISBN: 083-411-0776
083-410-8429 (set)

Printed in the United States of America

Unless otherwise indicated all scripture quotations are taken from *The Holy Bible, New International Version* (NIV), copyright © 1978 by the New York International Bible Society, and are used by permission of Zondervan Bible Publishers.

Permission to quote from other copyrighted versions of the Bible is acknowledged with appreciation as follows:

New American Standard Bible (NASB), © The Lockman Foundation, 1960, 1962, 1963, 1968, 1971, 1972, 1973, 1975, 1977.

Modern Language Bible, the *New Berkeley Version in Modern English* (NBV), copyright © 1945, 1959, 1969 by Zondervan Publishing House.

New English Bible (NEB), © The Delegates of the Oxford University Press and The Syndics of the Cambridge University Press, 1961, 1970.

New Testament in Modern English (Phillips), Revised Edition © J. B. Phillips, 1958, 1960, 1972. By permission of the Macmillan Publishing Co., Inc.

Revised Standard Version of the Bible (RSV), copyrighted 1946, 1952, © 1971, 1973.

Weymouth's New Testament in Modern English (Weymouth), by Richard Francis Weymouth. By special arrangements with James Clarke and Co., Ltd., and permission of Harper and Row Publishers.

ASV refers to American Standard Version

KJV refers to King James Version

All references designated ECH in this volume refer to *Exploring Christian Holiness,* volumes 1 and 2.

Beacon Bible Commentary is indicated by BBC.

10   9   8   7   6   5   4   3   2   1

Contents

Introduction

This portion of our three-part study is an attempt to present the doctrine of holiness systematically, as a coherent whole. It thus differs from the synoptic exegesis of volume 1 and the historical survey of volume 2. In such a presentation it is necessary to touch many other doctrines, but only a full-fledged systematic theology could discuss these adjunct doctrines thoroughly. They will be woven into this study only as they bear upon our main theme, *holiness.* Even justification and regeneration, as well as such themes as evil and providence, are treated primarily in their relationship to holiness. The book includes a study of the Atonement, yet no complete exposition of the Atonement is attempted. To search out these subjects in depth one must resort to H. Orton Wiley's three volumes of *Christian Theology* or to a similarly comprehensive work.

Many of the themes in the principal development could profitably become separate monographs, such as holiness and social ethics, and certainly holiness and culture. Some psychological aspects of holiness deserve more careful attention. But if holiness is to be experienced as a privilege of grace, rather than be merely a subject of speculation, its centrality in the plan of salvation must be shown and the way made clear. Our method of treatment has had this as its constant and supreme objective.

For this reason also, holiness has been approached, not as an ideal to be praised, but as a relationship with God and a state of soul to be enjoyed. The key is not time but faith. Ideals (if they are any good) represent standards toward which we strive. The concept is relevant to growth in grace and maturity of Christian character. But holiness is an experience of the heart available—indeed, obligatory—*now.* That "holiness" which is pushed into the never-never land of ephemeral ideals soon becomes romanticized and humanized and ceases to be either evangelical or biblical.

One further word is necessary to provide the key to the general outline. The doctrine of holiness is unfolded along Trinitarian lines. We begin with the holiness of God. Out of the consideration of God as Creator emerges logically our anthropology and hamartiology—the doctrines of man and of sin. This is followed by a study of God the Son, in respect to the bearing of both His person and His mission on possibilities of grace for the sinner.

It is inevitable that we should move next to the special soteriological work of the Holy Spirit, the Third Person of the Trinity. He is "the great fountain of holiness to his church," says Wesley. He adds, "The Holy Spirit is the principle of the conversion and entire sanctification of our hearts and lives."[1] Therefore the regenerating and sanctifying ministry of the Spirit necessarily dominates the major portion of the development. The birth of the Spirit, Christ's baptism of the believer with the Spirit, and life in the Spirit become the lead themes, with such others as sanctification and perfect love subsumed under them. These are possible and meaningful only as they are ministrations of the Spirit and, as such, are integral to the redemptive provision of Christ.

A large degree of humility is appropriate when expounding doctrine, especially in the area of soteriology, because dogmatic formulations of Christian experience are attempts to describe how the implicit and explicit teachings of Scripture seem actually to work out. In Scripture itself doctrine and experience are interwoven, not only in the more historical portions, as in Acts, but in the more didactic portions, as in the Epistles. Creedal summaries of the stages and processes of experience grow out of a study of this composite of doctrine/experience data. The result is a descriptive doctrine that says, This is the way it happens.

To the extent that the Bible is explicit, theology can say, This is the way it *must* happen. For example, repentance must underlie faith, faith must be the basis for works, and so forth. But to the extent that the Bible's soteriology is implicit rather than explicit, theology can only say, This is the way it is *usually* experienced. The dogma then should be viewed as a guideline, not a straitjacket. It approximates the norm but cannot verbally describe every personal variation in experience from that presumed norm. It can pronounce judgment on experiences obviously non-Christian and nonbiblical, but it cannot put a rule on every detail concerning the way different people are led by the Spirit into holiness and beyond.

—RICHARD S. TAYLOR

---

1. *The Works of John Wesley* (London: Wesleyan Conference Office, 1872; reprint, Kansas City: Nazarene Publishing House, 1978), 11:420; hereinafter *Works*.

HISTORICAL ROOTS

The roots of the following theology of holiness can be found in numerous denominational soils. The ground includes the rich development of doctrinal understandings of the 19th century, but it also includes the Wesleys and their century. More than that, it includes the precursors of Wesley clear back to the apostles, as is shown in volume 2. Most importantly, it includes the Bible, as is seen in volume 1. But no statement more accurately epitomizes the positions of this volume than the following declaration of the mission of the Church of the Nazarene, founded in Los Angeles by Phineas F. Bresee, October 1895, as reiterated in the 1908 *Manual* of the newly formed Pentecostal Church of the Nazarene:

> These persons were convinced that they were called of God unto holiness, to teach others the doctrine, and to lead them into the experience of entire sanctification. They were convinced, both by the teachings of the holy Scriptures and by their own experience, that entire sanctification necessarily implies a second work of Divine grace to be received by faith in Christ and wrought by the Holy Spirit. That purity of heart, with holiness of life, is the will of God in Christ Jesus for and concerning all His children. They were convinced that believers thus sanctified will follow Christ's example of preaching the Gospel to the poor, to which work they felt especially called.[2]

2. *1908 Manual of the Pentecostal Church of the Nazarene* (Los Angeles: Nazarene Publishing Co., 1908), 11-12.

1

The Meaning of the
Holiness of God

In volume 1 the basic teaching of Scripture on the holiness of God has been presented. It remains to consider the wide-ranging import of God's holiness in His redemptive relations with men. Only as we see the divine holiness will we understand why man must be holy, or understand something of what this holiness in man is to be (Leviticus 18—19; Isa. 6:1-6; 1 Pet. 1:15-16).

In nature men may, if they will, see "God's invisible qualities—his eternal power and divine nature" (Rom. 1:20). The world around us, and certainly the heavens above, bear for the believer the imprint of a God whose power is beyond computation and whose activity is solitary and transcendent. The contemplation of such a God has always filled thoughtful persons with both awe and fear.

But to fill in the gaps of our conception and to understand God's personal character and His thoughts toward man, we must trace His words and deeds as recorded in the Bible. The climax and perfection of God's self-revelation is in Christ Jesus, the "exact representation of his being" (Heb. 1:3; cf. Col. 1:15-19).[1]

---

1. David L. Mueller interprets Karl Barth as teaching that "sound theology is that which again and again fixes attention upon the God of the old and the new covenants." *Karl Barth* (Waco, Tex.: Word Books, Publishers, 1972), 49.

While accurate knowledge about God does not assure personal acquaintance with Him, it is nevertheless essential. For it is inevitable that our ideas of God will shape our religious experience, with resultant soundness or distortion. "Show me your gods," quoted E. Stanley Jones, "and I will show you your men."

If our image of God is that of a cruel despot, an eagle-eyed policeman, an indulgent grandfather, or perhaps a whimsical goblin playing games, our feelings toward Him will be conditioned accordingly. Our twisted concept will breed either fear mixed with resentment, or presumption, irreverence, and flippancy. On the other hand, to see God as He truly is, as revealed in the Scriptures and reflected in Christ, will foster both awe and love, total respect and total adoration. The truth is, we must learn reverence before we are entitled to learn intimacy. Therefore we need to contemplate God. "Know before whom you stand."[2]

I. HOLINESS THE PRIMAL ATTRIBUTE

A. Holiness and Other Attributes

Is holiness as a divine attribute, coequal and alongside other attributes? Most theologians think not, but see holiness as the moral quality of all God's attributes.[3] H. Orton Wiley says, "We may say then, that holiness belongs to the essential nature of God in a deeper and more profound sense than merely as one attribute among others."[4] In all that He is within himself and in His relations, He is pervasively and perfectly holy. This is so basic that P. T. Forsyth could say, "God's holiness is the fundamental principle not of our worship only, but of his whole saving revelation and economy of love. It is the moral principle of both love and grace. It is love's content."[5]

---

2. Motto on the chapel wall of Hebrew Union College, Cincinnati.

3. William B. Coker reminds us that the seraphim never cry out, "God is love!" but "Holy, holy, holy, is the Lord God Almighty" (Rev. 4:8; Isa. 6:3). He adds, "Whatever else we may say about God, that He is light, that He is love, that He is compassion, certainly standing at the root of everything we may say about Him is that He is holy" (Sermon preached at Asbury College, Fall, 1978; recorded by Radiant Cassettes, Vancleve, Ky.).

4. *Christian Theology* (Kansas City: Nazarene Publishing House, 1940), 1:370.

5. Quoted by John H. Rodgers in *The Theology of P. T. Forsyth* (London: Independent Press, 1965), 32. Elsewhere Forsyth says, "Any conception of God which exalts His Fatherhood at the cost of His holiness, or to its neglect, unsettles the moral

B. Holiness as Righteousness

The Old Testament conception of the divine holiness as *radiance, separation,* and *purity* has been discussed in volume 1. At this point it is necessary to stress again the ethical nature of God's holiness. It would be possible to conceive of radiance, separation, and purity amorally. Even an earthly potentate could have the "holiness" of great splendor, of unapproachableness, and even "purity" in a ceremonial sense, all without essential goodness in moral character. But as Turner points out, the Bible never permits such a morally empty concept of God's holiness.[6] More radiant, separate, and pure than any other being, God is primarily radiant goodness, separate from evil, and pure in absolute righteousness. The ethical perception of God is inescapably pervasive in the Old Testament. Harold B. Kuhn writes:

> It does not answer to the realities of Old Testament usage to contend that "holiness" was originally a morally neutral category, connoting some vague "numinous" or mysterious quality that elicited a sense of awe. Such a view as this, given classic form in Rudolf Otto's *Idea of the Holy,* rests upon a radical reinterpretation of the history of Israel's religion, a readjustment that is far from being evidently justified.[7]

But is God's holiness voluntary self-subjection to inherent rightness that He *finds* in the "nature" of things? If this were true He would be subject to authority outside of himself, and His absoluteness would dissolve in some form of metaphysical dualism. Gordon H. Clark says:

> Plato and Leibnitz attempted to conceive God as subordinate to independent moral principles. Then they limited God by a reality external to him. No such view is countenanced in the Bible. The highest norm of morality is the law of God. It is God's command that makes an act right or wrong.[8]

---

throne of the universe. Any reaction of ours from a too exacting God which leaves us with but a kindly God, a patient and a pitiful, is a reaction which sends us over the edge of the moral world. . . . It is a conception which tends to do less than justice even to God's love. It tends to take the authority out of the Gospel, the sinew out of preaching, the insight out of faith, the stamina out of character, and discipline out of the home" (Lyman Beecher Lectures, Yale, 1907, quoted in *Positive Preaching and Modern Mind* [New York: George H. Doran Co., n.d.], 354).

6. George Allen Turner, *The Vision Which Transforms* (Kansas City: Beacon Hill Press, 1964), 17-20.

7. *God: His Names and Nature* (monograph published by *Christianity Today,* n.d.), see chap. 1, 6-17.

8. *Baker's Dictionary of Theology* (Grand Rapids: Baker Book House, 1960), 241.

Yet it would be placing too great a stress on the ethically definitive power of the divine will to imply that God's will creates right
or wrong capriciously or arbitrarily. God's will is always the expression of the totality of His nature, which includes wisdom, justice,
truth, and love. There is an inner coherence and harmony defining
the divine nature. God will not—and even in a sense cannot—act
contrary to himself. While therefore we may say that what is right
is what God commands, we may equally say He commands it
because it is right. "Will not the Judge of all the earth do right?"
argued Abraham (Gen. 18:25).

The holiness of God is such that it is inviolable. Furthermore
there is a moral intensity in God's holiness that makes tolerance of
unholiness an impossibility. For "our God is a consuming fire"
(Heb. 12:29, NASB; cf. Deut. 4:24; 9:3; Isa. 33:14; 2 Thess. 1:7; Heb.
10:27, 31). *It is this intolerance of all evil that is the ultimate ground
for the necessity of atonement on the one hand, and the requirement of
real holiness in created moral beings on the other.* "You shall be holy,
for I am holy" is the unalterable logic of the divine nature (1 Pet.
1:16, NASB; cf. Lev. 11:44-45; 19:2; 20:7).

C. Holiness and Sovereignty

Sovereignty is not only God's inherent right to rule but also
the continuous, unimpeded exercise of that right. God's sovereignty remains uncompromised even by its voluntary self-
limitation, a limitation that accommodates itself to that free agency
in man which God's very sovereignty has ordained. God elected,
therefore, to create a moral being capable of independent moral
action (either creative or destructive), and to sustain with that being a flexibility of relationship marked by full respect for those
created and delegated powers.

This does not mean, however, that God has relinquished or
even diminished His throne rights. He claims sovereignty over the
creature, the free being as well as the nonfree. In this claim He
demands and expects obedience. Such sovereignty is exercised in
the giving of laws for the governing of man's behavior. It is equally
manifest in God's prerogative of judgment, in calling the creature
to account for the way he either accepts the Creator's sovereignty
or rebels against it.

Self-limitation, therefore, does not consist in a voluntary
abridgment of God's rights, but in refraining from enforcing those

rights by universal compulsion. Man will be called to account, and rebellion will bring punishment. But the punishment is after the event; that is, it presupposes that the culprit acted in freedom. The gift of freedom is sovereignly given, as also are the terms (in the form of covenant) imposed for its proper exercise, including the rewards for proper use and penalties for misuse. The freedom itself is real, yet the freedom in no sense constitutes an impairment of God's sovereignty. Thus can the concepts of creaturely freedom and divine sovereignty be harmonized.

But the holiness of God determines and assures the reliability of these basic notes in the divine sovereignty. Holiness is that integrity which renders unthinkable an unpredictable sovereignty. Sovereignty that is not holy could become tyranny by capriciously altering the terms, either canceling the freedom or changing the rewards and sanctions. The result would be chaos in moral government.

Wherever theology makes divine sovereignty the keystone of its system instead of divine holiness, it goes astray. Mere sovereignty engenders not the joyous freedom of the children of God, but the abject, voiceless bondage of servitude.

If the association of the idea of tyranny with God seems blasphemous, it can only be because we intuitively presuppose God's essential and absolute goodness. We sense that sovereignty is as truly a derivative of God's holiness as it is of His creation rights. A sovereignty not based on holiness would be for all created beings an unthinkable tragedy. A creature who cannot worship God as holy cannot lovingly obey Him as sovereign. The mind cannot rest in the contemplation of an obedience without love or fear without devotion. Fortunately we are spared this pain by the assurance, "Thy throne, O God, is for ever and ever: a sceptre of righteousness is the sceptre of thy kingdom" (Heb. 1:8, KJV), and "He is the Rock, his work is perfect: for all his ways are judgment: a God of truth and without iniquity, just and right is he" (Deut. 32:4, KJV; cf. Rev. 15:4).

II. HOLINESS AND CREATION

The doctrine of creation, fundamental to Christianity, is the affirmation that the universe and all things in it owe their being directly to the power of God alone. This is true equally of the material universe and the spiritual universe—that is, personal being. The latter category extends to angels, demons, men, and any other intelligent entities that may exist.

A. The Natural Order

It would be inconceivable for God's creative power to be exercised in a manner incompatible with His holiness. This means that what God would create would reflect His own character. The symmetry, balance, wholeness, integrity, benevolence—all attributes of God's own holiness—would be transmitted to the natural order. When, therefore, we read that at each stage of creation "God saw that it was good" (Gen. 1:4, 10, 12, 18, 21, 25, 31) we are to understand this to be more than mechanical or organic perfection, but invested worth. God saw the reflection of himself. The primeval order was good in its *purpose*, which was to glorify God and to provide a suitable habitation for man. And it was also good in its *purity*, that is, its freedom from discord or imbalance.[9]

B. The World of Personal Being

It is evident from the Scriptures that God created not only man but also spirit beings called angels. It is just as evident that there are in the universe malevolent spirit beings called demons. God's holiness rules out the creation of evil beings. If therefore either man or spirits are evil, such evil must have been self-induced since God completed His work. Furthermore, this defacement cannot in any sense be blamed on God.

This forces into the picture the concept of sin, as the antithesis of holiness. It also helps us to begin with certain basic axiomatic truths of a biblical religion. (1) God and His creation are interrelated but are not to be confused or identified one with the other. The Christian view is neither deistic, pantheistic, nor panentheistic, but theistic: that is, God is Wholly Other and truly transcendent, yet just as truly immanent (near and in)—"I am God, and not man; [I am] the Holy One in the midst of thee" (Hos. 11:9, KJV). Furthermore, (2) the world of things, man, and spirits is not the product of a cause and effect mechanism, but the creation of the

---

9. Adam Clarke comments that "everything was formed to the utmost perfection of its nature, so that nothing could be added or diminished without encumbering the operations of matter and spirit on the one hand, or rendering them inefficient to the end proposed on the other" (*Commentary* [New York and Nashville: Abingdon Press, n.d.], 1:39).

divine fiat proclaimed in complete freedom. Creation is not an eternal necessity. And (3) creation is under God's holiness, which is to say, related to God in terms of moral government. There are clearly prescribed mandates. Only thus could the forces that we call sin and redemption ever arise.

III. HOLINESS AND PROVIDENCE

Heb. 1:2-3 ascribes both creation and providence immediately to the Son: "through whom he made the universe . . . sustaining all things by his powerful word." The first phrase speaks of creation, while the second speaks of providence. Neither the beginning of the material order nor its preservation is the product of any kind of automatism built in. God did not create either a "perpetual motion" *mechanism* or a *bios* that had within itself its own powers of development and continuance—so that God could stand by and let the "machine" work or the vitalism unfold. Rather, the direct action of God is responsible for each stage of creation and equally responsible for its ongoing operation and maintenance—"sustaining" is the English term, or "upholding" (KJV).

A. The Freedom of God's Action

In Genesis, the bringing into being is by means of fiat—the spoken word. "Let there be" is the recurring refrain, with existence as the response. In Hebrews, providence also is seen as the action of the word. The significance of tracing both creation and providence to the divine word—instead of to the divine ingenuity or divine hands (to use an anthropomorphism)—is incalculable. The concept preserves at once the ideas of freedom in God's action, the radical discontinuity between God and His creation, and the ultimate in power. To fashion preexistent materials with one's clever hands, or to keep them running by manual tinkering, does not compare with the breathtaking, incomprehensible power of being able to speak into existence or control by a word. We may manufacture and exercise remote control over a television set, but the forces at work are quite traceable and manipulatable. Man's creative and controlling abilities are not comparable with God's.

But while the dependence of the universe on God's providence, involving His immediate and constant power, eases some difficulties, it further complicates others. Miracles can constitute no theoretical problem if the usual, nonmiraculous order is also the continuous action of God. The God who every moment sustains the intricate interplay of forces in patterns that we call laws can adjust these patterns if needed for a special display of His power. This can be either to get human attention or to serve human need. And He can do this without the miracle disrupting the system. God places too much value on order and reliability to allow the pattern to become askew.

B. The Morality of God's Methods

The real difficulty is in harmonizing God's loving holiness with the postulate of divine immediacy in natural disasters, such as earthquakes, hurricanes, and tornadoes. But the relation of the larger calamities to God's providence is no more difficult than explaining poisonous reptiles and insects, mildew, blight, and disease. A certain degree of dislocation was implied by God in cursing the ground and expelling man from the Garden. God allowed the natural order to become an obstacle instead of a ready-made paradise. This could have included a multitude of subtle changes, all the way from insect imbalance, to meteorological disturbance, and to aggravated activity such as the shifting of the earth's plates and continental shelves.

1. *The Curse a Moral Response*

As the earth was created and prepared as a suitable habitation for man, so likewise the earth's distortion was God's response to man's sin. For apart from man there is no problem. Earthquakes and violent windstorms are not necessarily disastrous in themselves; we see them as evils only because man is hurt by them. The natural tendency is to ask why a good God would have built such hazards into a world designed for man. A biblical doctrine of providence would reply that they were not built in, and the original design was for man in holiness and obedience to be spared from them. But the clear penalty announced in advance for disobedience was death, both physical and spiritual. It was appropriate that the material forces, both in man's body and in his environment, which had been designed to be instruments of life, should now become instruments of death.

We must not lose sight of the truth that it was God's *holiness* that mandated an adjustment in the natural order to match the disaster in the human soul. The physical upheaval—in some sense even cosmic—was essentially moral, by no means haphazard, and certainly not immoral. This is hard for rebellious, unbelieving people to grasp, for their very unbelief and rebellion prefer to see any loss of human life as cruel and needless destruction.

A truly immoral natural order, in respect to man, would be one that was totally indifferent to man's relationship to God, in which the violation of God's laws would bring no suffering in terms of natural consequences. Just as it is really a mark of benevolence for a burn to hurt, so it is a kindness for the universe to be against us when we are against God. For the universe is not independent, it is God's instrument in forwarding moral ends, and by means of it God can show either His approval or disapproval.

Therefore there are unpleasant consequences to human disobedience, whether the disobedience be to a positive divine command to Adam, or to God's laws written in the fabric of nature. Getting sick when we violate the rules of health is a simple example of this basic morality in the nature of things. Whether we call these consequences natural or penal makes little difference, for in truth they are both—except that the consequence of violating a positive command is primarily penal while the consequence of violating a hidden law is primarily natural.

2. *A Benevolent Necessity*

To repeat—God's holiness dictates this kind of providence. This becomes clearer when we look more closely at the loving objectives of the curse. Only by exposing fallen man to a world of hazards would man be kept reminded of his frailty and dependence. Only by experiencing the grief and pain and sorrow incident to death—whether it be by a disaster or by a disease—could man be made aware of his sin and his need of mercy on the part of a transcendent Power. Only by the necessity of labor and toil, to extract sustenance from the soil, could man be kept from total decay.

The very necessity of conquering nature and of overcoming obstacles made invention necessary. Thus was preserved in man some measure of the divine image, as seen in creativity and ingenuity. Man's technological progress was not born in the idyllic arbors of lush South Sea Islands, but in the harsh necessities of rugged lands with violent climates. But even more germane: It has been a community of suffering that has kept alive man's best side—his capacity for caring and compassion—and kept man from being totally inhumanized by his own selfishness.

And finally, it is the suffering and uncertainty of life that is the prime tool of the Holy Spirit in making man receptive to the gospel. The history of missions is packed with evidence of this. In the Fiji Islands, for instance, it was a terrible epidemic on the small island of Ono, plus the total impotence of pagan priests to alleviate it, that conditioned the people to receive the message of the one true God and to renounce their idolatrous practices.[10] But finding examples at a distance is not necessary. Every pastor knows that adversity, sorrow, and pain are his chief allies. The hardest to reach are those who are healthy, happy, prosperous—and smugly satisfied. Trouble is God's entrée into the human heart.

The purpose therefore of pain is disciplinary—"that we might be partakers of his holiness" (Heb. 12:10, KJV). While we are in this world we must at the same time be weaned away from it. If there had been no curse following sin, and if life now were not dangerous and disciplinary; if man could have disobeyed and remained in the Garden without ill effects; if the race could have continued in sin with unbroken prosperity, unalloyed happiness, and unlimited health, man's confirmation in sin and commitment to it would have been virtually absolute. The difficulty in bringing about repentance would have been compounded manyfold. Such a consideration justifies the action of God in permitting natural evil, and dissolves any seeming difficulty in reconciling suffering with the divine holiness.

C. Divine Holiness and Personal Providence

A more difficult area of the doctrine of providence in relation to God's holiness pertains to the interweaving of events in one's personal life. Every life is composed of a tapestry of contingency and necessity. There is the interplay of (1) seemingly accidental circumstances, (2) the actions—including sins—of others, and (3) the conjunction of a thousand vectors of influence. Where is God in all of this? How much is He involved in the detail? Does He ordain or merely allow? The answer must include God's love, which means His active concern and personal involvement in all

---

10. Robert Hall Glover, *The Progress of World-Wide Missions,* rev. J. Herbert Kane (New York: Harper and Brothers, Publishers, 1960), 440-41.

that happens. Certainly the God who observes the fall of a sparrow and knows the number of hairs on our heads cannot be an absentee God in our calamities.

But the answer also must include the *righteousness* of God's involvement, and this righteousness must mean the rightness not only of God's purpose but also of God's respect for human freedom. God is in a living relationship with man in which He allows man to hurt himself, and He refuses to cancel consequences or spare him from the complications that are of his own making. Yet He can overrule where He does not rule and can assimilate into His plan what should not have been, so that literally all things *do* work together for good to those who love Him (Rom. 8:28). Toward those who do not love God He can make all things work together for that blending of punishment and protection that has as its undeviating end their awakening and salvation. In all of this God's holiness steers His providence between total determinism on the one hand and total detachment on the other.

However, no matter how fascinating it would be, this is not the place to attempt to solve all the riddles of personal providence or to develop a full theodicy. It is enough to know that life is not a helpless ship adrift on an uncharted sea with an incompetent pilot. We are not victims of caprice or chance. We are in touch with a God who is both holy and almighty. The almightiness is our assurance that God is big enough for all our needs. The holiness is our assurance that all God's providences—all of His methods and principles of operation—are righteous. The universe is on the side of righteousness because it was created by a righteous God. What happens to us is never outside His knowledge and never apart from the core morality of His methods. We are in *moral* relationship with a holy God. In this knowledge is our security and our peace (cf. Rom. 11:22).

IV. HOLINESS AND JUDGMENT

God's holiness is the guarantee not only that His providential dealings will be right but also that at the heart of His love will be judgment. God's love is not soft or morally indifferent. As Harold B. Kuhn says, "Holiness . . . in action implies both strict rectitude and an aggressive form of justice."[11] God's love as holiness will

---

11. *God: His Names and Nature*, 19.

require that sin be treated according to its intrinsic demerit—which is to say, the sinner will be treated as he deserves. But God's holiness as love will impregnate the judgment with benevolence in spirit and purpose.

Neither love nor holiness can be neutral or indifferent to wrongdoing. Love does whatever must be done to achieve reclamation, which often includes the infliction of pain. Holiness demands the preservation and vindication of right itself. For holiness not to react vigorously and judgmentally toward unholiness would mean its own destruction.

To take a negative view of divine judgment proves an already inadequate view of sin. It is impossible for us to see the enormity of sin as God sees it—its blight and devastation—without recognizing the moral necessity of radical response. We must see sin as that which desecrates God's creation and debases man, God's crowning masterpiece. It spreads its deadly poison like a contagion, defying God's sovereignty and threatening the integrity of His very kingdom. It takes a choking grip on all the tomorrows and eternity itself, aiding and abetting the kingdom of Satan, archenemy of God and of a harmonious universe. For God to treat sin mildly, as if it were a passing peccadillo, would be grossly unholy.

A. Requirements Imposed by Holiness

The holiness of God requires that His judgment—

1. Be Fair

God "leans over backward" to be fair. A perfect synthesis of mercy and justice constitutes the vanguard of divine judgment. This is exemplified by God's refusal to drive out the Canaanites in Abraham's day—"The sin of the Amorites has not yet reached its full measure" (Gen. 15:16). God's exile of the Hebrews to Egypt was His deliberate determination to be fair, by giving to the Canaanites another four centuries to clean up (Jonah 4:2; 2 Pet. 3:7-9).

2. Show Concern for the Weak

God's judgment champions the wronged and oppressed. Repeatedly the Bible affirms that God is against those who do evil, and is the Protector of the weak who have been victimized by the strong (2 Kings 8:31-32).

3. Be a Model for Man

God's judgment serves as a model for human judges who, biblically, are to see themselves as God's deputies. The standard of the ideal judge described in the Old Testament is meaningful only because this is the kind of judge God is (2 Chron. 19:5-7). If earthly judges are to be fair and impartial, if they are to accept no bribes, or be intimidated by the strong, if they are to punish the guilty and acquit the innocent, then it is inconceivable that God would do less. The difference between God as Judge and man as judge would be not in moral obligation but in fallibility and infallibility. No matter how honest, a human judge may misjudge, but God never. And judge He will.

4. Uphold Law

God's judgment upholds the integrity of His own law. The moral government of the universe demands this much. When God declares that certain acts will bring certain consequences, His very *holiness* must see that those acts *are* followed by those consequences. His own word is at stake. The law is written deep in the nature of things because back of the nature of things is the holiness of God. "Do not be deceived: God cannot be mocked. A man reaps what he sows" (Gal. 6:7). In the offer of mercy and grace, says Harold B. Kuhn, God "will not violate the norms set by holiness."[12]

5. Punish Redemptively

God punishes sin while yet seeking the reclamation of the sinner. Love, which is holy, knows that sin must be punished (do not even wise parents know this much?). Holiness that is loving yearns to restore the sinner to holiness. Hence all divine judgment in this life is disciplinary and redemptive.

But hence also, all divine judgment upon nations and persons points to Calvary. The Cross gathers up into itself supremely the moral stress inherent in the tension between judgment and mercy. While holiness seeks reclamation, it cannot, at the deepest level, waive punishment. Even if a sinner turns, his sins must be covered; they cannot be ignored. Herein lies the rationale for the total Old Testament sacrificial system. But more importantly, herein lies the rationale for the Incarnation and the blood Atonement on the Cross—that God might be *just* (in punishing sin) and the *justifier* (giving mercy and pardon) of those who believe (Rom. 3:26). *Full* punishment would be eternal and rule out mercy. But sin punished vicariously and symbolically through the substitutionary death of

---

12. Ibid.

Christ enables God to save on a moral basis. That is to say, the punishing is not at the expense of His holiness.

It is God's love that prompts the Cross (John 3:16), but it is His holiness that is the ground of its necessity. Herein is the kingpin of all Christian theology. This is why H. Orton Wiley could say, "Propitiation, therefore, becomes the dominant idea of the atonement."[13] In an eloquent and moving passage Wiley says:

> The atonement is grounded in the nature and claims of the Divine Majesty. The nature of God is holy love. . . . Love is that by which He communicates Himself, or wills a personal fellowship with those who are holy, or capable of becoming holy. By His very nature, He could have no fellowship with sinful beings; and yet His love yearned for the creatures which He had made. Sin rent the heart of God. . . . His holiness prevented sinful man from approaching Him, while His love drew the sinner to Him. Propitiation became necessary in order to furnish a common ground of meeting, if holy fellowship was again to be established between God and man.[14]

The taproot of a redemption based on atonement is the holiness of God.

Finally, the holiness of God requires that His judgment—

6. *Respect Human Freedom*

The Atonement is a ground for mercy, not a basis for setting aside man's freedom by *imposing* mercy. Whatever else holiness means, it means that God's relationship with man at every step and every stage is thoroughly moral. Apart from a response by man that at the "bottom line" is free, the very terms holiness and sin lose their meaning. Both a coerced holiness and a necessary sin are a contradiction of terms. Therefore a decision by man *not* to accept God's offer has the backing of God just as much as has a decision to accept it. God's holiness must guarantee that an ultimate decision by man shall stand. Sharp and pointed is the verdict of the Scripture: "God 'will give to each person according to what he has done' [Ps. 62:12; Prov. 24:12]. To those who by persistence in doing good seek glory, honor and immortality, he will give eternal life. But for those who are self-seeking and who reject the truth and follow evil, there will be wrath and anger" (Rom. 2:6-8). And the wrath and anger will be eternal and irremediable. Its appeasement was provided at Calvary; if that is passed by, there will be no other

---

13. *Christian Theology,* 2:283.
14. Ibid., 273-74.

way of escape found later on (Heb. 10:26). As C. S. Lewis has been quoted, "There are only two classes of people: those who say to God, 'Thy will be done,' and those to whom God says, 'Thy will be done.'"

B. The Divine Mode of Judgment

How is God's judgment exercised?

1. By Rebuke

Judgment is first pronounced, and is borne to our conscience by the Holy Spirit in the form of a sense of condemnation. The Old Testament prophets were God's mouthpieces in declaring His wrath and warning of His impending actions.

2. By Natural Law

God allows the operation of the laws that govern the working of the human body, the human psyche, and of society. When violated they impose their own penalty. The body will become ill, the psyche deranged, and the group distressed and ultimately destroyed. For instance, hatred wreaks its own havoc in the body and soul of the hater.

3. By Special Providence

This takes many forms. God may use a conjunction of events or circumstances to get one's attention and call a halt. Too often we glibly brush aside the query of the sick person or the accident victim: "Why did God do this?" by the easy palliative: "You mustn't think that this indicates anything wrong in your life; probably God had nothing to do with it." Such well-intentioned comfort may circumvent what God is trying to do and flies in the face of such passages as, "The Lord disciplines those he loves, and he punishes everyone he accepts as a son" (Heb. 12:6; cf. Exod. 15:26; Jer. 2:19, 30, 35; 4:18; John 5:14; 1 Cor. 11:29-32).

It would be better to say: "God has a purpose in allowing this, and in due course He will let you know what it is. Just pray, 'Father, I trust You. If You are trying to say something to me, give me ears to hear.' And you may be sure that whatever it is God is wanting to say or do, this has happened not because He does not love you but because He does."

Or the judgment may take the form of the larger calamity that falls on a community or a nation. Rain or drought, famine, hail, locusts, hornets—all were instruments of God in Old Testament history. Haggai puts his finger on the explanation for the dire straits of the Israelites: "You expected much, but see, it turned out to be little. What you brought home, I blew away. Why? . . . Because of my house, which remains a ruin, while each of you is busy with his own house. Therefore, because of you the heavens have withheld their dew and the earth its crops. I called for a drought" (Hag. 1:9-11; cf. Mal. 3:9-12). God is still sending judgment in such form, but people are too dulled by their scientism to perceive what is happening. The increased disturbances in the natural order of recent years is not blind chance. God is trying to speak to modern man (Matt. 24:7-8; Rev. 6:12-16).

Or, God's judgment through special providence may take the form of human violence. When Israel backslid from God, He sent the sword; when Israel repented, God held her enemies at bay. Of Solomon God promised David: "When he does wrong, I will punish him with the rod of men, with floggings inflicted by men" (2 Sam. 7:14). On the other hand, "When a man's ways are pleasing to the Lord, he makes even his enemies live at peace with him" (Prov. 16:7). To deny God's involvement in the rise and fall of nations, and His utilization of man's depredations as forms of divine judgment, is to repudiate the entire Bible, for this mode of judgment is part of its very warp and woof.

4. *By Eternal Punishment*

Neither love nor holiness will permit heaven to be contaminated and corrupted by willful impenitence. As J. Paul Taylor has said, "There must be a holy God, with one heaven of holiness and one hell of unholiness, or an unholy God with two hells and no heaven."[15] Therefore the Bible speaks of "outer darkness," eternal punishment, the lake of fire—the "second death" (Rev. 20:14-15). There is in God's holiness a frightful and awesome moral imperative that in the end becomes a cosmic either/or. Satan as the enemy will be forever silenced and inactivated, and with him all who have chosen his side, whether angels or men. For it has already been pointed out that God will respect man's free agency. "Then the end will come, when he hands over the kingdom to God the Father after he has destroyed all dominion, authority and power" (1 Cor. 15:24).

---

15. *Holiness, the Finished Foundation,* unabr. ed. (Winona Lake, Ind.: Light and Life Press, 1963), 18.

2

Holiness in Man

Man cannot properly speak of having a "spark of divinity" in any pantheistic or theosophical sense. He is not a fragment of God and can never achieve such a mystical union with God that the Wholly Otherness of God on the one hand, and the unique distinctiveness of man on the other, are blurred. It is not the destiny of men to become gods, as the Mormons teach. God will forever be infinite and man forever finite; God always the Creator, man ever the creature; God omnipotent, omniscient, and omnipresent, man relatively feeble and dependent, limited in knowledge, and even more limited by both time and space. He is and forever will be unipresent, not omnipresent.

I. Man's Nature and Destiny

A. A Unique Being

Man, for all his finiteness, is the most godlike being on earth, and perhaps in the universe. So radically is this true that he is not just superior, but different in kind from all other forms of life. While he shares with the lower animals a common *bios* that is dependent on water, air, and food, his essential nature is in a class by itself. There is almost an infinite qualitative difference between a human being and the most intelligent animal. For when God said, "Let us make man in our image, in our likeness" (Gen. 1:26), He was announcing a radical innovation. The symbolic act of breathing "into his nostrils the breath of life" (2:7) means that man's nature is akin to God uniquely. He belongs to earth, for from its dust he was fashioned. But he equally belongs to the spirit order of being. He is thus different from either animals or angels, indeed, "made in God's likeness" (James 3:9).

B. Man's Destiny

Man was created for an inexpressibly lofty destiny. The Psalmist was overwhelmed by man's smallness in comparison to the universe:

> When I consider your heavens,
>   the work of your fingers,
> the moon and the stars,
>   which you have set in place,
> what is man that you are mindful of him,
>   the son of man that you care for him? *(8:3-4).*

Yet even as he felt overawed by the vastness of the overarching heavens, the Psalmist sensed in man a grandeur that counterbalanced mere immensity. He would have understood the young man who was taunted by the skeptic. After impressing him with the wonders of astronomy, the skeptic challenged, "In relation to all of this, what is man?" To which the quiet reply came, "Why, sir, he is the astronomer." The Psalmist, too, knows that the truth does not rest in a question mark, for he goes on—

> You made him a little lower than the
>   heavenly beings [or, *than God,* margin]
> and crowned him with glory and honor.
> You made him ruler over the works of your hands;
>   you put everything under his feet *(8:5-6).*

Yet the "glory and honor" and the earthly authority (prompting Eric Sauer, in his book title, to call man *The King of the Earth*) were the gifts of God and to be returned to God. Man's destiny was related to God and could be fulfilled only in God. When the Westminster Catechism raises the question, "What is the chief end of man?" the answer is crisp and ringing: ". . . to glorify God and to enjoy Him forever." Could anything be higher?

To glorify God is to magnify God and increase His honor in the universe. Since honor is possible only when there are personal beings to observe, we are compelled to see that God's creation of man was with other beings in view. As far as we know, the only other such beings that exist are angels—unfallen angels and fallen angels, which are opposite forces locked in combat. Satan and his kingdom of evil spirits represent the epitome of everything that is anti-God—hatred, deceit, violence. Satan's sole objective is to dishonor and even dethrone God. What God calls good, Satan contrives to twist and make evil. Where does man fit into this kind of a cosmic struggle?

Perhaps the answer may not be too far removed from the saying of Oswald Chambers, "God created man to counteract the devil." At least God created in man a being who could and would become involved in the struggle. The most startling conception is to see man as God's master stroke, the one being who in the end would tip the scales decisively toward total, terminal victory.

How more could man glorify God than that? The angels would watch this being in wonder, and demons would attack him only to be defeated. Here is a *creature*, earthbound and feeble, finite in knowledge and wisdom, yet with a moral capacity to choose ethically and align himself with right in spite of odds. And in the end he will be God's instrument in bringing about Satan's downfall and the complete destruction of the kingdom of evil. Man's behavior in this conflict, and the struggle between God and Satan with man as the prize, is the story of the Bible. It is a breathtaking conception and a thrilling drama.

C. The Divine Image

Man's capacity both to glorify God and to enjoy Him forever is the interface of the divine image in man. What is that likeness which creates a bond between God and this biped, a bond totally unavailable to all other earthly beings?

1. Personhood

The first respect in which man was made like God was the possession of personhood, with all the attributes pertaining to it. This implies self-*awareness*, or consciousness of one's own identity, with the capacity to study it objectively, and also to study consciously and objectively the environment that is not self. Animals have consciousness but not this kind of self-consciousness.[1] They experience pleasure and pain, and evidence even some degree of selective reaction, but this falls short of man's capacity for self-study and non-self-study. With this self-consciousness and individuality are memory, reason, imagination, inventiveness and creativity, and the capacity to project oneself into the future. There is no evidence that animals ever experience the thought of "tomorrow."

Furthermore, man's created personhood is like God in its *power to act.* This includes an ability to move at will, including the fulfillment of a predesigned scheme of action. It also includes an ability to react to stimuli, not merely spontaneously but intelligently and volitionally. It also includes the ability to exercise some degree of control over the environment rather than be its passive and helpless victim.

Finally, personhood is like God in its capacity for *awareness of other persons,* and in its *ability to communicate with them.* It is this that constitutes the basis for communication between God and man. For true communication is two-way and necessarily interpersonal. There can be no real communication between personal and nonpersonal entities. A teenager may talk to his car and even develop a "feeling" for it, but there is no *shared* awareness. The car cannot enter into his master's joys or sorrows. One may talk more freely to a dog and get real feedback; but if we want satisfying communication, we must turn to other persons. In fact, we will find ultimately that if the communication is ever to be totally satisfying, the other person must be God.

2. *Immortality*

If the catechism is correct, and man's destiny is to "enjoy Him [God] forever," he must have been created with a "forever" kind of being. Death was not included in the blueprint; but even its intrusion does not reduce man to temporary existence. For the Scriptures see death not as the extinction of being but as its alteration and transposition (to a higher or lower key). The traditional way of saying this is that man has (or *is*) an immortal soul. More precisely,

---

1. "Men, cats, trees, rocks all *are;* they have being, we come across them in the world. But so far as we know, only man is open to his being, in the sense that he not only is, but is aware *that* he is, and aware too, in some degree, of *what* he is" (John Macquarrie, *Principles of Christian Theology* [New York: Charles Scribner's Sons, 1966], 54).

he is a spirit inhabiting a physical body as a temporary and probational mode of existence. He is a spirit that while always beginning in a body can ultimately transcend the body. The dissolution of the body does not spell the end of the person.[2]

That God's plan includes a new body to replace the old—one that is impervious to the hazards of *bios*—is also the teaching of Scripture. There is nevertheless an individuality, a personal identity, that is a continuum. This is the entity by which the two bodies are related to one person instead of constituting two persons. As Rufus Jones is quoted, "I once had a pair of boots. Over the years I resoled them three times, and put new uppers on them twice—but they were the same pair of boots." Yet this analogy falls short of illustrating the concrete personal identity that abides unchanged through successive changes.

3. The Moral Image

Everything said so far about man's nature belongs to what we call the natural image of God in man. As has already been said, this is the ground of communication. But two persons may communicate without either enjoyment or fellowship. If there is to be spiritual unity, there must also be, in addition to the likeness of personhood, a fundamental character likeness. Since God is holy in moral character (as well as in the other ways unique to Deity), man also must be holy. This is called the *moral* image of God in man. We turn now to a deeper inquiry into this holiness that men may share.

II. HOLINESS IN MAN AS CREATED

A. Holiness and Human Nature

1. *Natural yet Amissible*

Holiness may be said to be native to human nature in two respects. First it is so fundamentally *natural* to man that he cannot function properly without it. Only a holy person is a normal hu-

---

2. Such modern scholars as Oscar Cullmann, in their repudiation of the Platonic doctrine of immortality, have tossed truth out with error, and swung to an extreme view of an indissoluble body-soul unity, which cannot be biblically sustained. Admittedly Plato's idea of a pure, preexistent spirit being contaminated by its conjunction with a vile material body, and immortality as the soul's escape from its prison house, does not do justice to the biblical view of the body's sanctity. But

man being as God intended; to whatever extent he is unholy he is abnormal and corrupted.

This leads to a significant qualification in respect to man's nature and holiness. While personhood could not be lost without man ceasing to be, the same cannot be said of holiness. Man without holiness may be maimed, but he is still man. Therefore, while holiness is natural to human nature it is not inseparable from human nature. It is not an attribute of manness per se. For there is in human nature (in its probational form) one attribute even more endemic than holiness—the capacity to change. Man's nature in its primitive state was not locked into holiness in a deterministic sense. In *Paradise Lost* Milton ascribes to God the words,

> I made him just and right
> Sufficient to have stood, though free to fall.

God could not conceivably become unholy and remain God, but man can become unholy and remain man. Man's holiness, therefore, because derived and dependent, and because a fragile quality of a finite free agent, is amissible. It may be lost. But this qualification does not annul the *natural* affinity of human nature for holiness. It is sin that is foreign and unnatural, therefore destructive.

2. Holy, Not Neutral

The second respect in which holiness is native to man is in the fact that he was created holy, not neutral. This is a watershed proposition from which whole systems of thought flow in opposite directions. Let us examine this more closely.

B. Original Holiness

Man was created holy, not merely with a capacity for holiness, as Pelagius taught. The holiness was created with the creation of the person, rather than a special gift following creation *(donum superaddituum)* as the Roman Catholics teach. They came to this conclusion on the grounds that since it could be lost, it must not have been an original element of man's constitution. Pelagius, on the other hand, stumbled over the paradox of moral character, the

---

that man's essential spiritual being survives physical death is assumed throughout the Scriptures. See "Immortality," "Soul," in *Beacon Dictionary of Theology* (Kansas City: Beacon Hill Press of Kansas City, 1983); also see Purkiser, Taylor, and Taylor, *God, Man, and Salvation* (Kansas City: Beacon Hill Press of Kansas City, 1977), 256-63.

product of choice, being created. The error in both extremes is the failure to distinguish between created holiness and ethical holiness—about which more will be said later.

1. *A Spontaneous Bent* 5'

Man's first self-awareness included an awareness of God and his personal relationship to God. It could not have been long after creation that God articulated the prescriptive terms of their relationship in terms of (1) assignment, and (2) restriction. The announcement of the covenantal obligations, by which man's subordination to God was spelled out, found no resistance in the primal pair. Their acquiescence was glad and natural, for they intuitively perceived the inherent rightness of the arrangement. In other words, there was no prior perversity to overcome, as is true in the case of grace functioning toward fallen man.

H. Orton Wiley says:

> This created holiness consists in a spontaneous inclination or tendency toward the good—a subjective disposition which always answers to the right. It is more than innocence. Man was created not only negatively innocent but positively holy, with an enlightened understanding of God and spiritual things, and a will wholly inclined to them. When, therefore, we speak of Adamic holiness, we mean thereby simply the spontaneous inclination, or positive disposition which belonged to him by virtue of his creation.[3]

Sound condition must underlie and be prior to sound moral action. Such was Wesley's insistence in his debate with the Unitarian John Taylor. Taylor, because he had no concept of either holiness or sinfulness but the fully ethical, denied both inbred sin and original holiness. He insisted that "righteousness is right action." To which Wesley replied, "Indeed it is not. Here . . . is your fundamental mistake. It is a right state of mind; which differs from right action, as the cause does from the effect. Righteousness is, properly and directly, a right temper or disposition of mind, or a complex of all right tempers."[4]

Obviously a concept of either sin or holiness that is *exclusively* volitional cannot claim Wesley for support! Wesley's (and Wiley's) position is that Adam's holiness was a state or condition before it

---

3. *Christian Theology,* 2:44-45. See A. M. Hills, *Fundamental Christian Theology* (Pasadena, Calif.: C. J. Kinne, 1931), 1:373-82.
4. *Works,* 9:342.

could be expressed in concrete choices and ethical situations. This state was a moral preconditioning, an original disposition to do right. There was in Adam a native affinity for God, an inward harmony with God's will, and a contentment with God's law. Adam found in himself no impulse to rebel and no sense of loss or injustice in living within the divine guidelines.

2. A Living Relationship

Yet, while holiness relates to *being* first, it also is a matter of a righteous relationship. Adam and Eve were in a triple relationship that was kept happy because holy. It included relationship *(a)* with God, which was the primal relationship; *(b)* with each other; and *(c)* with their environment.[5] The second and third were normal and happy as long as the first remained so. This primal relationship was also threefold: *(a)* man worshiped God as his Creator; *(b)* he served God as Owner/Sovereign; and *(c)* he enjoyed fellowship with God as Father.

Fellowship with God was man's crowning privilege and his supreme source of joy and satisfaction. "Deep calleth unto deep" (Ps. 42:7, KJV), and man was created with a spontaneous desire for God. The love of God perfectly matches the spiritual hunger of man. Without this unity with God, the soul of man is forever restless. This is simply the way his nature functions. While right relationship with God is amissible, the need is not. Human nature is so geared for God—and this is so endemic to human nature per se—that without God human nature is inescapably crippled and deformed.

Not only, therefore, did original holiness consist of a delightful naturalness and ease in loving and obeying God, but it included also the practice of that same loving and obeying in a continuing, daily relationship.

3. A Relationship Through the Holy Spirit

In view of the Wholly Otherness of God, intimate fellowship would be possible then, as now, only as mediated by the Third Person of the Trinity, who bears this peculiar office and function. As William Burt Pope says, "The Holy Trinity must be connected with every stage of the history of mankind. As the Protoplast was formed in the image of the eternal Image—a son of God, after the

---

5. Man's stewardship under God was reciprocal to his right relationship with his environment. Ecology begins not with man as end, but with God.

likeness of the ONLY-BEGOTTEN SON—so he was under the spiritual and natural government of the Holy Spirit proceeding from the Father and the Son."[6] He further expresses the view that the "LORD GOD of the garden was the Holy Ghost in the human soul."[7]

Yet he immediately adds a wise caution, "The Spirit in man's spirit must not, however, be confounded with the image of God as such." The spontaneous bent of man's original holiness found its perfect counterpart in the fellowship of the indwelling Spirit, who molded, moved upon, and taught man. Adam's receptivity and response was a balance between passive pliancy and free and willing cooperation. But though the Holy Spirit must not be equated with the moral image of God in man, any discussion of original holiness must include the activity of the Holy Spirit.

Hence original holiness must be seen as that relationship within which man began. It was comprised of *(a)* the native affinity for God and right; *(b)* the living personal relationship; and *(c)* the indwelling Holy Spirit as the divine Agent or Bearer of the relationship. God's is the initiative totally; man's is the response. Man's holiness is preserved in the matrix of this relationship only as he continues in willing partnership—not as a coequal, but in the subordination of a creature to its Creator, a steward to the Owner, and as a son to his Father.

C. A Subethical Holiness

A created proclivity toward God is a truly holy state; this was Wesley's insistence. But such a native holiness is not complete; it is not yet fully ethical until tested. In this the Pelagians were right. They felt that holiness must somehow be an acquired moral character—the product of choice—as well as a natural bent. At this level of definition Wesley would have agreed. But Wesley saw that the truth of holiness as a state or condition is not canceled by the

---

6. *A Compendium of Christian Theology* (London: Wesleyan Conference Office, 1880), 1:427. He further comments, "He [the Holy Spirit] did not add the moral image, but He guided the principles of action of man's soul created in that image" (ibid.). Wiley also distinguishes between "the moral rectitude of Adam's nature as a subjective state" and "the presence and agency of the Spirit," but insists that the two must be conjoined in any true doctrine of primitive holiness (*Christian Theology,* 2:47; cf. 47-50).

7. Ibid., 1:428.

truth of holiness as moral choice. For the concepts of original sin and original holiness are counterparts. Original sin cannot be understood except in the light of original holiness. Both are prevolitional and therefore subethical. The categories of ethical holiness do not fully apply to primitive holiness, and neither do the categories of ethical or actual sin apply to original sin. *To a great extent, a consistent theology of sin and holiness hinges on this fundamental distinction.*

Ethical holiness, then, may be defined as that kind of love and loyalty to God that has been consciously chosen and decisively established in the face of contrary possibilities and pressures. We do not know how long Adam and Eve walked with God in unbroken communion. It would not be correct to say that during this time they were like programmed missiles or moral sleepwalkers. They walked willingly, but without a crisis in which they were confronted powerfully by a seductive temptation. Only by such a temptation could their native goodness be either corrupted or confirmed. A right choice not only would have confirmed original holiness, but in the process also would have elevated it to the fully ethical level. Apart from such ethical holiness the pair were less than their potential as persons and as moral agents.

1. *The Desirability of Ethical Holiness*

Because ethical holiness involves both nature and character, it would naturally have greater intrinsic value than untested, primitive holiness. Life affords many analogies. Do we not get a greater thrill when our dog turns a deaf ear to a stranger's whistle in order to respond to ours than we do from his placid following because no one else is around and there are no options? Or—on a higher level—is not the tearful hug and "I love you" of an eight-year-old who has just been spanked more ethically significant than the cooing of a baby who has no self-awareness and is making no hard decisions? Or is not the loving loyalty of a husband and wife after 20 years of testing through daily stress and contrary enticements more valuable and more mutually satisfying than the flush of "puppy love"? Ask the "puppy" and he will say no; but ask the mature couple and without hesitancy they will say yes.

Therefore ethical holiness is to the greater glory of God. For man to be tested and in the test confirm his choice of God would have immeasurably enriched the relationship. It would have been lifted from the childhood level to the manhood and womanhood level. For God to create a human who loved Him naturally and spontaneously was a wonderful thing; but how much more would God be magnified for this pair to choose to love Him against severe odds.

2. The Cosmic Issues

The greater glory to God should not, however, be seen in its intrinsic truth only or merely in the abstract, but also in the larger relationships and issues that hung in the balance. The world would have escaped the curse, and thousands of years of carnage and needless suffering, both among men and sensate creatures, would have been avoided.

But even more far-reaching would have been the effects in Satan's domain. Satan would have been defeated decisively and his depredations forestalled. The vanquishing of Satan accomplished later by the Second Adam at much greater cost would have been accomplished by the first Adam. Admittedly this is a complex area of theology, and many difficult questions remain. But Adam's fall brought both the race and the planet into Satan's sphere of influence and in some sense even established a kind of legal right—a hold that took the death of God's Son (like the death of Aslan in Narnia)[8] to break (Heb. 2:14-15; John 12:31; 14:30; 16:11; 1 Cor. 2:6; Eph. 2:2; 6:11-12; Rev. 12:10-11).

III. HOLINESS IN MAN AS REDEEMED

The moral necessity of holiness in man as a condition for ongoing fellowship with God has never been abrogated. Nor could it be. Even the doctrine that affirms the imputation of Christ's righteousness is an acknowledgment of this necessity. But such is a doctrine of despair, because it does not do credit to the power of grace. It substitutes a legal fiction by which God *sees* the believer as holy even when he is not. But no such surrogate righteousness is needed. Christ did not come into the world to become a token holiness in man's stead, but to make real holiness again possible.

---

8. C. S. Lewis, *The Lion, the Witch, and the Wardrobe* (New York: Collier Books, 1976 [copyright 1956]).

A. Its Inner Substance

But what is the inner nature of this holiness? Since this question is really the subject of the balance of this book, only a concise preview is needed here.

1. A Reconciled Relationship

Holiness must begin with man's getting right with God. The rebel must cease his rebellion and sue for peace through the Son. The prodigal must come home and confess his wrong in complete self-humbling. He must know the relief of forgiveness, and sense the kiss of acceptance. This brings peace with God. This is that justification by faith (Rom. 5:1) by which the repentant and trusting sinner enters into covenant relationship with God and by which the lost sonship is restored. This is where holiness begins, and where the holiness that belongs to redemption must forever be grounded. No future holiness is possible apart from one's continuous dependence on the primal ground of acceptance—pure mercy through Christ (never merit).

Concomitants of justification are regeneration, adoption, and initial sanctification. (See pp. 138-41.)

2. A Recovery of the Moral Image

The reconciliation with God that comes in justification clears away the moral impediments of the past that hitherto have alienated man from God. The objective is to recover the lost fellowship by which the redeemed can enjoy God not only forever but also now (Rom. 5:11). But sinfulness will destroy this fellowship after conversion as surely as before. Therefore there must be a subjective change—a "real" change—to match the forensic or relative change. A stolen and wrecked car needs not only to be recovered and returned to its rightful owner but also to be restored to its rightful condition. A man condemned to die for a crime but also dying with cancer needs a twofold salvation—both pardon and healing. A preserved communion with God demands a moral likeness to God. Therefore a great saying is Rom. 5:9-10, "Much more then, being now justified by his blood, we shall be saved from wrath through him. For if, when we were enemies, we were reconciled to God by the death of his Son, much more, being reconciled, we shall be saved by his life" (KJV).

This "life" is the power for holiness that the resurrected Christ shares with us through the Holy Spirit (2 Thess. 2:13). He is adequate not only to make us right but also to keep us right by making us holy. Almost immediately following this good news (Rom. 5:9-10), Paul launches into his exposition of that sanctification which is the counterpart of justification and by which the problem of "the sin" has its thorough and radical solution. Wesley is thus thoroughly Pauline when he says:

> Ye know that the great end of religion is, to renew our hearts in the image of God, to repair that total loss of righteousness and true holiness which we sustained by the sin of our first parent. Ye know that all religion which does not answer this end . . . is a poor farce. . . . Know your disease! Know your cure! . . . By nature ye are wholly corrupted: By grace ye shall be wholly renewed.[9]

It is apparent, therefore, that the question of holiness is centrally and inextricably related to mankind's loss and recovery of the moral image of God. This is indeed the heart of redemption. To miscontrue holiness as a secondary or unimportant fancy, or some kind of a bypath from the main road, is to betray one's failure to grasp the primary end of revelation. It is to miss the central purpose of the Incarnation, the Cross, the Resurrection, and Pentecost.

This recovery of God's moral image is essentially experienced in two distinctly different crises. Each of these crises is governed by definable moral terms, and there is an inherent logic in their separateness and in their sequence. Moreover, this recovery must not be viewed as defective simply because the holy character is still subject to development, deepening, and strengthening. Nor is it to be considered inadequate because the complete restoration from the racial scars incident to the Fall must await the next life. For the *essential* image is the total inner adjustment to the holiness of God, manifest in an artless disposition to love and obey. It is not to be confused with maturity, knowledge, or skill. Nor does it mean freedom from infirmities of the flesh—any more than native holiness in Adam consisted of his mental prowess in naming the animals. This would be a confusion of the moral image with the natural image.

3. The Reinhabitation of the Spirit

This supreme objective is reciprocal to the correction of man's nature. No relationship could have been more intimate and real, or so completely unmarred by a discordant note, than Adam and Eve's walk with the Spirit. When this unity was lost through sin

---

9. *Works,* 6:64-65.

and rejection of the Spirit, man's nature could not but become twisted, bereft, and lonely; and the human race has struggled with loneliness and emptiness ever since. But from the moment of man's defection, God's dealings with him have had as their supreme objective the recovery of this lost estate. In the fullness of time Christ came, born of a woman, not just to save us from the terrible guilt of committed sin and its consequences but to make possible the return of the Holy Spirit to the human heart, both as Resident and as President.

This is conceivable only on the basis of a subjective change in man himself by which the discordant elements, which would prevent the Spirit from being at home, are removed. They are removed by the Spirit in answer to man's petition; they are kept out by the Spirit as long as the Spirit is honored by the human agent. For the Holy Spirit and the human spirit never merge into one entity; they remain two distinct personal beings. (See pp. 189-90.) Therefore the Spirit's indwelling is a covenant relationship, not a metaphysical fusion. To stress the fullness of the Spirit apart from the renovation of human nature is to lose sight of this fact. But by means of both the sanctifying action of the Spirit and the sanctification of the receptive human spirit, man's relationship with God is normalized.

4. An Ethical Holiness

The plan of salvation is essentially God's provision for man through Christ to attain the ethical holiness the primal pair failed to attain. For them it would have been relatively easy, for they already had the support of original holiness. In contrast, today we confront the options with every disadvantage. The human environment now is hostile to holiness. But the real drag is within. We do not come into the world with native holiness—innocence, yes, but not holiness. Our nature leans away from God, not toward God. It is easier to hide, run, and rebel than to come, bow, and submit. Yet God has initiated an available grace to enable us to turn the tide on the downward drag both within and without. He has made it possible for us to become not only reconciled but also attached to God with the love of confirmed, continuous, and established choice (Titus 2:11-14). It is not the unity of a ventriloquist and his dummy but the thoroughly volitional and responsible communion of friend with friend.

In every respect, the ethical element of an available holiness in

Christ must be the dominant note at each step and stage of our pilgrimage. It is ethical in the sense that it is consciously volitional and in the sense that the volition is related to right and wrong. For a moral act to be fully ethical, there must be not only the *ethical issue* but also the *purposive decision* in the face of contrary possibilities. A wrong decision is ethically sinful, a right decision is ethically virtuous.

Let us apply this. Christian life begins in repentance, which is the conscious and sincere repudiation of sin and commitment to holy living. The subsequent deeper cleansing of the nature is ethical inasmuch as it is not an arbitrary miracle performed in one's sleep. It is, rather, a grace received on clearly defined moral terms and conditions that the Christian accepts and meets as a very active participant. The subsequent life of holiness is ethical inasmuch as it requires ever-new choices and reaffirmations of the basic commitment to God and right. But this daily commitment is no longer a daily struggle against the deepest grain of our nature, but a natural bent, made natural by grace, so that our service of obedience can be rendered in freedom and with joy.

Gradually this ethical holiness will take on all the advantage of original holiness. There will develop an artlessness, spontaneity, and naturalness, until our pattern will be so confirmed as to be virtually irreversible. The irreversible pattern enjoyed with perfect ease in heaven will be but the extension of the pattern established through the Spirit while yet in this world of probation.

B. The Formal Aspect of Holiness

We are still discussing that holiness which is available to man as redeemed. We have already delineated its material or essential nature. The term *formal* is sometimes used to designate secondary qualities or external marks in distinction from this inner content. If we describe Christian holiness in this way, we must attach to it four propositions: It is (1) a twofold work of grace; (2) a state of heart; (3) a way of life; and (4) a progressive imperative.

1. *A Twofold Work of Grace*

Evangelical holiness is from beginning to end the accomplishment of divine grace. This is in contrast to its being any kind of a *humanistic,* do-it-yourself affair. Our own resolvings, discipline, prayer programs, or culture of the soul do not make us holy. Holiness is a gift of grace offered in Christ and inwrought by the

Spirit. This contrasts it also with a *moralistic* holiness, which is simply an external keeping of rules. It is to contrast it further with *ceremonial* holiness, which is a matter of performing the correct rites in the correct way.

Furthermore, this means more than simply an acknowledgment that all the movements of redemption stem from God's gracious initiative. We need to affirm it very concretely. Regeneration is a *work* of grace: It is an inner quickening by the Spirit that is sheer miracle and can in no sense be wrought or duplicated by psychological means. Likewise, entire sanctification is a very definite *work* in the soul, a further subjective change accomplished by the Holy Spirit. While it is not apart from the active involvement of the believer, it is more than the sum total of what the believer does. It cannot be explained totally in terms of the believer's surrender, or some kind of a psychological breakthrough.[10]

2. *A State of Heart*

John Wesley, in his controversy with John Taylor, insisted on the necessity of a state of holiness as the ground of holy action. But he later became wary of the word *state* when he saw the peril of complacency in a static experience. Yet he never ceased his affirmation of a *real* holiness rather than a mere imputation. While our holiness is in Christ, in respect to its moment-by-moment source, it is nevertheless also a personal quality of character.[11]

If the heart is the seat of sin, as Jesus taught (Mark 7:21-22), the heart must also be the focus of cleansing. Only a soundness of heart (the pure heart for which David prayed) can provide genuineness and credibility to a holy life. External holiness not flowing from the heart would be sheer hypocrisy and illusion. An element of comfort here is that a holy heart is always seen by God as such, even though it may not be apparent to critical observers who see only the blunders of the head and the hand. Holiness is not only inward, but sometimes hidden. This will pose no problem as long as we define holiness as purity rather than maturity.

---

10. At times this insistence on divine works of grace has been impugned as belief in "magic." Magic is the attempt to manipulate supernatural power by means of formulas or incantations. There is not the least savor of this in the affirmation of the miraculous element in these changes. The fact that we do not know how the Spirit works or what the exact nature of the change is, in no way weakens the certainty of the basic experiential reality.

11. See his sermon "On the Wedding Garment," *Works,* 7:311.

3. A Way of Life

While there is a doctrine of holiness to be believed, holiness fundamentally is an experience to be enjoyed and a life to be lived. "But just as he who called you is holy, so be holy in all you do" is the command (1 Pet. 1:15). A holy person never willingly or knowingly makes allowance for sin. Rather he chooses to "put on the Lord Jesus Christ, and make no provision for the flesh in regard to its lusts" (Rom. 13:14, NASB).

Nor is this inconsistent with the primary inwardness of holiness. For no heart is bottled up; it is necessarily the dynamic source of the life-style. Jesus said, "Make a tree good and its fruit will be good, . . . for a tree is recognized by its fruit" (Matt. 12:33).

The working out of our salvation into our way of life and our ethics is our responsibility (Phil. 2:12), and it requires a degree of intelligence as well as grace. Because of this, there may be a time lag in matching the outward with the inward. The performance may be sufficiently flawed by infirmity as to make us targets for snipers. But the honesty of the effort should be obvious enough to assure credibility in the eyes of the fair-minded.

However, although time is required to perfect the outward man in the fine print of the Christian life, certain observable marks belong to any true holiness from the beginning: genuine spiritual-mindedness, a strong moral concern, and a highly visible religious life-style. The church, the Bible, prayer, and witnessing will constitute the polarities of the daily routine. Holiness is a life structured by an all-consuming devotion to God, and such a devotion cannot be hid. It may be possible to be religious without being holy, but it is not possible to be holy without being religious or without religion being the pervasive dynamic of life.

4. A Progressive Imperative

Holiness is a universal imperative and is the irreducible standard for all moral agents anywhere in the universe. Furthermore, it is always an imperative *now*. The obligation to be holy is a present obligation. Deferred holiness is preferred unholiness.

But the imperative extends to holiness as an ongoing, unfolding, and developing walk with God. To be holy is to keep on "walking in the light" (cf. 1 John 1:7). Since the light will be progressive, the walk must be progressive. Static holiness is an impossibility. Stale piety is impiety. At the heart of an authentic holiness is a lively dialogical relationship with the Lord involving two-way communication, instruction, rebuke, restraint, direction, discovery, and excitement. Moral decisions are being made. Temptations are being resisted. Adjustments of habit, manner, interpersonal relationships, spending, recreation, or, most of all, *attitudes*, are the day-by-day response to the tutoring of the Spirit. And if and when the Spirit is grieved, the quick resort always is to the Blood, which alone remains the basis of our justification.

Yet this is not essentially a becoming more holy, in the sense of purity or entire sanctification. It is character development. It is a progressive walk with God, not toward, but *on* the highway of holiness.

3

Man's Unholiness

Thoughtful men are not as optimistic in their confidence in science and education as they once were. A recent study uncovered prevailing dishonesty among college students.[1] Shoplifting and employee pilfering have reached epidemic proportions. Political corruption is both rampant and blatant. The moral debauchery vies with dissolute Pompeii. The stubborn refusal by the academic world to face the obvious sinfulness of man prompted one of the world's most famous psychiatrists, Karl Menninger, to write a book of rebuke titled *Whatever Became of Sin?* He was not meaning that sin had disappeared but that it was high time professionals got their heads out of the sand and acknowledged its stark reality.[2]

Sin is a religious word, implying the existence of divine law and willful, responsible wrongdoing in defiance of a holy God. It belongs to the vocabulary of ethics viewed from a religious standpoint. Unfortunately, wherever men are, sin is. Men universally do wrong—a simple empirical fact.

The Christian who learns to think biblically will see sin as the root of all other ills and dislocations of men. Every twinge of pain, every stabbing sorrow, every vacant chair and occupied grave, ev-

---

1. Carnegie Foundation's Council on Policy Studies in Higher Education, as reported by Tom Braden, May 19, 1979.
2. *Whatever Became of Sin?* (New York: Hawthorn Books, 1973).

47

ery tear of brokenhearted grief, all loneliness and injustice and cruelty and violence, every shattered friendship, every tattered and torn ideal, every broken home, every family quarrel with hurt children looking on with anguished eyes, every jail, every prison, every war, can be traced directly or indirectly to sin. "Fools mock at sin" (Prov. 14:9, NASB). Only fools will!

Sin is therefore the problem that makes the quest for holiness necessary. If it is essential to sound theology to understand the holiness of God and the nature of man, it is equally essential to understand sin. Just as a right view of the divine holiness will give sure direction to our view of sin, so likewise the reverse is true; our view of sin will shape our ideas of God, of Christ, the Atonement, indeed of salvation itself.[3] For our doctrine of sin will necessarily affect every other doctrine in our theology of redemption. We cannot go further therefore in our study of holiness until we have examined very carefully the problem of unholiness.

I. THE PRIMEVAL SIN

It is impossible to retain a coherent Bible except on the premise that not only the human race but also human sin began with Adam and Eve in the Garden. This is the kingpin of everything that follows in the Scriptures. While the inspired account comes to us clothed in rich metaphor and symbol, it is nevertheless to be accepted as sober history—that in a space-time setting the original pair were allowed to be tempted, and that they fell, dragging the race down with them. The history of the race confirms that if "man was perfectly holy in his moral nature, as God made him, there has been a disastrous fall."[4]

A. Why the Temptation?

1. *The Necessity of Self-rule*

God deliberately set up a government over man that demanded at its very core man's rule over himself. That would not have been true if God's orders had stopped with the command, "Be fruitful, and multiply, and replenish the earth, and subdue it" (Gen.

---

3. Cf. Richard S. Taylor, *A Right Conception of Sin* (Kansas City: Nazarene Publishing House, 1945), 9.

4. J. Paul Taylor, *Holiness, the Finished Foundation,* 20.

1:28, KJV). This could have been obeyed by self-indulgence and self-assertion. But God added a prohibition that required self-restraint. This is a far deeper test of our subjection to God. It is now a competition between God and self for the final and supreme allegiance of the soul.

2. *The Prohibition*

A test would not have been possible if there had been no declared boundaries. Therefore a single restraint was placed upon man. "The Lord God took the man and put him in the Garden of Eden to work it and take care of it. And the Lord God commanded the man, 'You are free to eat from any tree of the garden; but you must not eat from the tree of the knowledge of good and evil, for when you eat of it you will surely die'" (Gen. 2:15-17).

Obviously a single restraint in the midst of otherwise limitless privileges could not be a ground for complaint. It constituted no burden or deprivation. But it represented man's subordination to God's authority. Adam had to have restrictions placed on his dominion. He needed to be reminded perpetually that, though he was a king, he was also a subject. If the world was subordinate to him, he was subordinate to God. Only such an imposition of law could forestall a false sense of independence and maintain in Adam a healthy awareness that, though he was above the animals, he was not God, but a creature in between, who while exercising authority in one direction needed ever to be humble in another. "Adam's lordship," says Raymond Spencer, "was predicated on his servanthood."

3. *A Moral Necessity*

The possibility of disobedience, confronting man directly, was essential to the making of a moral decision in full awareness. That such a decision must be made if Adam's original holiness was to become ethical has already been pointed out (chap. 2). Moreover, the contrary possibility must be sufficiently attractive to be desirable, or it would not be a real test. If in the eyes of Adam and Eve the fruit of the tree seemed ugly or dangerous, avoidance could be due to self-love, rather than to a desire to please God. Obedience is only perfect when it involves self-restraint and self-denial from something that looks good, wholly because the desire is to please God rather than self. When Adam therefore would be confronted with such an attraction and in the face of it made a conscious choice to obey God, he would become ethically holy. The law therefore was a means to moral character—and with it the inheriting of eternal life.

4. *The Particular Tree*

The prohibited object was called "the tree of the knowledge of good and evil," not because it was instrinsically different from any other tree—any tree would have served the purpose—but because God tagged this tree it became the occasion for obedience or disobedience. If man obeyed, he would gain *experiential* knowledge of moral good; if he disobeyed, he would possess experiential and ethical knowledge of moral evil. A knowledge of good is necessary to human happiness, but not a personal knowledge of evil. God designed that some forms of knowledge be intellectual only. Information about poison is needed for our welfare, but not personal experimentation. Only a fool will not learn from others but must find out for himself.

B. Why the Serpent?

1. *The Involvement of Satan*

The Genesis account does not imply that Satan was the tempter and that he merely used the serpent as a means of communication. Rather, the action is ascribed to the fact that the serpent "was more crafty than any of the wild animals the Lord God had made" (Gen. 3:1), as if this creature were capable of initiating such a confrontation totally on its own. But if so, it had a moral nature and was evil, not "good" as had already been pronounced (1:31).

It is better to see this as one of the symbolic elements in the account. The serpent was Satan's mouthpiece. This takes on credibility when we remember that in the temptation of the Second Adam the identity of Satan as the tempter is clearly stated; and elsewhere he is called "that old serpent" (Rev. 12:9; 20:2).[5]

2. *The External Source*

But far deeper than the question of the identity of the serpent is the question, Why was a third party permitted to enter the picture? Because it is important to see that the temptation did not arise from any evil inclination or moral defect in Adam and Eve. The very contentment with God's will that marked original holiness suggests that apart from an unexpected seduction from an outside

---

5. For a discussion of Satan, demons, and the origin of evil see Wiley, *Christian Theology*, 2:66-81. For comment on the serpent, see ibid., 56, including footnote.

source, the sin would not have been probable. A real temptation developed only when the wily serpent was able to create a measure of dissatisfaction, out of which could spring naturally a curious desire for the forbidden object.

Furthermore, the native goodness of the pair was proved by the fact that to be successful the temptation had to be deceptive. There was a clever and sophisticated rationalizing that made wrong seem right; "as Eve was deceived by the serpent's cunning" is the way the Word puts it (2 Cor. 11:3).[6]

All of this is obvious with Eve. What about Adam? His sin also was prompted by persuasion from without and did not arise from a prior disloyalty in his own heart. While the element of deception was less, if not altogether absent (1 Tim. 2:14), the element of persuasion was greater—his own wife. The "social environment" had become contaminating.

C. The Psychology of the Fall

Sin entered the human race by unbelief, which explains why it can only be banished by faith. That *doubt* was the opening wedge, leading to unbelief and culminating in disobedience and rebellion, becomes clearer when we trace the psychological steps in the Fall.

In actual fact there were three restraints Eve brushed aside in order to partake of the forbidden fruit: the restraint of faith, the restraint of love, and the restraint of obedience. The first restraint was imposed by the mind, the second by the affections, and the third by the will.

1. *The Restraint of Faith*

The restraint of faith said, "God has said . . . and God's Word is true. Believe it!" If Eve had respected this restraint—this block in her path—she would have taken no more steps. When the serpent raised the insidious question mark, "Yea, hath God said . . . ?" then cast aspersions on God's integrity by the flat denial, "Ye shall not surely die" (Gen. 3:1, 4, KJV), Eve should have retorted, "This is what God has said, and I believe it, and that settles it"—maybe

---

6. The question might arise, If Eve was deceived, then how could she be blamed? She was deceived because she accepted the serpent's word as superior to God's. This was an optional reaction on her part, neither automatic nor necessary. For this she was blameworthy.

stamping her foot! That would have been the end of that. But she pushed aside the restraint of faith by accepting the serpent's question mark, and in doing so opened the door to sin.

She now stood on the side of doubt. Doubt soon became unbelief, which is a rejection of God's word as *Truth*. Having first allowed doubt to shake her confidence in the all-sufficiency of God's word, she next replaced God's word by her own faculties as the judge of truth. He who really believes that what God says is true is content to leave it at that; he doesn't have to go searching for himself. But when one begins to doubt God, one is shut up to believing himself. He must now trust his own judgment as being better qualified to perceive truth.

Therefore Eve examined the tree for herself. She felt the need to see for herself because she no longer could take the word of God for granted. Her own faculties seemed to confirm the word of the serpent. She saw that it was "good for food and pleasing to the eye, and also desirable for gaining wisdom" (Gen. 3:6). Now her unbelief became settled disbelief, as she felt "compelled" to the logical conclusion that God's word was not to be taken too seriously, at least not without proving it first. In this case it didn't seem to prove out.

But what *kind of sin was this?* It was self-separation from God as absolute Authority for Truth, and the enthronement of human reason in God's place as authority for truth. This is the genesis of rationalism, and the root of ethical relativism. Men ever since have been searching for truth by means of the test tube of their own faculties—their own reason and senses. [*Unbelief* therefore is the sin of the mind in rejecting the Word of God as the sole standard of ultimate meaning, and replacing it with man's own unaided intellect.]

2. *The Restraint of Love*

The second restraint guarding the forbidden fruit was love. True love desires to please its object and to preserve happy relations at all cost. In Eve's case love would have said to her, "God's fellowship in the cool of the day is the sweetest and most important thing in your life. Be content with it, and with the gifts of His love in this garden; don't grieve Him by coveting for more than He has given."

But Eve had allowed the serpent to plant a suggestion in her mind, "Your eyes will be opened, and you will be like God, knowing good and evil" (Gen. 3:5). She should have indignantly rejected this seed of dissatisfaction by saying, "I don't want to be anything but what God has made me. If He is satisfied, I am. If He had seen that I needed that fruit, He would have given it to me." Thus *trust*, that element in love that is perfectly sure of the other's goodness and motives, would have saved her. But love was stabbed by suspicion and ambition. She accepted the suggestion that maybe she could be more important than she was, and she wanted that self-elevation. At the same time the ugly thought entered that God was cheating her and her husband, that He was "holding out" on them. Thus was love poisoned by both ego-exalting ambition and sullen resentment. We might call this *Pride*.

As Unbelief rejected God's Word as Truth, so now does Pride reject God's approval as supreme value. Love wants nothing more than God and what He desires us to have. Pride with its exaggerated self-importance imagines that it deserves more; contentment gives place to resentment, then hostility. Man is now by nature "averse to God," as the creed says.

This is sin in the sense of self-separation from God as supreme value, and enthronement of self as supreme value. It is not only pride but also idolatry. From this stem all forms of humanism, which place man in the center as the "measure of all things." And thus the sin of Lucifer in wanting to usurp the throne of God is duplicated. From this preening self-importance comes all the strife that has separated men (including the pre-Pentecost bickering of the disciples and the fussing of the Corinthians).

In this also can be seen the progress of sin. Eve began by doubting the reliability of God's word. She then proceeded to doubt the goodness of God's intentions. This destroyed love. We cannot love God if we doubt that He is seeking our highest happiness and that all His mysterious dealings with us are to this end. But when we cease loving God we supremely love self and all the toys that self has invented and the treasures it has accumulated. Thus the affections become twisted and idolatrous.

3. *The Restraint of Obedience*

The third restraint that Eve cast aside was obedience. This represented submission to God as Sovereign. The actual disobedience, in its awful finality, could still have been avoided, if she had stopped to reflect: "God has forbidden this fruit. I do not understand such a rule, for the tree looks harmless to me. What is more,

I don't like it, and think it is a stuffy restriction. But even so, God is God, and His word is law, and I will obey."

As Unbelief rejects God's word as Truth, and Pride rejects God's approval as supreme value, so Rebellion rejects God's authority. The first may be said to be the sin of the mind, the second the sin of the affections, and this the sin of the will. At this point is made the final decision to commit or not commit the overt act. Eve took this fatal step.

In this act sin is seen as self-separation from God as Lord and Ruler, and the enthronement of self as king. It is now "my rights." This rebel wants complete autonomy, without interference. His song is "I did it my way," and his refrain is, "No one can tell me what to do." God-rule is rejected for self-rule. Submission is replaced by self-will. An obedient heart says, "I will mind God, even if I do not understand His ways." But self-will says, "Even if God is right, and regardless of the consequences, I demand my way!"

But following the doubt, distrust, discontent, and disobedience, swiftly come disillusionment, disenfranchisement, depravity, and death. Actually while we theorize that the downward plunge could have been halted before the point of overt action, the sequence of sin is such that once doubt has been accepted, resistance is broken, and successive stages follow in rapid succession almost inevitably. If the domino theory is true anywhere, it seems to be true in the unfolding of the sin syndrome.

D. Satan's Great Swindle

God put Adam and Eve in a situation of maximum freedom and minimum restraint. They ended with minimum freedom and maximum restraint.

1. The Lost Freedom

The sly serpent succeeded in deluding our first parents into imagining that by rejecting God's boundaries they would be increasing their freedoms. They found to their sorrow that the exact opposite was the result. They lost the freedom of an ideal environment and found themselves under the necessity of hard work if they were going to eat. They lost the freedom of perfect health; they were now limited by weariness and pain. They lost the freedom of innocence; now they were aware of abnormal and disorderly appetites, which they had to discipline—as symbolized by the wearing of clothes. They lost the freedom of communion with

God and now found themselves under the bondage of fear. They lost the freedom of peace—freedom from strife and tears—and discovered the crushing, heavy agony of murder even in their own family. Nothing turned out as they thought. Their few remaining freedoms were like a man living within walls that were relentlessly being moved inward a little at a time. Their options became fewer and fewer until finally the walls closed in on them.

What happened in the Garden of Eden was Satan's Great Swindle, or, "The Great Delusion." Mankind is still being deceived by it. This is the folly of supposing that freedom is destroyed by law, and therefore our freedom lies in escape from law. But "absolute freedom," says Eldon Trueblood, "is absolute nonsense." It seems incredible, but the newspapers reported a group of church women activists in New York City sitting in a circle chanting praises to Eve for "committing the first free act." Praise for disobeying God? Disobeying God a *good?*

Such irrational, twisted thinking constitutes incontrovertible evidence of a depraved mind. Eve's disobedience was an act made in freedom indeed, but not thereby praiseworthy, any more than a murder is virtuous simply because it is voluntary and deliberate. It may have been the first supremely ethical act—but hers and his were also the last entirely free acts. Every subsequent moral action by Eve or Adam or any of their descendants has been circumscribed and hemmed in by the consequences of their first dual disobedience.

2. *The True Nature of Freedom*

What Satan obscured from their view was the reality built into the nature of life itself: that freedom's maximum realization, its optimum expansion, and its eternal preservation can be found only in perfect subjection to God. This is the paradox of moral reality, and the most profound truth of life. Only out of perfect submission comes perfect self-realization; only out of obedience comes liberty. "I will walk at liberty," testifies the Psalmist, "for I seek thy precepts" (Ps. 119:45, KJV).

Man's nature is so created that it will function properly only within the framework of God's rule. When he defies God his nature breaks down, and his freedoms both internal and external are diminishing and vanishing and his chains are thickening and multiplying. Today man is lashing out for freedom as a man gasping for air. But he is like a frantic dog that has tangled itself in its rope and only entangles itself all the more with every circle around the tree. If he would only stop barking and stop racing, and let the Master come and help him![7]

E. Personal Effects of Sin

1. *The Loss of Innocence*

Eating of the tree did make Adam and Eve "wise," but in a surprising way. Their eyes "were opened, and they realized they were naked." Their knowledge now included the distressing consciousness of guilt and shame. It was not a pleasant or advantageous enlargement. They now knew sin, but they no longer knew the peace and joy of holiness, for holiness was destroyed. What the serpent had not told them was that they could not gain experiential knowledge of evil and at the same time retain possession of goodness.

2. *Guilt and Alienation*

As children who have secretly disobeyed are uncomfortable in the presence of their parents, so Adam and Eve "hid themselves from the presence of the Lord God" (Gen. 3:8, KJV). The Presence that had been in them was now external to them, and they were afraid of it. This was a profoundly tragic disruption of the divine-human fellowship. The loving, joyous confidence they had enjoyed was now replaced by fear and uneasiness. Their consciences rebuked them, and they knew they were no longer entitled to God's loving favor. Sin always brings an inner sense of estrangement from God and His kingdom.

3. *Spiritual Death*

God had warned them, "When you eat of it you will surely die" (Gen. 2:17). The serpent had scoffed, "You will not surely die" (3:4). But now death had come in its awful reality. True, they did not at once cease to live physically and mentally in their earthly sphere. Neither would they ever cease to exist as self-conscious, distinct persons. But a death did occur the very moment they disobeyed, unutterably tragic, beside which the latter physical death

---

7. Wise are these words: "There is at the core of every freedom a grain of prohibition which insures the existence of the freedom itself. Yet we, so mad to be free, can sometimes center down on that one grain of prohibition and try to cast it out . . . forgetting that it may be the crucial element which makes the whole operate freely . . . There are some things I cannot do and be free" (author unknown).

was but a feeble echo. Holiness, innocence, perfect love, mastery over self and nature, inner tranquillity and happiness, joyous affinity with both Creator and creation—in short, *spiritual life*, in all its rich facets, was extinguished. The third dimension was blotted out, and man became a two-dimensional creature, with nothing left of the former fullness but a dormant, shriveled capacity, and feeble flickerings of longing. Sin had certainly not expanded life; it had contracted it.

II. The Meaning of Sin

It will be seen that a reasonable philosophy of sin, per se, conforms perfectly to what actually occurred in the Garden of Eden. *Sin is accountable wrongness before God.*

A. The Essential Notes of Sin

1. *Before God*

As has already been pointed out, sin is a religious concept. If there were no God, there could be no sin (crime, perhaps, which is violation of society's laws without necessary regard to a Supreme Being; Communists talk of crime but not of sin). Furthermore, "before God" means in His eyes. He is the Evaluator of all moral actions. Where He sees no sin, there is none.

2. *Wrongness*

As trite as it may seem, it is nevertheless necessary to say that wrongness is deviation from rightness. If there were no rightness, there could be no wrongness. Furthermore, recognizable wrongness would be impossible without a known and recognizable standard of rightness. No matter how many liberties a carpenter may take in building a house, he cannot be said to be wrong if there are no blueprints or specifications.

Generally, there are three basic philosophies of rightness and wrongness: *(a) Ethical anarchy*—that every man is a law unto himself. *(b) Ethical relativism*—that rightness and wrongness are determined either by the society in which one lives, or the ethical situation itself (or a combination of both); and therefore there may be many ethical systems, each equally "right" within its cultural framework. This approach presupposes a denial of moral absolutes. *(c) Ethical absolutism*—that morality is rooted in God; that His authority in the realm of ethics is absolute and final; that the elementary essentials of rightness and wrongness before God are unchanging and universally valid; and that God has revealed His standards of right and wrong, and this revelation is available. This does not exclude a degree of legitimacy in the concept of relativism, if kept subordinate to biblical absolutism.

The final implication is that violation of God's standard is sin; conformity is rightness (holiness).

But so far we have "legal" sin, that is, the bare fact of discrepancy between performance and the objective standard. This is called legal because the performance fails to fulfill the letter of the law or measure up to an absolute standard; therefore it must of necessity be disapproved, and needs to be corrected. The so-called sins of ignorance (Lev. 4:2; 5:14-17; Num. 15:27-31, cf. KJV) would belong to this category. Legally the speed limit is violated when exceeded even if the driver is unaware of his violation. But such an unintentional *hamartia* (falling short) is not sin per se, or "properly so-called" (Wesley), because it lacks the one element necessary to make sin *wicked*—evil willing. This alone makes sin a moral evil that requires *condemnation* as well as disapproval. And in this is to be found the distinction between a legal concept of sin and an ethical concept. Therefore we must include another term:

3. *Accountability*

When we say that a person is accountable we mean that he is sufficiently responsible as an intelligent moral agent to justify being held responsible for his deeds by both God and man. But this implies blameworthiness, if the deeds are wrong; that is, it is proper to blame him and impose on him penalties. If he is not responsible, he is not blameworthy. This pinpoints the most essential element of sin, per se: *demerit*. Without demerit, or true *guilt* (as distinguished from mere guilt feelings), sin loses its exceeding sinfulness. It may be

—just an accident: pitiable, but not punishable; or
—merely a misfortune: again pitiable, but not punishable.

The elements of accountability have already been implied but perhaps should be isolated for more detailed consideration. The first is *intelligence*: idiots cannot be held accountable, nor can infants. This is why we can properly speak of the "age of accountability." The second element is *knowledge*: men cannot justly be held accountable for knowledge they do not have and have had no

Sin is → willful transgression of a known law of God by a morally responsible person

opportunity to acquire.[8] The third element is *freedom:* where there is no personal option there can be no accountability. It is impossible for pure determinism to speak meaningfully of either sin or virtue.

As A. W. Tozer says:

> Where there is no freedom of choice there can be neither sin nor righteousness, because it is of the nature of both that they be voluntary. However good an act may be, it is not good if imposed from without. The act of imposition destroys the moral content of the act and renders it null and void.[9]

A child may be justly punished for running away, but not for being kidnapped. Lying is blameworthy; being honestly mistaken is not. Sin, then, is possible only to moral agents; machines, robots, or puppets cannot sin. And sin can occur only within a context of intelligence, knowledge, and freedom.

A fourth element is *volition.* The first three elements of accountability can be called the subjective prerequisites by which sin is a potentiality. But now the potential becomes actual. Within the matrix of freedom (which, while admittedly limited, is nevertheless real) there must be the exercise of the power of choice. This does not mean that only premeditated actions can be sinful. Sins of weakness and impulse are blameworthy also, for they could have been prevented by greater care, and in the doing of them there was a consent. Sometimes, it is true, the moral agent is tricked into sinning by his carnal mind against his better wishes and intentions (Romans 7); these are "surprise" sins of passion or unchristlike reaction. Nevertheless there is a subtle volitional involvement, and the consequence is a feeling of condemnation and blameworthiness.

Such sin may take various forms: It may be committed in the mind, without overt action (Matt. 5:22, 28). It may be either commission or omission. It may be a sin of the flesh, such as sexual irregularity or intemperance; or it may be a sin of the spirit, such as covetousness, ill will, or envy.

But in all these forms the underlying elements of sin as bibli-

---

8. In some situations we are responsible for our ignorance. The saying "Ignorance is no excuse before the law" implies that we could and should have become informed. But absolute ignorance, which is also innocent ignorance, is an excuse before God (Acts 17:30).

9. *That Incredible Christian* (Harrisburg, Pa.: Christian Publications, 1964), 30.

cally conceived are present. In these elements we distinguish the Christian view of sin from (a) the Gnostic, which tends to define sin as *ignorance*; (b) the existential and neoorthodox (e.g., Reinhold Niebuhr), which tend to trace sin to man's *finiteness*, implying that his culpability is diluted by the inherent weakness of his nature; and (c) the Calvinist and Lutheran views, which so stress the legal concept of sin that it is overextended to include amoral shortcoming; and which also so stress man's irremediable depravity that no deed can ever completely escape sin's taint. These latter are not profounder views of sin (as often claimed) but shallower, for they minimize man's true culpability, on the one hand, while at the same time postulating an inherent defect beyond the reach of corrective grace.

Therefore in our definition of sin the word *accountable* must be present; otherwise we are locked into a mechanically legalistic perception of sin. Herein also lies the infinite qualitative difference between sin and error, or unintentional mistake. To confuse sins with mistakes is to cancel all moral distinctions. "To label everything sin, . . . is to all intents and purposes to make sin of no particular account."[10] On the same basis of moral distinctions can be seen the qualitative difference between *sinfulness* and *infirmity*.

In short, when the term *sin* is used of wrongness to which attaches no accountability, therefore no guilt, it is used in an accommodated, subethical sense. When sin is thus defined exclusively in terms of the objective standard, the result is either legalism and despair or carelessness and indifference.

Yet the converse peril requires a word of warning. The ethical

---

10. W. T. Purkiser, *Beliefs That Matter Most* (Kansas City: Beacon Hill Press, 1959), 45. It has been claimed that John Wesley had a threefold conception of sin: (1) as the voluntary transgression of a known law; (2) as inherited or original sin; (3) as any failure or falling short of the perfect law of God. This latter is questionable. While he acknowledges that all such failure needs the blood of Christ to cover it, he refuses to concede that when inadvertent or unknowing it can properly be called sin. He insists that many shortcomings from a perfect standard are in "no way contrary to love," therefore are not "in the Scripture sense, sin." Later he says, "Such transgressions you may call sins, if you please; I do not." And, "Let those who do call them so, beware how they confound these defects with sins, properly so called." Then he queries, "But how will they avoid it? How will these be distinguished from those, if they are all promiscuously called sins? I am much afraid, if we should allow any sins to be consistent with perfection, few would confine the idea to those defects concerning which only the assertion could be true" (*A Plain Account of Christian Perfection* [1872; reprint, Kansas City: Beacon Hill Press of Kansas City, 1966], 51-67).

view of sin must not be pressed to the point of forgetting that objective standards do exist and must be accepted. When sin is defined exclusively in terms of the subjective factors (as if *intention* is all that matters while the *standard* is unimportant), the resulting tendency will be relativism in ethics, antinomianism in theology, and superficiality in religion.

Obviously the sin of Adam and Eve was fully ethical. It was accountable wrongness before God. They had been given a clear standard, which was understood by them. They acted in freedom, as fully responsible persons. They willfully disobeyed. They sinned.[11]

B. The Verdict of Scripture

The normative conception of sin in the Bible is thoroughly ethical. This can be shown in two ways:

1. *Definitive Passages*

Four texts in the New Testament, while not full definitions technically, are definitive in nature, and all refer obviously to ethical sin.

a. "But he who doubts is condemned if he eats, because his eating is not from faith; and whatever is not from faith is sin" (Rom. 14:23, NASB). Conduct not in harmony with faith in the sense of "strong conviction in the light of his relation to Christ and his enlightened conscience"[12] is sinful, in a thoroughly accountable sense, for it is conduct that tampers with conscience. It reveals a willingness to take moral risks. That frame of mind that is more concerned about personal satisfactions and liberties than personal righteousness is a sinful frame of mind, for it is not the frame of mind that belongs to faith.

b. "Anyone, then, who knows the good he ought to do and doesn't do it, sins" (James 4:17). Here is willful neglect of known duty, or else willful rejection of what is perceived to be the right course of action. Clearly this is ethical to the core.

c. "All unrighteousness is sin" (1 John 5:17, KJV). The word

---

11. L. Harold DeWolf clearly distinguishes between legal and ethical sin but uses the terms *formal* sin for ethical and *material* for legal. *A Theology of the Living Church* (New York: Harper and Brothers, Publishers, 1953), 182.

12. Archibald Thomas Robertson, *Word Pictures in the New Testament* (New York and London: Harper and Brothers, Publishers, 1931), 4:416.

here is *adikia*, which in New Testament usage is far more than simple not-rightness such as an error, but a willful rejection of the truth in affection and action; it is wrongness in opposition to the truth.[13] The *adikia* that is "not unto death" is the sin that, while observable to the brethren, is not final; it is not complete apostasy (cf. Gal. 6:1).

d. "Everyone who practices sin also practices lawlessness; and sin is lawlessness" (1 John 3:4, NASB). The word *anomia*, "no law," does not mean a state *without* law or of ignorance of the law, but of insubordination to the law. This is thoroughly ethical.[14]

2. *Biblical Terms*

An attempt to analyze Hebrew and Greek terms for sin is of limited value. This is due partly to the sheer number, literally scores of terms designating unacceptable behavior. But the effect would be complicated by the necessity of studying each use of the term in its immediate context, for the same word does not always carry precisely identical nuances. An in-depth word study therefore is the task of a full book[15]; in this volume we must content ourselves with a very brief overview of some of the primary New Testament terms.

a. *Hamartia*, literally, a missing of the mark. However, while this etymological meaning should never be completely lost sight of, it is not a reliable key to New Testament usage. Instead *hamartia* is the primary term for sin, found at least 175 times, plus the verb form *hamartanō*, and a variant *hamartēma*. It is used for the sinful nature, "the inward element producing acts" (Vine), for example, Rom. 3:9; 6:1-2; 7:7, 8, 9, 11, 13, and others. It is also used to personify sin as an organized governing power, as in Rom. 5:21; 6:12; 7:20; 8:2; 1 Cor. 15:56; Heb. 3:13; James 1:15; and others. It is used for sin generically, referring to sin in the abstract; but at times it refers to a specific evil deed, for example, Matt. 12:31; Acts 7:60.

---

13. Cf. Rom. 1:18; 2 Thess. 2:10-12; John 7:17-18; 1 John 1:9. See W. E. Vine, "Unrighteousness," *Expository Dictionary of New Testament Words* (Westwood, N.J.: Fleming H. Revell Co., 1966); also Cremer; Arndt and Gingrich.

14. Supporting passages are (a) John 9:39-41, which implies that guilt is determined by light; (b) Rom. 5:12-13, which declares that sin is not imputed (i.e., charged against one *as sin*) when there is insufficient light; (c) 1 John 3:6-10, which excludes sinning from the Christian life even as a possibility: obviously that which is morally impossible for Christians to practice could only be ethical sin. See ECH, 1:225-26.

15. Cf. C. Ryder Smith, *The Bible Doctrine of Sin* (London: Epworth Press, 1956).

In a few instances also the word probably is intended to convey its original literal sense, and should be translated "shortcomings" or "faults" (Luke 11:4; 1 Pet. 4:8; possibly also James 5:16). The most significant usage is with the article, *the sin*, some 28 times in Rom. 5:12—8:4, where Paul discusses the sin principle in relation to sanctification.[16]

b. Paraptōma, primarily a false step, which could be a disloyalty leading to apostasy, as in Heb. 6:6; or a less serious blunder, as in Gal. 6:1—"Brethren, if a man is overtaken in any trespass . . ." (RSV). It is very probable the sense of human shortcoming and inadvertency is at least included by Jesus' use of *paraptōmata* following the so-called Lord's Prayer: "For if ye forgive men their trespasses [blunders], your heavenly Father will also forgive you: but if ye forgive not men their trespasses, neither will your Father forgive your trespasses" (Matt. 6:14-15, KJV). Jesus' use of this word helps us to understand His intended meaning in using *opheilēmata*, debts, in the prayer itself: "Forgive us our debts, as we forgive our debtors" (v. 12, KJV). This certainly should include volitional and culpable failures, but it could also refer to unintentional shortcomings. At least the prayer cannot be construed as proof that continuous ethical sinning is to be for the Christian the usual order of the day.[17] However, the prayer is always an appropriate reminder that at best we are dependent on divine mercy, forever in debt to God's grace, since we fall short of the absolute standard of Christlikeness.

c. Apistia, unbelief. This sometimes is a definite and sinful "unfaithfulness," as in Rom. 3:3 (RSV). Generally it is willful lack of faith, or a refusal to believe the gospel (Mark 16:14; Rom. 4:20; 1 Tim. 1:13; et al.). Occasionally it may mean a weakness of faith that yet marks unsanctified Christians (Matt. 17:20 [some MSS] and Mark 9:24). If without "faith it is impossible to please God" (Heb. 11:6), unbelief is obviously displeasing to Him. Since we are saved by believing "on the Lord Jesus Christ" (Acts 16:31, KJV), to disbelieve is to remain unsaved. Unbelief is sin now for the same reason it was the initiating break with God in the Garden: At heart it is a libel on God.

---

16. William M. Greathouse, "Romans," *Beacon Bible Commentary* (Kansas City: Beacon Hill Press of Kansas City, 1968), 8:114; hereinafter BBC.

17. The use of *hamartias,* "sins," in Luke 11:4 does not disprove this possible flexibility, since we have already noted the imprecision of *hamartia.*

d. Apeitheia, "the condition of being unpersuadable, denotes obstinacy, obstinate rejection of the will of God" (Vine). This is clearly thoroughly ethical and culpable, as seen in such passages as Eph. 2:2; 5:6; Rom. 11:30, 32; Heb. 4:6, 11. The fact that the KJV sometimes translates the word "disobedience" and sometimes "unbelief" is understandable, for the condition is not due to a real intellectual difficulty or an inability to believe, but a willful refusal to believe because of an unwillingness to obey.

e. Parakoē, hearing amiss, a refusal to hear. This, too, may be an act of disobedience. In Rom. 5:19 this is the term used to designate the kind of sin of which Adam was guilty—"one man's disobedience" (KJV). Such sin fully deserves punishment (2 Cor. 10:6; also Heb. 2:2).

f. Parabasis, a going over, a definite transgression of law; "the breach of a definite, promulgated, ratified law" (Thayer), as in Rom. 4:15; 1 Tim. 2:14. The word is used only seven times, but very significantly. Whereas *hamartia* could apply to "sins of ignorance," not so with *parabasis,* which is always a known violation of a known law, matching precisely Wesley's definition of sin "properly so-called." *Hamartia* is not imputed *as sin* when full knowledge of the law is lacking, which means that the *hamartia* that prevailed between Adam and Moses was less fully ethical than the *parabasis* of Adam—his deliberate transgression of a known law (Rom. 5:12-14).

g. Anomia, lawlessness, 15 times plus 9 times for *anomos* and *anomōs.* Generally translated "iniquity" (KJV), this word speaks of the wickedness of rebellious man in wanting to overthrow not only law but also the Lawgiver. Speaking of 1 John 3:4, Vine says, "This definition of sin sets forth its essential character as the rejection of the law, or will, of God and the substitution of the will of self." He further says that this will culminate in the appearance of the "lawless one" (2 Thess. 2:8) who will "attempt by the powers of darkness to overthrow the Divine government."[18] When believers tolerate any vestige of the carnal mind, which is "hostile toward God" (Rom. 8:7, NASB), they are to that extent in Satan's camp. If alive when the Antichrist begins to exalt himself, these persons will be startled to find within themselves an unexpected sympathy with him and at least a partial blindness to what is really going on.

---

18. Vine, *Expository Dictionary,* 2:317.

h. Adikia, also translated "iniquity" (six times, KJV) but usually "unrighteousness" (KJV; cf. Luke 16:9; Rom. 1:18; 6:13; 2 Thess. 2:10; Heb. 8:12; 2 Pet. 2:13; 1 John 1:9; et al.). Once Paul uses this term subethically, but ironically, with his tongue in his cheek (2 Cor. 12:13). Apart from this its usage is thoroughly ethical and expresses not only specific wrong acts but also (and normally) a settled commitment to wickedness, a pleasure in sin, which can be nothing less than a fundamental bent of personal character (cf. Rom. 1:29; 2:8; 3:5; 2 Thess. 2:12). The distinction between sins that need to be forgiven and an inner twist of soul that needs to be cleansed is very clear in 1 John 1:9, "If we confess our sins, He is faithful and righteous to forgive us our sins and to cleanse us from all unrighteousness" (NASB).

i. Asebeia, plus verb and adjective forms, 14 times: "ungodliness." Arndt and Gingrich say, "godlessness, impiety in thought and act." This is also a pattern of life and quality of soul. Ungodliness is not primarily what men do but the fundamental mark of their life-style; they not only are without God but also do not miss Him.

Summary

It is apparent that the conception of sin found throughout the Scriptures is virtually the interface of the conception developed from a careful study of the tragic event in the Garden. In other words, a doctrine of sin developed solely from Genesis 1—3 would match essentially a doctrine of sin developed solely from the balance of Scripture. Fundamentally, sin is disobedience to God, which is the free action of a free agent, fully accountable for his decision. But this disobedience contains within itself four moments: *(a)* Preparatory stages within the heart of *unbelief* and *pride; (b)* concomitant guilt, condemnation, and alienation; *(c)* a resulting mind-set of self-sovereignty (or *self-idolatry*)[19] and rebellion; and *(d)* a progressively cumulative inversion of values, moral blindness, enslavement of the will, and general deterioration. Sin as an act has effects that are both relational and subjective. Sin thus be-

---

19. In *Hardness of Heart* (Garden City, N.Y.: Doubleday and Co., 1955), E. La B. Cherbonnier develops the thesis that the essence of sin is idolatry.

comes a matter not only of record but also of character, even of nature. It is to this racial kind of sin that we now turn our attention.[20]

Appendix: Dispositions and Practices Condemned in the New Testament

The following is a list of evils (based on KJV) that the New Testament identifies as sinful. Only one reference, generally, is given for each item, though in many cases the term occurs frequently. No claim is made that this list is flawless or exhaustive. But it does serve to provide a remarkably comprehensive summary of the kind of behavior and interpersonal relationship that is irreconcilable with the Christian life.

1. Adultery, Mark 7:21
2. Anarchy, Rom. 13:1-4
3. Apostasy, Heb. 6:6
4. Backbiting, Rom. 1:30
5. Bitterness, Eph. 4:31
6. Blasphemy (slander against God), James 2:7
7. Blasphemy (slander against men), 2 Tim. 3:2-3
8. Boasting, Rom. 1:30
9. Clamor, Eph. 4:31
10. Covenant breaking, Rom. 1:31
11. Covetousness, Mark 7:22
12. Debate, Rom. 1:29; cf. Phil. 2:14
13. Deceit, Rom. 1:29
14. Despitefulness, Rom. 1:30
15. Disobedience, Col. 3:6
16. Drunkenness, 1 Cor. 6:10
17. Duplicity, 1 Tim. 3:8
18. Effeminacy, 1 Cor. 6:9
19. Emulations, Gal. 5:20
20. Envy, evil eye, Mark 7:22

---

20. For further word studies see Wiley, *Christian Theology,* 2:82; Turner, *The Vision Which Transforms,* 27-32, 99-107; Carl G. Kromminga, "Sin," *Baker's Dictionary of Theology,* 486.

For further study of the doctrine of sin generally, see Purkiser, Taylor, and Taylor, *God, Man, and Salvation,* Chaps. 4; 7; 16—17; Richard S. Taylor, *A Right Conception of Sin;* Donald S. Metz, *Studies in Biblical Holiness* (Kansas City: Beacon Hill Press of Kansas City, 1971), 52-85; *especially* Wiley, vol. 2, chaps. 18—19.

21. Evil concupiscence, Col. 3:5
22. Evil speaking, Eph. 4:31
23. Evil surmisings, 1 Tim. 6:4
24. Evil thoughts, Mark 7:21
25. Extortion, 1 Cor. 6:10
26. Eyeservice, Eph. 6:5-7
27. Fearfulness, Rev. 21:8
28. Fierceness, 2 Tim. 3:3
29. Filial disobedience, Rom. 1:30
30. Foolish talking, Eph. 5:4
31. Fornication, Mark 7:21
32. Gluttony, Titus 1:12 (RSV)
33. God-hating, Rom. 1:30
34. Greediness, Eph. 4:19
35. Hatred, Gal. 5:20
36. Heresy, Gal. 5:20; cf. 1 Tim. 4:1-5
37. Hostility to goodness, 2 Tim. 4:1-5
38. Hypocrisy, 1 Pet. 2:1
39. Idolatry, 1 Cor. 6:9
40. Implacability, Rom. 1:31
41. Indifference to human need, Matt. 25:41-46
42. Inhumanity (no natural affection), Rom. 1:31
43. Insincerity, 2 Pet. 2:1
44. Jesting (ribaldry, vulgarity), Eph. 5:4
45. Judging, Matt. 7:1
46. Lasciviousness, Mark 7:22
47. Lesbianism, Rom. 1:26
48. Love of pleasure, 2 Tim. 3:4
49. Love of the world, James 4:4
50. Lukewarmness, Rev. 3:15-16
51. Lust, Rom. 7:7-8
52. Lying, Rom. 13:9
53. Malice, Rom. 1:29
54. Malignity, Rom. 1:29
55. Murder, Mark 7:21
56. Neglect, Heb. 2:3
57. Partiality and social snobbery, James 2:1-4, 9
58. Perjury, 1 Tim. 1:10
59. Presumption, 2 Pet. 2:10
60. Pride, Rom 1:30; cf. 2 Tim. 3:4

61. Railing, reviling, 1 Cor. 5:11
62. Rebelliousness and insubordination, 2 Pet. 2:10
63. Revelings, Gal. 5:21
64. Secularism, Heb. 12:16
65. Seditions, Gal. 5:20
66. Seduction, 2 Tim. 3:13
67. Self-hardening, Heb. 3:15
68. Selfishness, 2 Tim. 3:2
69. Self-willfulness, 2 Pet. 2:10
70. Sloth, irresponsibility, 2 Thess. 3:11
71. Sodomy, 1 Cor. 6:9
72. Strife, Gal. 5:20
73. Theft, stealing, Mark 7:22
74. Treachery, betrayal, 2 Tim. 3:4
75. Unbelief, Heb. 3:12
76. Unbridled tongue, James 1:26
77. Unclean conversation, Eph. 4:29
78. Uncleanness, Rom. 1:24
79. Unfaithful stewardship, Matt. 25:25-30
80. Unforgiving spirit, Matt. 6:15
81. Unmercifulness, Rom. 1:31
82. Unruliness, 1 Thess. 5:14; cf. disorderliness, 2 Thess. 3:11
83. Vainglory, Phil. 2:3
84. Variance, Gal. 5:20
85. Vengeance, Rom. 12:17, 19
86. Whispering, Rom. 1:29; cf. Phil. 2:14, grumblings, murmurings (NASB)
87. Witchcraft, Gal. 5:20
88. Wrath, Gal. 5:20

4

The Racial Effects
of the Fall

The universality of sin is pivotal to Paul's theology. The presence of sin, not just in every culture but in every *person*, is a linchpin premise of his gospel: "We have already made the charge that Jews and Gentiles alike are all under sin" (Rom. 3:9); since "all have sinned and fall short of the glory of God" (v. 23). But this is not a new doctrine of man; it only echoes the Old Testament Scriptures:

> We all, like sheep, have gone astray,
> each of us has turned to his own way (Isa. 53:6).

The universality of sin, therefore, can hardly be a matter of serious debate. As L. Harold DeWolf says, "When we are fully aware of the whole breadth and subtlety of sin we find it hard to escape the conviction that the Scriptures speak truly to the condition of us all in portraying us as sinners, every one."[1] The problem therefore that remains to be considered is: How is this universality of sin to be explained?

I. Theories of Racial Sin

A. Environmentalism

This is the belief that individual wickedness is the product of an evil environment. The systems and structures of society are

---

1. *A Theology of the Living Church,* 189.

wrong. A moderate sociological expression of this is found in Reinhold Niebuhr's *Moral Man and Immoral Society,*[2] which supposes that society by its very nature is violent, coercive, and immoral, so much so that there is no escape for the individual from guilty involvement. Moreover, the problem is without remedy. "There is an impersonal and brutal character about man's collective behavior which belongs to the order of natural necessity and can never be brought completely under the dominion of reason or conscience."[3]

A psychological form of environmentalism would be typified by Floyd Martinsen, who says, "Human nature as we know it in the actions of men in society is acquired after birth."[4] The root of this view may be in John Locke's idea of tabula rasa—a baby is a blank tablet: "give him planned experiences and he will become anything that the planner desires."[5] Ronald Gray suggests that the "popularity of environmentalism may well be a pragmatic expedient. . . . Man can do something about his environment, but he can do little to affect his heredity."[6]

But as an explanation for the universality of sin, environmentalism leaves much to be desired. It fosters an unrealistic optimism in educational theory. Especially do parents labor under the illusion that if they can only surround the child with the right influences, the production of a good person will be assured. The theory also engenders a naive faith in the potential of social engineering to achieve behavioral modification by controlled conditioning. The problem is, who are to be the social engineers? If they too are sinners, then who will condition *them?* And how can hu-

---

2. New York: Charles Scribner's Sons, 1932.

3. Explanatory comment by William Kimmel and Geoffrey Coine, eds., *Dimensions of Faith* (New York: Twayne Publishers, 1960), 434. Cf. Macquarrie, *Principles of Christian Theology,* 240, who speaks of "individual beings sucked up into the world and carried along with it." See also E. La B. Cherbonnier, *Hardness of Heart,* 136.

4. *Marriage and the American Ideal* (New York: Dodd, Mead, and Co., 1960), 403-4.

5. Ronald F. Gray, "The Psychological Bases of Christian Education," *Exploring Christian Education* (Kansas City: Beacon Hill Press of Kansas City, 1978), 120.

6. Ibid.

"If universality of sin is caused by evil environment. What is Cause of evil environment?

The Racial Effects of the Fall / 71

man personality be manipulated without reducing persons to puppets of the system?[7]

Furthermore, the theory is simplistic, for it implies that to solve the sin problem we need only provide an ideal environment. But it is sin—selfishness, greed, dishonesty, lust, and injustice— 𝒜 that creates the nonideal environment. The environment is the product, not the cause. The theory fails to account for the delinquent child of an ideal home, or the quick decay of new housing provided for the poor. As the realists know, getting people out of the slums does not get the slums out of the people. And society collectively would not need to deprive people of liberties, and use often nonideal methods of coercion, if lawlessness in the populace did not create the necessity of restraining misbehavior by force. Always, therefore, the question remains—if the universality of sin is due to evil environment, what is the cause of the evil environment?

B. Finitism

2B

This is the assumption that man's sin is due to his finitude. Since the spirit in man glimpses possibilities beyond the existent, it naturally seeks escape from the chains of limitations. The disposition of human nature to combat obstacles (implied in the commission to "subdue" the earth [Gen. 1:28, KJV]) becomes the impulse to transcend these limitations and reach for new levels of freedom and power. At the same time the finitude of knowledge and understanding makes self-delusion not only possible but probable, by blinding man to the perils of excessive freedom and improper grasp of power. Inordinate self-assertiveness results. On this reasoning the "fall" is not just Adam's, but every person's, upon reaching the level of personhood where self-assertion becomes the norm.[8]

---

7. The more fruitful forms of psychotherapy have been developed by such persons as Gordon Allport, Kurt Lewin, Hadley Cantril, and Carl Rogers. While these men differ, they have one presupposition in common, that the individual is not the helpless pawn of impersonal forces but is a responsible and choosing reactor. If, therefore, he is sinful, the cause must be found in himself as well as in his environment.

8. This seems to be the basic position of Reinhold Niebuhr in his two-volume work *The Nature and Destiny of Man* (New York: Charles Scribner's Sons, 1949)—that while man's finiteness does not make sin necessary, it nevertheless makes it inevitable.

No Free Will

The answer to such an explanation for sin's universality is to be found in the unlikelihood that God would create a being with a nature that made sin inevitable.[9] Such a nature could hardly be pronounced "good," and any subsequent punishment for simply being natural would be monstrously unjust. To recognize the potentiality of sin in creation is altogether different from viewing creation as in any sense the cause.

There is nothing inherently incompatible between human finiteness and holiness. It was obvious that in dealing with Adam and Eve, God assumed the possibility of obedience to His command, and that such obedience was in no sense an unreasonable expectation. When they fell, God's reaction was judgmental, not exonerative, as would have been expected if they had merely been following out the action inevitable to their nature.

C. Developmentalism   *Perhaps maturity*

This explains sinning by the fact that in an infant the development of the senses has a head start over the development of the reason. As a consequence, when the age of moral accountability is reached, the will is already conditioned to please self. This was the position of Charles G. Finney. He wrote:

> The sensibility acts as a powerful impulse to the will, from the moment of birth, and secures the consent and activity of the will to procure its gratification, before the reason is at all developed. The will is thus committed to the gratification of feeling and appetite, when first the idea of moral obligation is developed.[10]

The consequence of this prior habit pattern is the choice of self-indulgence: "This selfish choice," he says, "is the wicked heart—the propensity to sin—that causes what is generally termed actual transgression."[11]

A more modern variant of developmentalism accents the child's need for freedom as the occasion of the "fall." Before a child can make moral choices, says L. Harold DeWolf, "he must awaken to the possibility of making them; that is, he must discover his

---

9. Or that slandered creation with the Buddhist dictum, "Thine own existence is itself a sin" (from E. La B. Cherbonnier, *Hardness of Heart*, 114).

10. *Finney's Lectures on Systematic Theology* (reprint, Grand Rapids: Wm. B. Eerdmans Publishing Co., 1951), 253.

11. Ibid., 254.

freedom."[12] But this he can discover only by asserting himself; and because his understanding lags far behind the strength of his will, he will assert his rebellion excessively, which is to say, sinfully. In the evolution of sin in "the individual and in societies large and small," says DeWolf, "the mistaking of freedom for unconditioned, absolute autonomy such as no finite creature could have has had an important part."[13] This theory is similar to finitism, except that it explains the process in terms of the child's natural development —from instinctive behavior as a creature of its senses, to semi-moral discovery of the possibilities of freedom, to immoral assertion of self-will.

At base this is as deterministic an explanation for sin as finitism. For in either case a real freedom of choice is ruled out. If the structure of life is so rigged that one *cannot* know enough to lock the barn door until after the horse is out, then how could the loss of the horse be avoided? Where there are predictable consequences from a set of given conditions, and when those conditions are objectively determined for us, obviously there are no real options, and without options freedom is an illusion. Moreover, sin's universality here also could be ascribed to a bungling in creation—which is to say, bluntly, sin is God's fault. For He created a race subject to this kind of procreation and development: infancy preceding childhood, and childhood preceding adulthood. If this system cannot but cause sin in every individual, the system itself must be faulty.

Furthermore, neither environmentalism, finitism, nor developmentalism escape the criticisms made against the doctrine of inherited sinfulness. What is the real difference between the rise of sin in the individual being traced to a proclivity within himself inherited from Adam, and the same sin being traced to some physiological, psychological, or environmental condition? In either case the root of sin is *prevolitional* and therefore *premoral.*

D. Augustinianism

This term refers to that general system of doctrine traceable to Aurelius Augustine (A.D. 354-430), bishop of Hippo in North Africa. Its imprint can be found in Roman Catholicism, Lutheranism,

---

12. *A Theology of the Living Church,* 195.
13. Ibid.

Calvinism, and Arminianism. This influence is especially pronounced in hamartiology.[14] According to virtually all forms of Augustinianism, the sole and sufficient explanation for the universality of sin is the transmission of sinfulness from Adam to his descendants. Not one child has ever come into the world with a moral nature either good or neutral, but with a defective nature. The defect is both negative (a weakness), and positive (a dynamic proneness to evil). This condition is called original sin.

A Lutheran description is: "All men . . . are born with sin; that is, without the fear of God, without trust in Him, and with fleshly appetite."[15] The Anglican statement is:

> Original sin . . . is the fault and corruption of the nature of every man, that naturally is engendered of the offspring of Adam; whereby man is very far gone from original righteousness, and is of his own nature inclined to evil.[16]

When John Wesley abridged the Anglican creed into the Methodist Articles of Religion, 1784, he copied this statement, verbatim, except that he added, "and that continually."

The Five Arminian Articles, 1610, speak of "the fallen, sinful race of men." The Westminster Confession, 1647, specifically declares that from "this original corruption, whereby we are utterly indisposed, disabled, and made opposite to all good, and wholly inclined to all evil, do proceed all actual transgressions."

The following contemporary form is an obvious adaptation of the Anglican/Methodist statements:

> We believe that original sin, or depravity, is that corruption of the nature of all the offspring of Adam by reason of which every one is very far gone from original righteousness or the pure state of our first parents at the time of their creation, is averse to God, is without spiritual life, and inclined to evil, and that continually.[17]

---

14. For fuller discussion of Augustine's teaching see ECH, 2:87-108.

15. Augsburg Confession, A.D. 1530.

16. The Thirty-Nine Articles of the Church of England, 1563 (Latin), 1571 (English), rev. 1801.

17. *Manual, Church of the Nazarene,* 1980. The Free Methodist statement reads: "Original sin standeth not in the following of Adam, as the Pelagians do vainly talk, but it is the corruption of the nature of every man that naturally is engendered of the offspring of Adam, whereby man is very far gone from original righteousness, and of his own nature inclined to evil and that continually." The Wesleyan Church statement is identical.

The philosophical presupposition of all these formulations of an Augustinian doctrine of sin is that back of existence is *esse*, *becoming* is rooted in *being*, and *relationships* not only affect our *state* but also reflect it.

Not that Augustine "invented" the doctrine of original sin. The concept of birth sin or inherited depravity underlay the systems of Origen, Tertullian, Irenaeus, right back to the apostle Paul.[18] But Augustine developed a more thoroughgoing and systematic statement of it. While seeing sin per se as willful disobedience, Augustine saw the consequences of Adam's deliberate sin as a universal bondage of the will, which only the sovereign infusion of converting grace could break. His doctrine did not originate in his controversy with Pelagius, but the debate forced him to hone it into a razor-sharp dogma, refining in the process the more radical implications. There were two.

1. *The Element of Guilt*

The infant was not only depraved but also fully guilty; so truly guilty as to be properly under sentence of eternal punishment. Only baptism could remove this guilt and assure the infant of salvation should it die before the age of personal choice. This curious aspect of the doctrine is explainable on the basis of what is called realism: Because the human race was seminally in Adam, the entire race participated in his sin. Therefore all sinned; Adam's sin was not just his, but literally theirs.

2. *The Totality of Moral Impotence*

The inherited depravity was so complete that no descendant of Adam would have in himself the least vestige of either inclination or ability to turn to God. This natural *inability to do good*, including repenting and believing, and total proclivity to do evil, has been a standard bulwark of any truly Augustinian hamartiology.

The apparent corollary was fully embraced—namely, that salvation could only be the sovereign action of God upon this impotent will, regenerating it "out of the blue," so to speak, thus *creating* both the ability and the inclination to repent, believe, and obey. Since obviously God did not do this universally, the failure to so convert any sinner could only be because God chose not to. So

---

18. Cf. Otto W. Heick, *A History of Christian Thought* (Philadelphia: Fortress Press, 1965), 1:127-28.

we have predestinarianism as an inevitable further corollary. Naturally the logical extension will demand limited atonement and unconditional security of the elect. It is a perfectly logical, watertight system.

Such is the Augustinian concept of sin and grace: grace totally objective and monergistic, as the necessary counterpart of total depravity. Because it is monergistic, it is necessarily _irresistible_. Since the operation is on the will, the miracle consists in inclining the will to submit. A *resistant* will would only prove that the miracle had not been performed. Obviously, therefore, a resistible grace would be a contradiction in terms.[19]

It was against such a one-sided, closed concept of grace that Pelagius reacted. He thought he saw this as the cause of _failure to pursue personal holiness._[20] Many since Pelagius have sensed that those doctrines of sin and grace carried within themselves the seeds of antinomianism.[21]

E. Pelagianism

Pelagianism is the view of human freedom in relation to grace advanced by a British monk in Rome, Pelagius, in the early fifth century. Shocked by the moral laxity among Christians, he thought the cause was in Augustine's one-sided, all-or-nothing doctrine of grace. Personal moral endeavor had come to be understood as a matter of indifference, for in no sense would it have a decisive bearing on one's ultimate salvation. Human depravity was so total that any spasm of moralism would prove grossly inadequate, while the operation of grace on the elect would be so effectual as to accomplish its end infallibly without the sinner's effort. Therefore personal striving was superfluous. The result was the deadening of any sense of moral responsibility.

In a later age, Finney would protest a similar lassitude among

---

19. What Calvinists call "common grace" is quite different. It is the divine restraint on man's wickedness for the common good, even the prompting of some degree of benevolence and virtue. But such grace is not necessarily intended to save but only to preserve the race from utter corruption.

20. Moreover, in all fairness to many liberals who have vigorously repudiated the doctrine of original sin, it must be noted that it was the Augustinian form that they were renouncing, which included transmitted guilt, unrelieved inability, and the arbitrary selectivity and irresistible action of grace.

21. The doctrine that grace frees the believer from any obligation or necessity of keeping the law.

New England Calvinists who made no effort to repent on the grounds that their moral inability was so complete that they were helpless until God in His sovereignty chose to come upon them overwhelmingly.

Pelagius therefore really desired to achieve a revival of true righteousness. He sought to reinvest moral meaning in the concepts of holiness and sin by relating them to personal volition and responsibility. He saw no way to do this but to affirm the ability of every person to choose right or wrong. Such ability implied complete freedom, which was not reconcilable with that doctrine of original sin that implied the loss of such freedom. Therefore he repudiated the doctrine of original sin.

H. W. Johnson explains:

> Spiritual death is not the inherited consequence of Adam's sin, but comes to each individual will which misuses its power of free choice by choosing to sin. All men by virtue of their reason and free will have the power to avoid making this unrighteous choice. If in the exercise of his free and morally responsible will man so chooses he may grasp the external aid of divine grace which is bestowed according to man's merit.[22]

The desire of Pelagius and his followers to rescue religion from a stultified monergism, which destroyed incentive and undercut personal responsibility, was commendable. And actually they only made explicit the view of freedom and accountability that had traditionally prevailed.[23] But they established human responsibility by minimizing both sin and grace. From Augustine's absolute divine monergism they swung to an almost equally one-sided *human* monergism, which turned out to be a kind of moralistic humanism. They wanted a moral religion, but their theories resulted in a severance of the moral man from Christ as an absolutely indispensable Savior. This, of course, was far from authentic Christianity.

As Augustinianism foundered on the rock of practical determinism, so Pelagianism foundered on the rock of an unreal perfectionism. It was unreal because it could not account for the universality of sin. Theoretically an unbiased will, enjoying the equilibrium of native freedom, should choose rightly part of the

Man was essentially good.

---

22. Vergilius Ferm, ed., *An Encyclopedia of Religion* (New York: Philosophical Library, 1945), 569-70.

23. Heick, *History of Christian Thought,* 1:195.

time—even (mathematically) 50 percent of the time. Also, there should be as many examples of good persons, who had consistently chosen virtue, as evil persons. In fact the Pelagians at times asserted that "many heathen and Jews had lived a perfect life."[24]

But according to Heick, Pelagius himself could not maintain this stance but blamed the "apparent universality of sin" to (a) man's "sensual nature which, although entirely innocent in itself, became the occasion for temptation and sinning," *and* to (b) "the attraction of evil examples."[25] Thus we have elements of both *developmentalism* and *environmentalism*. Why evil example is so attractive is unexplained; Pelagius merely calls attention to the powerful and pervasive influence of long-established custom—which only evades the problem by pushing it farther back.

According to Heick,

> Pelagius is compelled to admit the necessity of sinning. This is a very significant admission! The universality of sin is explained by a sinful condition in the human race which defeats the original assertions of the goodness of nature.[26]

But to talk about "a sinful condition in the human race" is virtually to throw in the towel.

Though Pelagianism has consistently been declared heretical by the Church, it has repeatedly reappeared in various forms. Environmentalism, finitism, and developmentalism are all forms of Pelagianism. Many textbooks in religious education have been Pelagianistic in their major premise of the essential goodness of man.[27]

---

24. David Broughton Knox, "Pelagianism," *Baker's Dictionary of Theology*, 400.

25. *History of Christian Thought*, 197-98.

26. Ibid., 198.

27. For a scholarly exception see A. Elwood Sanner and A. F. Harper, eds, *Exploring Christian Education* (Kansas City: Beacon Hill Press of Kansas City, 1978), 105-10, 119-23.

The new face of Pelagianism is the current emphasis on sin and holiness as strictly relational, and the corresponding discounting of sinfulness as a condition of human nature (as fallen) and holiness as a restored state of nature. Behind this school of thought are motifs of both existentialism and process theology (stemming from process philosophy à la Whitehead). In this approach the locus of reality is not *being* but *becoming;* therefore the interest is in *change* rather than *state*, in *growth* more than a specific identifiable *condition*. It has great difficulty trying to accommodate itself to such Wesleyan concepts as inbred sin, the "carnal nature," instantaneous cleansing, and "works of grace."

F. Wesleyan-Arminianism

Both Jacob Arminius and John Wesley were thoroughly Augustinian in the following respects: *(a)* The race is universally depraved as a result of Adam's sin; *(b)* man's capacity to will the good is so debilitated as to require the action of divine grace before he can turn and be saved.[28]

1. Guilt and Prevenient Grace

In respect to inherited guilt, John Wesley was semi-Augustinian. He taught the guilt of infants, but with two very radical and significant differences:

a. The guilt was legal rather than personal. That is, Adam was the legal *representative* (or federal head) of the race. When he fell, the race was implicated, not because they sinned in Adam, but because they shared the legal liability to sin's consequences. The guilt therefore was not a personal culpability but a liability to suffering and rejection. Infants thus were under condemnation, not for anything they had done, but because of what Adam had done, and because their depraved condition made them unfit for heaven and, therefore, unacceptable.

b. But the most radical departure—which proved to be a watershed difference—was in Wesley's contribution to the concept of prevenient grace. This he saw as the total answer to the guilt question. Infants were absolved by prevenient grace, as an unconditional and universal benefit of the Atonement. If all were born in sin, therefore, they were also born under grace, which from the moment of birth becomes a counteracting influence against their inborn evil inclination.

2. An Enabling Influence

Yet prevenient grace is not a certain or *determining* influence, only an *enabling* influence. The impairment of moral ability in the Fall is sufficiently restored to make the exercise of free agency once again possible. In his controversy with Perkins, Arminius affirmed (in the words of Carl Bangs) that "the act of believing is a choice of the free will which has been brought from its addiction to evil to a point of flexibility by grace."[29] The Arminian Articles later plainly affirmed that this grace, while absolutely necessary, and chro-

---

28. See *The Five Arminian Articles,* 1610, Art. III.

29. *Arminius: A Study in the Dutch Reformation* (Nashville: Abingdon Press, 1971), 221.

nologically prior to man's response, is "not irresistible." The grace, therefore, that unmodified Augustinianism saw as all-or-nothing *regeneration,* the Wesleyan-Arminian school sees as awakening and conviction. These are preparatory works of grace and have full salvation as their objective, but they do not constitute regeneration.

In regard to the disease of sin, we may summarize:

Pelagianism does not admit the sickness and therefore sees no need for a radical cure.

Augustinianism affirms the sickness but denies the possibility of a cure in this life.

Wesleyanism (not necessarily Arminianism) affirms the disease and equally affirms a possible cure.

In respect to the doctrine of grace, Pelagius insisted on personal righteousness, freely chosen, but in such a way that in the end grace was merely ancillary. Augustine insisted on the supremacy of grace, but in such a way that in the end righteousness was secondary, even dispensable. They were both right and both wrong. The truth must of necessity lie in a harmonizing key that neither one found. That key is the Wesleyan development of the doctrine of prevenient grace.

II. EVIDENCES OF INBORN SINFULNESS

A. Biblical Evidence

The same Bible that so clearly holds the sinner responsible for his own sinning also teaches an inherited corruption of nature that prompts him to sin. This is paradoxical. Indeed it is a great stumbling block, so much so that many who cannot endure any seeming incoherence strive to deny, or at least minimize, the biblical evidence for this. But just as we found it important to establish the ethical nature of sin per se, so must we just as carefully face up to the fact of inherited sinfulness. Only as we do this will we be able to grasp the full depths and scope of saving grace.

1. *The New Testament*

It has already been pointed out that the Bible's assumption of sin's universality is incontestable. Every person, Jesus taught, needs to be born again, since "that which is born of the flesh is flesh" (John 3:6, KJV). He means that human nature *as is*—as procreated from generation to generation—is spiritually dead. Parents are not procreating new members of the kingdom of God, but members of a fallen race whose inherited condition makes them incapable *(ou dunatai)* of perceiving spiritual realities; therefore the *universal* need for a birth from above. Clearly Jesus is implying not an individually acquired condition, created by individual sinning, but a condition now universally and natally human.

When Paul sought to explain the stubborn pervasiveness of sin, he *(a)* traced man's corruption to Adam as the ultimate cause (Rom. 5:12-19), then *(b)* proceeded to pinpoint the "dwelling-in-me sin" as the immediate cause (7:7-23).

His problem was: What makes me act this way, when as a rational being I disapprove of what I do? In his answer he exonerates the law, since that is "holy, and just, and good" (v. 12, KJV). He also exonerates human nature as created, which was not inherently defective. But this normal human nature has been "sold under sin" and as a result has become "carnal" (v. 14, KJV).

There is now an enemy, an inner abnormality, which can appropriately be called "a law, that, when I would do good, evil is present with me" (v. 21, KJV)—a law not in the sense of a commandment but a principle of action. He *finds* it, he does not create it; therefore he is not responsible for its presence. Moreover, it antedates moral accountability, for he was "alive without the law once" (through prevenient grace, in infancy), but when the commandment came, the inborn perversity was activated ("sin revived," or sprang into life) and he "died," that is, he forfeited the safety of prevenient grace (v. 9, KJV).

Clearly Paul is describing a condition in human nature that is the real cause of sinning and the real explanation for sin's universality. It is not endemic to human nature as created, but now normal to human nature as fallen. It is thus a *natural* proneness to evil that is at the same time *unnatural.* As such, it is *(a)* subvolitional and *(b)* disorganizing and debilitating.

There can be little doubt, moreover, that when Paul reminded the Ephesians that by "nature" they were "children of wrath, even as others" (Eph. 2:3, KJV), he was referring to a universal state in which they were born. Furthermore the "new man, which after God is created in righteousness and true holiness," is the antithesis of the "old man, which is corrupt according to the deceitful lusts," which is to be put off (4:22-24, KJV). This language seems more appropriate for a described transformation of nature than as an intended reference merely to a change in life-style. Also the ascribing by Jesus of all forms of expressed evil to an inner depravity of heart (Mark 7:21-22) strongly suggests a state of heart that is antecedent to the making of conscious moral choices.

2. Old Testament

The New Testament presupposition of universal sinfulness of human nature as fallen simply echoes the Old Testament. It is the heart that is "deceitful above all things, and desperately wicked" (Jer. 17:9, KJV). This is a generic description, not a concession that *some* people are deceitful in heart. And while many have sought to play down the significance of David's self-analysis, it is really quite impossible to miss his thesis, that before his evil *doing* was his evil *being*—"I was shapen in iniquity; and in sin did my mother conceive me" (Ps. 51:5, KJV). Not that he is hiding behind this as an excuse, but rather this humiliating recognition of birth sin is part of his confession. Commenting on this, Purkiser says, "Sinful tendencies and dispositions go back to a racial pollution, part of man's liability as springing from a fallen race."[30] And David not only sees the need for a cleansing deeper than forgiveness, but in faith he dares to ask for it.[31]

Aaron accurately diagnosed the sickness of human nature (including his own!) by reminding Moses of the *proneness* of the Israelites to defect—a proneness so ingrained that 1,400 years of history constituted a perpetual demonstration of it (Exod. 32:22; cf. Deut. 9:6-7, 24, 27; Hos. 11:7). It was the same proneness that prompted the postdiluvians to defy God by building a tower that would outwit any future judgment by flood. Obviously the polluted stream had not been cleansed by Noah, in spite of his own personal rise above his sinful nature to be a righteous man. What was common after the Flood was only more of that which occasioned the Flood—the total depravity described in the indictment, "that every imagination of the thoughts of his heart was only evil continually" (Gen. 6:5, KJV).

If, therefore, *environment* was the explanation before the

---

30. BBC, 3:256.

31. To suppose that David was implying that his mother conceived him out of wedlock is to reach for a farfetched escape; even more so would be to read into his phrasing an indictment of marital intercourse as being in itself sinful: such would not be in harmony with the total Old Testament view of sex matters.

Flood, what was the explanation after the Flood, when Noah and his family went forth to a purged world, beautiful and untainted, without the sight or sound of evil anywhere? No—God understood well; for His promise not to destroy the world again by a flood was His solemn testimony that such a purgation did *not get at the real problem*—"for the imagination of man's heart is evil from his youth" (Gen. 8:21, KJV).

The evil virus goes right on back, all the way to a jealous Cain, who in his rage killed his brother. After describing the horror of two fighting brothers, a correspondent asked, "Is it natural for brothers to fight?" to which the columnist replied, "Look at Cain and Abel." Yet our inner being revolts at the concept of fighting between brothers as being *natural*. Monstrous nature! Every vestige of reason protests the slander, declares the inherent naturalness of brotherly love, and insists that where fighting has become "natural," some terrible calamity has perverted nature.

No, Adam procreated sons and daughters "in his own likeness, after his image" (Gen. 5:3, KJV), and that image was now marred. No infant has ever been born (except Jesus) with a perfectly normal human nature. Every descendant has been adversely affected in his congenital makeup by what Adam was.

But does not the story of Cain and Abel imply that only Cain was sinful? The clear answer to that is in Heb. 11:4, where we read that Abel obtained witness that he was righteous by his "more excellent sacrifice," which he offered "by faith" (KJV). The total biblical frame of reference does not permit uncertainty concerning the implied meaning of this. Abel's righteousness was not self-inherent, it was evangelical justification by grace on the basis of his sacrifice offered in faith. His sacrifice was his confession of need.

B. Empirical Evidence

The underlying premise is that if environmentalism is inadequate as an explanation of sin's pervasiveness, we are compelled to look within man himself—every man—for the cause. J. Glenn Gould cites one of his college professors attempting to account for the chicanery of 19th-century European politics, then adding the significant comment, "The theologian may have dismissed the idea of original sin; but the historian must call it back from limbo in order to understand an otherwise inexplicable situation."[32] But this could be said of any period of history since Adam.

The theological liberal who has an optimistic view of human nature is totally at a loss to explain the moral insanity reflected daily in the newspaper. The perpetual astonishment is the seeming inability of otherwise intelligent people to think rationally about moral issues. Wrong is made to appear right, and right wrong. The degree of exception is determined almost totally by the degree to which people are still conditioned by the Judeo-Christian ethic, which for centuries impregnated the thinking of Western civilization.

John Henry Newman eloquently describes the inevitable distress and mystification of one who begins with the premise of God, then looks at the world. "The world seems simply to give the lie to that great truth of which my whole being is so full," he says. He then draws an analogy from a boy with promise and refinement who as a man is alienated. He says:

> I should conclude that there was some mystery connected with his history, and that he was one of whom, for one cause or another, his parents were ashamed. Thus only should I be able to account for the contrast between the promise and the condition of his being. And so I argue about the world; *if* there be a God, since there is a God, the human race is implicated in some terrible aboriginal calamity. It is out of joint with the purposes of its Creator. This is a fact, a fact as true as the fact of its existence; and thus the doctrine of what is theologically called original sin becomes to me almost as certain as that the world exists, and as the existence of God.[33]

There are several aspects of the empirical evidence.

1. *The Irrational Aversion to God*

The creed says that man by nature is averse to God; Paul says the carnal mind is "enmity against God" (Rom. 8:7, KJV; "hostile," RSV, NIV, NASB). These words precisely describe what is everywhere observable. It is seen in the avidness with which men embrace materialistic science. Chance, says Tournier, "is the last word of any scientific explanation of the world. 'The classical theory of science,' writes Lecomte de Nouy, 'simply replaces God with

---

32. *The Whole Counsel of God* (Kansas City: Beacon Hill Press, 1945), 39.
33. *Apologia Pro Vita Sua*, 241-43; quoted by Olin Alfred Curtis, *The Christian Faith* (Grand Rapids: Kregel Publications, 1956), 190.

chance'"[34]—the desperate, irrational expedient of men who do not "like to retain God in their knowledge" (Rom. 1:28, KJV). We see it further in the emotional fever of the anti-God professor. Sören Kierkegaard even perceived this spontaneous hostility in the readiness of scholars to accept destructive higher criticism.[35] David A. Redding expounds his meaning:

> "The Bible is a mirror," he says, but instead of assisting us to see ourselves in it more clearly than ever, criticism tends to distract us. We exhaust our energy and interest, dating the mirror, measuring it, counting bubbles and cracks. . . . We do everything to the Bible but look in it and shout, "Hallelujah, it is He!"[36]

The telltale evidence is our willingness to be distracted. We seize anti-God "proofs" eagerly and face up to theistic proofs reluctantly. We find in ourselves a readiness to blame God, to accuse Him of inaction or injustice, to erect walls of bitterness that keep God out. The fact that the Holy Spirit at the same time is drawing us, creating a hunger, only proves the point. The Holy Spirit is pulling against an inner drag. If by nature we were pro-God, why would there be a struggle, and why would the "Hound of Heaven" have to pursue through so many years? There is in every human heart a self-recognition in Francis Thompson's lines:

> *I fled Him, down the nights and down the days;*
> *I fled Him down the arches of the years;*
> *I fled Him down the labyrinthine ways*
> *Of my own mind; and in the midst of tears*
> *I hid from Him, and under running laughter.*[37]

This always latent and often overt aversion to God, alongside the ever-present hunger, is too deep to be blamed on external influences; it is a veritable state of the *self.* Fortunately some yield to Christ in childhood, and the chase is not literally a tragedy of years; yet even they remember their postconversion struggles with latent hostility still lingering in their hearts, always poised to spring in fresh rebellion—until finally cleansed by the Holy Spirit.

---

34. *A Whole Person in a Broken World* (New York: Harper and Row, Publishers, 1964), 33.

35. *For Self Examination* (London: Geoffrey Cumberlege, Oxford University Press, 1946), 50-58.

36. "Neurosis of Defiance," *Christianity Today,* Jan. 15, 1965.

37. James Dalton Morrison, ed., *Masterpieces of Religious Verse* (New York: Harper and Brothers, Publishers, 1948), 57.

② Moral Impotence

Karl Menninger shares, he says, the bewilderment of Socrates, who wondered how it is that "men know what is good, but do what is bad."[38] The fact is acknowledged by Paul: "For the good that I would I do not: but the evil which I would not, that I do" (Rom. 7:19, KJV). That's my case, says the human race. There "is a profound sense," says Olin Curtis, "in which a man is, as he comes into the world, totally depraved." He explains this depravity as man's complete inability to "organize his life under the demand of conscience."[39] Through education, self-discipline, and training he may achieve a certain moral character, which leaves untouched the inner impotence. He adds:

> The greater his development in moral personality the greater the impossibility of that adjustment which secures wholeness and peace in manhood. It is this inorganic condition of a man's fundamental, individual being which I understand to be depravity. Every man comes inorganic into the world.[40]

This is the only explanation of that strange moral lag that students of developmental psychology have observed. Speaking of the extensive research by Hartshorne in the '20s, and May in the '30s, Gary Collins says, "The results of this careful study were startling. As children grow older their knowledge of right and wrong increases, it was found, but so does their tendency to be deceptive. Indeed there was no correlation between knowledge of right and wrong and moral behavior."[41] This phenomenon is explainable only on the basis of a moral nature that lags behind intellectual growth because of a diseased condition that inhibits normal growth.[42]

---

38. *Whatever Became of Sin?* 230.
39. *Christian Faith,* 200.
40. Ibid.
41. *Man in Transition* (Carol Stream, Ill.: Creation House, 1971), 62.
42. Arnold Toynbee calls this the "morality gap," which, he says, "has always been." It is the gap between man's "giftedness for science" and his apparent inability to apply the same intelligence to moral issues. The cause of the gap, he says, is "human egocentricity," and he claims that all religions "have been concerned, first and foremost, with the overcoming of egocentricity." From *Surviving the Future* (London: Oxford University Press, 1971), quoted by Menninger in *Whatever Became of Sin?* 227.

The obverse of moral impotence is the observable *positive affinity* with evil. The modern advertising and entertainment industries are aware of this and exploit it to the hilt. "So our screens," says Max Rafferty, "whether in the movie houses or in your family room, are glowing with putrescence and reeking with filth" (syndicated column, *Los Angeles Times Service,* Nov. 12, 1980). This is what rakes in the profits.

3. The Result of Being "Natural"

If man's moral nature were perfectly normal, the child would naturally develop into an adulthood marked by maturity and integrity. On the contrary, if such development is to occur, it will only be achieved by multiple and continuous restraints of nature, applied both internally and externally. Modern psychologists recognize anger and the tendencies of willfulness and rebellion even in preaccountable infants. It is this proneness, obviously inborn, which produces the tantrums at two and the kicking and slapping at three.

A feeble attempt is made to label such behavior as "natural," as if it were a necessary stage in a child's maturation. But if so, then the process should not be blocked by any interference whatsoever. Logically, if the process were left to itself, the development would result in a healthy, balanced, altruistic, and socially oriented personality. Yet the whole world knows this does not happen; maturity occurs only when all along the way, from early childhood on, there has been consistent restraint, and *training* toward patterns of behavior that are not "natural" but must be learned.

The ease of evil and difficulty of goodness is universally recognized in all socieities and religions. "Man is the only being coming within our knowledge who has a nature that is plainly unnatural," writes William Arthur.[43] "There is not a beast of the field but may trust his nature and follow it, . . . but as for us, our only invincible enemy is our nature: were it sound, we could hold circumstances as lightly as Samson's withs; but it is evermore betraying us."[44] There is both irony and truth in his reminder that men do not seek help to do wrong, for this is easy and "natural"; but they intuitively sense the need for special help when they resolve to do right. And in rearing children we have to teach truthfulness, not lying; purity, not impurity; industry, not indolence; self-control, not rage. This would not be true if nature were not out of joint with right itself.

On this rock of man's perverted "naturalness" breaks the logic of humanism. Humanism glories in the natural and with sanguine optimism supposes that "doing what comes naturally" is a trustworthy philosophy of life. So nudity is espoused, for nudity is natural; clothes are artificial. The impulse to cohabit is natural,

---

43. *Tongue of Fire* (London: Epworth Press, J. Alfred Sharp, n.d.), 115.
44. Ibid., 115.

therefore should be followed. Repressions, the humanist claims, are not only inhibiting but destructive.

But to the extent that men follow this brand of humanism, chaos and confusion result. The premise is wrong. Humanism supposes that nature determines the norm and therefore can be safely followed. It does not take into account that since the Fall nothing is quite natural. Fallen nature is twisted, therefore it debases and distorts what might otherwise be innocent. If the human heart were as Adam's and Eve's before the Fall, nudity would indeed be safe, but in the presence of the sinful heart it is not. Because of sin all sorts of regulative barriers and inhibitions must be fostered to preserve any semblance of civilization.

4. The Tendency to Degenerate

"How long have you been in the family, Parker?" asked a visitor of an elderly butler.

"For three degenerations, sir."

And so it generally is. Improved material circumstances do not normally result in improved moral character; generally the opposite is true. Only much discipline, prayer, and watchfulness will counteract this tendency. Said a young man, "Religion for my grandfather was a way of life; for my father it was a tradition; for me it is a nuisance." Nowhere is the law of entropy more observable than in the religious life of society. Why are periodical revivals necessary? Only because of the inherent tendency to decay.

How easy it is to gravitate to the risqué, the avant-garde "new morality," the permissive life-style, the popular vices, the experimentation with drugs and sex. This cannot just be passed off as the normal desire to test for oneself; it is a perversion of this normal impulse. It is a recapitulation of the rebellion in the Garden, arising not now from the serpent without but from the serpent within.[45] Moreover, it is an inward affinity, deep down, with the world, not in its elevation but in its deterioration.

Sad is the phenomenon of the eroded ideal. Through prevenient grace young people often enter adulthood with fine dreams of altruistic service—dreams that gradually fade before the leeching grasp of reality. They do not plan to drift into callous greed and bitter cynicism, with the steady atrophy of the service motive; but apart from religious influences this is the prevailing

---

45. A recapitulation broken only by the Second Adam in His temptation.

one-way street of maturing years. Rare is the nonbeliever at 50 who is more than the shadow of his ideals at 20.

The problem is, as men soon discover, there are within themselves moral weaknesses and basic tendencies that they had little suspected but that grow stronger and more imperious with the years. Instead of these tendencies being mastered, they master. The decay of motivation, so universally observed, can be explained only by postulating original sin.[46]

In summary, it seems impossible to observe the moral wretchedness of the human race, then look honestly into one's own heart and back into one's earliest childhood, without the overwhelming conviction that the source of moral evil is within. "We, the people, are the environmental problem," said a sign on a California campus on Earth Day several years ago. And so we are. And the problem is natal.

III. THE NATURE OF INBORN SIN

The following are representative ways of defining original sin: "a positive bias of human nature toward evil";[47] "an inherent positive disposition toward sin";[48] "a positive evil . . . which arises as a consequence of the loss of the image of God";[49] "the total depravity of man, which means that although he is not altogether bad, every part of his nature became tainted by sin";[50] "a quality, predisposition, bias, twist, or state of the human personality from which rise all actual transgressions and all unchristian attitudes such as pride, selfishness, self-will, and enmity against God."[51]

46. Nowhere is this downward push of the human soul more perfidious than in the tendency to destroy the holy. The Grand Inquisitor reproaches Christ for not understanding that men will sell their souls for bread. This will be the secret of the Antichrist: "But dost Thou know that for the sake of that earthly bread the spirit of the earth will rise up against Thee and will strive with Thee and overcome Thee, and all will follow him crying, 'Who can compare with this beast? He has given us fire from heaven'" (Fyodor Dostoyevski, *The Brothers Karamazov*, trans. Constance Garnett [New York: Modern Library, Random House, n.d.], 262).

47. W. T. Purkiser, ed., *Exploring Our Christian Faith* (Kansas City: Beacon Hill Press, 1960), 238.

48. L. Berkhof, *Systematic Theology* (London: Banner of Truth Trust, 1941; reprint, 1963), 246.

49. Wiley, *Christian Theology*, 2:124.

50. Herbert Lockyer, *All the Doctrines of the Bible* (Grand Rapids: Zondervan Publishing House, 1964), 145.

51. Metz, *Studies in Biblical Holiness*, 85.

A. Terminology

It has already been noted that *asebeia*, ungodliness; *anomia*, lawlessness; and *adikia*, unrighteousness, refer not only to outward conduct but also to inward orientation. Also, as was pointed out in the previous chapter, *hamartia* is often used in reference to the sin principle, especially by Paul in Romans 5—7. Other biblical terms are graphic: "filthiness" (Ezek. 36:25; cf. 2 Cor. 7:1); "stony heart" (Ezek. 36:26); the "old man" (Rom. 6:6; Eph. 4:22; Col. 3:9);[52] "the body of sin" (Rom. 6:6); "sin that dwelleth in me" (7:17); "the body of this death" (v. 24); "the law of sin and death" (8:2); "the carnal mind" (v. 7); "the flesh" (vv. 8-9, 12-13; Gal. 5:17); "the sin which doth so easily beset us" (Heb. 12:1); "superfluity of naughtiness" (James 1:21); "ye double minded" (4:8, all KJV).[53]

B. Depravity from Deprivation

Original sin should not be thought of as a penal reorganizing of man's nature toward evil, but the inevitable decay of moral nature as the consequence of having lost the Holy Spirit, and through that loss, the moral image of God—or original holiness. When man ceased to be God-centered it was inevitable that he should be self-centered; but self-centeredness is an eccentricity, for the self was created for God as its true center. A circle that is off center is eccentric; when this is a cog in intricate machinery, the eccentricity creates a distortion in the whole system.

By nature man is an active, dynamic being. Activity not centered in God becomes centered in some non-God, which perverts and disorients the whole of the personality. Therefore depravity is more than deprivation and more than a weakness; it becomes, by the very nature of human personality, a positive derangement in the wheels of life. Connected with the deprivation, says Wiley, "is a positive evil also, which arises as a consequence of the loss of the image of God." He then quotes Watson's description of this state or condition as "the loss of spiritual life, followed by estrangement

---

52. Admittedly the import of these passages is sometimes debated. But of Rom. 6:6 Wesley says, "Coeval with our being, and as old as the fall" (*Explanatory Notes upon the New Testament* [1754; reprint, Naperville, Ill.: Alec R. Allenson, 1958]). J. Kenneth Grider interprets "old man" as the *old life* (*Entire Sanctification: The Distinctive Doctrine of Wesleyanism* [Kansas City: Beacon Hill Press of Kansas City, 1980], 131-32).

53. These are KJV terms; other translations vary.

from God, moral inability, the dominion of irregular passions, and the rule of appetite; aversion, in consequence, to restraint; and enmity to God."[54]

And while prevenient grace is operative toward the newborn infant, its action *in* him is not yet either regeneration or sanctification; therefore the eccentricity prevails, even though in incipient and latent forms.

C. Inability and Free Agency

In speaking of fallen nature as being a condition of "moral inability," Watson touches the nerve of an apparent paradox. How can we reconcile "moral inability" with the postulate of free agency? Free agency implies that man by divine design and gift is an autonomous moral agent, free to choose between moral alternatives, without being subject to external coercion. Sin has not abridged nor altered the fact of free agency but has impaired man's moral power to exercise his freedom in behalf of right. His inclinations are so pervasively evil that in perfect freedom he chooses the wrong. Even when aroused by prevenient grace to desire the right, he is unable in his own strength to sustain his resolution—"how to perform that which is good I find not" (Rom. 7:18, KJV). But this results from a vitiated moral nature, not from an abridgment or cancellation of free agency per se.

D. The Question of Guilt

Arminians generally tend to repudiate out of hand the idea of guilt being attached to original sin. What is not often understood is that such a stance is not strictly Wesleyan. The problem arises in seeking to account for the infliction of death *upon all* as a penalty for sin (including the infant's liability to death) if the *all* are in no sense implicated in the sin. As we have already seen, Wesley's solution was in the legal bond of Adam, as the representative, with the race he represented, just as an action of the head of a family or the president of a country may carry inescapably the entire corpus with it. When a husband defended his plunging into deeper and deeper debt via charge accounts by saying to his wife, "This is my problem, not yours," she quietly asked, "If you should die, would I be liable for those debts?" He dropped his head and said, "Yes."

---

54. *Christian Theology,* 2:124.

There is a certain legal solidarity in human relations that must ever be taken into account.

There is then a sharing of legal responsibility that involves suffering and the consequences of sin. However, it could be questioned if "guilt" is the right word for this. By definition the word denotes responsibility for an evil act. In courts of law, to "plead guilty" is to say, "I did it." Yet we have to make room for what Wesley and others have meant by their accommodated use of the term. They meant a *liability*, not strictly to punishment, but (a) to the suffering that properly belongs to another's sin, and (b) to the suffering of rejection because of condition.[55]

Wiley says, "The two ideas of responsibility for the act and liability for the consequences are not inseparable."[56] It is apparent, therefore, that the infant, too, needs a Savior, both for justification and for sanctification. Authentic Wesleyan-Arminianism does not say that infants who die are saved because they are innocent, but because they are covered by the blood of Christ through prevenient grace—which is quite different.

E. Moral and Amoral Depravity

 The core of original sin as a moral condition is an inherited bent to self-idolatry, tending to manifest itself in unbelief, pride, and rebelliousness. But since the Fall was so total, man's entire nature is affected adversely. The body "fell" too and became prey to consequences of the sins of the spirit. The mind is clouded, the will is weakened, appetites are deranged and ill-balanced.

1. *Definition—Restricted or Expanded?*

Some holiness scholars would differentiate between original sin per se and the outer layer of scars and effects that in themselves may be said to be morally neutral. "Original sin," says Richard E. Howard, "is a corruption of the inner man—man's heart." The depraved "outer man"—irregular "desires, passions, appetites, propensities" belong not to original sin itself but are consequences of original sin.[57] The advantage to this position is its clean-cut dis-

---

55. Like a defective part that is rejected because it cannot be fitted into its proper place.

56. *Christian Theology,* 2:126.

57. *Newness of Life* (Kansas City: Beacon Hill Press of Kansas City, 1975), 42; cf. Grider, *Entire Sanctification,* 110-13.

tinction between sin and infirmity, and the assignment, without confusion, of sin to the solution of entire sanctification, and of the remaining infirmity to the correction of growth in grace.

On the other hand, William Burt Pope defined original sin broadly, as an *individual* depravity that is eradicable, and as a *generic* condition that plagues even the sanctified.[58] With this Wiley would seem to agree. "We have seen," he says, "that the 'flesh' as St. Paul uses the term, includes both the spiritual and physical nature as under the reign of sin. The corruption extends to the body as well as the soul."[59] Yet he implies a clear moral distinction between the two forms of "fallenness":

> The depravity of his spiritual nature may be removed by the baptism with the Holy Spirit, but the infirmities of the flesh will be removed only in the resurrection and glorification of the body. Man in a general way has no difficulty in distinguishing between the soul and the body, but the fine line of demarcation, the exact arresting point between the spiritual and the physical, cannot be determined. Could we but know where this line of distinction lies, we could with ease distinguish between carnal manifestations which have their seat wholly in the soul, and physical infirmities which attach to his physical constitution still under the reign of sin. . . . Since mental strain often weakens the physical constitution, and physical weakness in turn clouds the mind and spirit of man, there is ever needful, a spirit of charity toward all men.[60]

In practical terms this suggests that an entirely sanctified person, cleansed of moral depravity of spirit, may yet be afflicted with abnormal appetites and tendencies, acquired or inherited, of which he may not be aware.[61]

If, therefore, the term *original sin* is to be stretched to include man's total ab- or sub-normalities, then we must distinguish between an inner spiritual core that is eradicable and an "outer layer" that is ineradicable but will only yield to the spiritual disciplines of growth in grace. Rather than so extending the term *original sin,* it would seem more consistent to differentiate it from the amoral scars of sin. Yet this must be done with great care, lest a Wesleyan

---

58. See ECH, 2:255-67.

59. *Christian Theology,* 2:140.

60. Ibid.

61. Are there, for example, no sanctified persons who habitually overeat who have not yet been made sharply conscious of the matter as a *stewardship* and therefore a moral issue?

brand of excused carnality be tolerated—even a dangerous affirmation of "freedom" that borders perilously close to libertarianism. For what may in itself properly be called amoral has explosive moral potential. Its rigorous discipline and mastery will be the acid test of any truly authentic sanctification.

2. *Concupiscence—Essence or By-product?*

That branch of the Christian church that has traditionally linked original sin too closely to the body, and hence is outraged by the very idea of "eradication," is discussed in volume 2. The emphasis is traceable primarily to Augustine, who first saw sin as pride, then expanded his conception of sin to include—even to stress—concupiscence, by which he meant the abnormality of the sex drive. This he saw as the one universal mark of a sinful race, containing within itself the seeds of all other vices.[62] It was almost inevitable that this should be the focal point of his attention, since it was the focal point of his struggling. A more biblical and wholesome view of both sex and marriage on his own part, lived out in a proper marriage, might have redressed the balance and saved him from excessive preoccupation.

There can be no doubt that sex becomes sinful *(a)* when it is made central in any person's life; *(b)* when it is uncontrolled and intemperate (even within marriage); *(c)* when it is indulged contrary to the biblical mandates and restrictions. Neither is there any doubt that it represents a weakness of fallen man so pervasive and powerful as to be the subject of more divine attention, judgment, and rebuke than almost any other form of sin. Furthermore, it is undeniable that the Genesis account implies a connection between excessive sex awareness and the Fall:

> The man and his wife were both naked, and they felt no shame *(Gen. 2:25).*
>
> Then the eyes of both of them were opened, and they realized they were naked; so they sewed fig leaves together and made coverings for themselves *(3:7).*
>
> The LORD God made garments of skin for Adam and his wife and clothed them *(3:21).*

Obviously, therefore, while in one breath we can insist that sex per se is not sinful but holy, because created by God as a gift of love for husband and wife and as a means of procreation, in virtually the same breath we must make a qualification: Sex since the

---

62. See ECH, 2:93-95, 207-8.

Fall has never been truly natural. There has been in the human body and in the human psyche a proneness to sex interest and excitability that exceeds what would have been the case if the Fall had not occurred. As a consequence both God and man have had to hedge the sex impulse in with numerous restrictions, involving clothes, public decency, marriage and divorce, laws relating to consanguinity and incest, and so forth, as a sheer necessity for the preservation of society and the prevention of total debauchery.

This situation pertains to man's sinfulness; of this there can be no doubt. The question is, is this weakness (which, of course, some feel more than others) the essence of original sin or a by-product of the Fall? If it is the essence, then obviously complete escape must await our deliverance from this body, for even those who claim an experience of entire sanctification find themselves at times beset by temptations of a sexual nature. The holiness movement learned early (after some moral tragedies due to presumption) that sanctification does not desexualize either man or woman. And in the light of this it is easy to understand the proneness of non-Wesleyans to identify too closely the sin principle with physical appetite.

The total biblical account would tend to support not Augustinianism, but Wesleyanism, which sees sin not as primarily a bodily matter but a corruption of soul, with the body as the occasion for temptation and a potential instrument of sin. When Paul said, "It is better to marry than to burn" (with sexual desire) (1 Cor. 7:9, KJV), and when he urged married couples to be fair with each other "that Satan tempt you not for your incontinency" (v. 5, KJV)—that is, lest they be subjected to excessive temptation—he was not implying that their sexuality was inherently sinful. And while the Corinthians were to perfect holiness (moral purity) by self-cleansing "from all filthiness of the flesh and spirit" (2 Cor. 7:1, KJV), celibacy was not held up as holier than marriage,[63] or a religious experience promised that would make them immune to the danger of falling.

The wiser conclusion, therefore, is to see that one of the scars coinherited with original sin per se is an appetitive organism, which has in it abnormalities that to some extent may plague the child, the youth, and the adult. These are controllable by grace but

---

63. 1 Cor. 7:32-36 must not only be interpreted in context, but in the light of 9:5; Eph. 5:22-33; Col. 3:18-21; 1 Tim. 4:3; 5:14; Heb. 13:4; et al.

not usually purged by grace. We must be careful, therefore, to define carnality as the Bible does, as a spiritual condition rather than as the appetitive nature itself. Spiritual Christians who are not "carnal" may yet be tempted within the context of their humanity.

F. The Genetic Problem

While the realistic and representative theories of the transmission of sin relate to the question of *guilt*, the genetic theory pertains solely to the inborn depravity itself. Conceivably one could have a belief in the transmission of guilt, yet be Pelagian in one's concept of birth nature. But equally, one may be a geneticist respecting the sin tendency itself and at the same time hold to the realistic or representative mode respecting guilt, *or neither.*

The major creeds assume geneticism. The Westminster Confession speaks of "corrupted nature" being conveyed to Adam's posterity "by natural generation." Wiley says, "So, also, Arminianism has made much of this genetic law in its explanation of native depravity."[64] He further explains, "Hereditary depravity, then, is only the law of natural heredity, but that law operating under the penal consequences of Adam's sin."[65] The common wording of the creed implies geneticism in the expression "the corruption of the nature of all the offspring of Adam."

1. Alternatives to Geneticism

Naturally geneticism implies traducianism, that is, the position that the soul (including the spirit) is procreated with the body. The alternatives are:

a. Preexistence. This view, held by Origen and more recently by Julius Muller, supposes that the body only as a biological organism is procreated and that at birth it becomes incarnated with a preexistent spirit, which in becoming fused with the animal life constitutes a human person. Thus, the sinfulness of this spirit can be explained only by a preincarnate fall, or else by its association with a sinful body. This position is essentially Gnostic.

b. Creationism. This view is similar to the above respecting the limitation of procreation to the biological. But it assumes that God incarnates the fetus (at what point is uncertain) with a spirit especially created for this particular body. In this case any inherited

---

64. *Christian Theology,* 2:118.
65. Ibid., 125

sinfulness would be wholly physical and the locus of sin would indeed be the body; *unless* we supposed that God in penal response to Adam's sin created each spirit with a sinful bias. Such a theory would not take seriously the moral impossibility of a holy God creating a sinful personal spirit. If the other horn of the dilemma is adopted—that sin is in the body—we again have the basis of a revived Gnosticism.

c. *Epiphenomenalism.* This is the position of naturalistic psychology, which denies the soul altogether, excepting as the self-consciousness that develops out of the biological organism and is totally dependent on it. But in this case man is merely animal, and death terminates existence. But if the soul is an illusion, so also is the "problem" of sin.[66]

2. *Not Unscientific*

To suppose that geneticism implies a substantive sin in the sense of lumpishness or measurable materiality is to draw inferences not necessarily present. To begin with, the modern knowledge of chromosomes, genes, and DNA confirms, more than disproves, the direct connection of every person with Adam. For the numerical characteristics and arrangements of chromosomes are unique to the human species, implying a continuity back to an aboriginal pair. Moreover, in each newly fertilized egg is the complete blueprint for the person that will unfold. This blueprint includes not only measurable traits, such as hair and eye color, but nonmeasurable, such as aptitudes and tendencies of a psychic nature. "The law of like producing like does not refer exclusively to the biological features of man's existence, but also embraces psychological qualities."[67] If the cluster of mental traits that will gradually develop in the child is in the cell, the presence of that mysterious entity, the soul, becomes a reasonable hypothesis.

---

66. For a contemporary scientific analysis of brain functioning in relation to the self, see *Brains, Machines, and Persons,* by Donald M. MacKay, research prof. of Communication and Neuroscience, University of Keele (London: William Collins and Co., 1980; and Grand Rapids: Wm. B. Eerdmans Publishing Co., 1980). While for every conscious experience or decision, "there is some correlate in the physical activity of our brains," MacKay says, he hastens to add, "Notice that we are not here saying, as some 'materialists' would, that my conscious experience is just an 'epiphenomenon' of the workings of my brain, as if my physical brain were the solid reality, and my experience just a ghostly or imaginary appendage" (82-83). See pp. 190-91.

67. *Exploring Our Christian Faith,* 239.

Out of the fertilized egg, therefore, will develop dispositions and capacities of a spiritual nature, including affection, conscience, and decision making. The blueprint is not fatalistic in the spiritual facets or levels of being, for while the chromosomes unavoidably determine some traits, they do not determine how the growing person will use these traits. The chromosomes may include an aptitude for music but will not determine that the individual will become a musician. For the potential for freedom is part of the original organism. The inherited functioning, which in time will become decision making, may develop into altruism or may develop into selfishness and brutality.

The doctrine of original sin simply says that since the Fall, the blueprint has in itself a racial defect that constitutes a negative effect on the psychic organization, creating an *abnormal* tendency for the psyche to develop inordinately around self. The science of genetics clearly recognizes the possibility of mutations creating transmissible degenerative traits. There is no logical reason, therefore, why the inheriting of a primitive psychic detriment leading to undesirable tendencies should be unthinkable.

G. A Subethical Sin

This strange, racial defect, spiritual in nature, yet transmitted by physical conception through biological carriers, can be called "sin" only in a very carefully qualified sense. It is the counterpart of original holiness, which as a spontaneous bent would presumably have been transmitted to the offspring of Adam and Eve had they not sinned. But as that would have been subethical in each infant, so must inbred sin be seen as subethical. By subethical is meant that the condition, either of original holiness or inbred sin, is not the product of conscious and volitional moral processes.[68] The state of a newborn infant—to say nothing of the embryo and the fetus—can hardly be called *ethically* unclean without violating our moral sense.

Yet the Church has frowned on semi-Pelagianism, which confessed the depravity of nature, in the sense of weakness, but denied that it was sin. Wiley asks, "If inherited depravity is not of the essence of sin, how can we understand such texts as the *Lamb of*

---

68. See pp. 37-39.

God, which taketh away the sin of the world? . . . To weaken our position on sin is to weaken it on holiness also."[69]

In what sense, then, can this inherited "inorganic" (Curtis) condition be called sin? Karl Rahner says it has "in an analogous sense the character of sin" because, at the very heart, it "is a state which ought not to be."[70] Furthermore, he reminds us that since the child comes into the world without that holiness God had designed for man, its condition is therefore unholy. But to say *unholy* is to say, in some sense, *sinful.*

To this we may add: This condition *(a)* is an aberration which if allowed to take its natural course will become antagonism toward God, and therefore *(b)* constitutes a subconscious but powerful proneness to the making of wrong decisions when the child begins to be confronted with moral options. Inbred sin is therefore "ethical insofar as its tendencies and manifestations are intrinsically wrong. But because it is not fully ethical, we may speak of it as semi-ethical or sub-ethical; possibly, in view of this, the term 'sinfulness' might be more appropriate than 'sin.'"[71]

H. The Substantive Versus Relational Question

A relational approach sees sin as a violation of relationships, and sinfulness as alienation. It stresses the volitional side of sin. A substantive approach sees sin not only in its relational and volitional aspects, but insists that back of these is a subvolitional bent of nature. It sees sin as a willful act but sees also a state or condition in the person constituting an abnormal proneness to such sinful acts, as depicted so graphically in Romans 7.

To pit the relational against the substantive, as if a theologian had to be one or the other, is foolish, futile, and even heretical. It is heretical because a denial of an inherited sinful bent, not the product of one's own choices but the product of the Fall, is Pelagianism, pure and simple, and needs to be labeled as such. And furthermore, it is certainly not Wesleyan. Authentic, normative Wesleyanism has always insisted that there was in fallen human nature a real predispositional and subvolitional sinfulness that needed a

---

69. *Christian Theology,* 2:121.

70. *Encyclopedia of Theology* (New York: Seabury Press, 1975), 1152.

71. Merne A. Harris and Richard S. Taylor, "The Dual Nature of Sin," *The Word and the Doctrine* (Kansas City: Beacon Hill Press of Kansas City, 1965), 112.

real cleansing. This cornerstone of Wesleyanism must not be suppressed or compromised.[72]

For professed Wesleyans to line up on one side or the other and say, "I'm a relationalist, but he's a substantivist," smacks more of superficiality than of theological sophistication. The relational and substantive aspects of sin are complementary, not contradictory. Relationships can be set right by repentance, forgiveness, and acceptance; but right relationships can be maintained with some degree of happy consistency only if the human relater is healed at heart.[73] If he is not cleansed from his basic selfishness and willfulness, disrupted relationships will tend to recur repeatedly.[74]

I. Inbred Sin and the Will

Similar to the substantive versus relational question is the question of the comparative weight to be placed on sinful nature versus the will.

While it is customary to speak of the will as the mainspring of both character and destiny (e.g., "The Battle for the Will," p. 137), this way of speaking can be dangerously misleading. The language implies a personification of the will, as if we were talking about some sort of independent agency or entity. There is no such entity.

---

72. Wesley's classic statement of the doctrine of original sin clearly shows the inner connection between its relational and "substantive" aspects: "Man was created looking directly to God, as his last end; but, falling into sin, he fell off from God, and turned into himself. Now, this infers [sic] a total apostasy and universal corruption in man; for where the last end is changed, there can be no real goodness. And this is the case of all men in their natural state: They seek not God, but themselves. Hence though many fair shreds of morality are among them, yet 'there is none that doeth good, no, not one.' For though some of them 'run well,' they are still off the way; they never aim at the right mark. Whithersoever they move, they cannot move beyond the circle of self. They seek themselves, they act for themselves; their natural, civil, and religious actions, from whatever spring they come, do all run into, and meet in, this dead sea" (*Works*, 9:456).

73. In the thought of Jesus *being* underlies *acting*, and flows out of it—Matt. 7:16-18; cf. 12:33-35.

74. Certainly the sin in human nature is not substance in the philosophical sense of independent being; this would be metaphysical dualism. Laurence W. Wood reminds us, "In Christian thought, evil is always parasitic; it has no absolute existence of its own. Only the good has true being" (*Pentecostal Grace* [Wilmore, Ky.: Francis Asbury Publishing Co., 1980], 162). Wood devotes eight pages to the concept of substance and provides a very erudite and helpful discussion. It is wise to keep in mind also the reminder of Harold H. Titus that a "substance . . . does not have to be material; it may be either material or nonmaterial" (*Living Issues in Philosophy*, 5th ed. [New York: Van Nostrand Reinhold Co., 1970], 149).

The will, as a thing in itself, *is* nothing and *does* nothing. We are rather speaking of the person *willing*—which is quite different. It is the total person—involving emotion, affections, motives, and values—that is making a decision. In relation to God he is submitting to God or resisting, or perhaps wavering and vacillating. He cannot say with technical correctness, "I can't seem to get my will on the altar." What he should rather say is, "At this point I am unwilling to yield myself wholly to God."

Why is this distinction important? Because an overemphasis on the will tends to minimize, if not ignore, the moral condition of the self, that is, the nature. Why is it difficult to yield to God? Not because there is anything wrong with this mythical thing called "the will," but because there is something wrong with the self who is making choices. He finds it difficult to make right choices because he himself is sinful—in disposition and subvolitional inclination (i.e., *nature*) *before* he is sinful in act. When he as a total person chooses to take sides against this inner reluctance, he places himself in a position wherein the Holy Spirit can alter this inner misalignment, so that total surrender is no longer a battle against the grain of his nature. This will make the difference between partial bondage and complete freedom; between heavy feet and "hinds' feet" (Ps. 18:33, KJV) on the highway of holiness.

It is this inner alteration of the nature (or cleansing of the heart) that is the sine qua non of an authentic Wesleyan doctrine of entire sanctification (cf. pp. 161-63).

SUMMARY

While sin per se may be defined as accountable wrongness before God, original sin may be defined as inherited and therefore unaccountable wrongness before God, in nature or moral disposition. This condition or state becomes accountable when its cure is neglected or rejected. The cure for this disease of the personhood or self is available in Christ. While accountable wrongness needs to be forgiven, this sinful state or condition cries out for cleansing. The provision for this cleansing is central to the saving action of Christ on the Cross and in the Resurrection, and its implementation is central to the ministry of the Holy Spirit. To this provision and this implementation we now turn.

5

God's Provision in Christ

Christ Jesus the Lord is man's sole Hope—his only means of escape from the morass of his own corruption, impotence, and death. "There is no other name under heaven given to men by which we must be saved" (Acts 4:12), affirmed Peter before the self-righteous Sanhedrin. This premise is the essence of Christianity.

The great, fundamental question challenging the world and the Church is: Is Jesus an adequate Savior? Does He save *in* sin or *from* sin? If from sin, is it *all* sin—now? The Bible says *from* (Matt. 1:21) and declares Christ's ability "to save completely those who come to God through him" (Heb. 7:25).

The Good News isn't good enough unless we can proclaim to groping humanity the power of Christ to heal at the heart. It is said that Mahatma Gandhi turned from a near-acceptance of Christianity when he was told by his host in England that Jesus could not save from sinning but saved only by the imputation of His own righteousness to the believer. Gandhi wanted to be saved from sin. He saw no advantage in exchanging one impotent religion for another.

Let us inquire, then, into the nature of our salvation in Christ.

I. HOLINESS DISPLAYED

A. Christ as an Exemplar

1. *What Holiness Is*

As we look at Jesus we see modeled before our eyes the very holiness He taught (see vol. 1, chap. 3).

a. It was *oneness with the Father*—a deep, all-embracing piety. Between Jesus and the other Members of the Godhead there was total harmony and unbroken fellowship. While the Incarnation included a metaphysical union unique to the God-man, the spiritual oneness displayed by Jesus is the standard for all. A motive for His prayer for the sanctification of His disciples is "that they also may be one in us" (John 17:21, KJV).

b. The holiness we see in Jesus is also *complete righteousness.* "Which of you convinceth me of sin?" is His challenge (John 8:46, KJV). This was not only outward blamelessness but also total inner rectitude—the very purity of heart necessary to "see God" (Matt. 5:8). There was coherence between His way of life and the law of God. He did what He ought. What He felt, said, and did matched what He perceived to be right. Not only were His actions right but so also were His motives. He did the right thing for the right reasons.

c. Furthermore, we see Jesus' holiness as a *demonstration of love.* Only in thought can we abstract this from oneness with God or from righteousness, for both belong to the very nature of love. Christ loved the Father; the love was the essence of the oneness. Christ loved His fellowmen; the love was the essence of His righteousness. Therefore, it was more than a legal, external propriety of action; it was an outflowing of concern. Jesus "was moved with compassion" for the multitude, "because they were as sheep not having a shepherd: and he began to teach them many things" (Mark 6:34, KJV).[1]

2. *Special Features of Holiness*

The display of holiness by Jesus was peculiarly that kind of holiness appropriate to man the creature. Holiness in man will include submissiveness, humility, obedience, and reverence, for these traits belong rightfully to man's status as creature and subject. In God, the exercise of sovereignty, including the drawing of the sword, is perfectly compatible with His holiness, for such sovereignty belongs to His person as Creator and Governor. God's demand for the throne of our heart, then, belongs to His holiness; our demand for that throne belongs to our iniquity.[2]

---

1. Yet His love was not a weak, indulgent tolerance; e.g., His cleansing of the Temple and His scathing denunciation of the Pharisees (Matt. 21:12-13; 23:13-39).

2. See "Some Implications in the Holiness of God for the Holiness Preacher," Richard S. Taylor, *Wesleyan Theological Journal,* Spring 1973, 33.

It is profoundly significant, therefore, that Jesus said, "I am meek and lowly in heart," and in so saying pointed to himself as our Pattern (Matt. 11:29, KJV). Holiness is Christlikeness, and Christlikeness of spirit will be marked—doubly in us—by sound self-appraisal. While not depreciating ourselves in a mock humility, we will have a deep awareness of our constant dependence on God and will therefore show a constant teachableness and pliancy.

As a youth Jesus subjected himself to His parents because He knew this to be the divinely ordained order. He humbled himself in public baptism in order to "fulfill all righteousness" (Matt. 3:15). He lived a life of prayer, of constant dependence and equally constant obedience. "For even Christ did not please himself" (Rom. 15:3).

The gulf between the holiness we see in Christ and our own natural disposition is painfully obvious. But the standard is clear: Our holiness, too, must not only accept the rule of God but be marked by an inner adjustment so thorough that we are happy in it. But if so, the root of enmity must be eradicated. Pride must be broken until we are willing to take the lowly place and serve God for His glory alone (Matt. 6:19-33).

3. *Compatibility of Holiness with the Common Life*

Jesus forever dispelled the notion that holiness requires withdrawal. In Him we see that holiness is not dependent upon environment but upon the Holy Spirit within. Jesus was the Friend of sinners but was uncontaminated by them. He shared the hospitality of the high and the low, and mingled with the throngs daily, but always redemptively. Too many Christian workers set out to change the world but in the end are changed by the world. Holiness, if truly Christlike, is that quality of spirit and inner divine resource that makes it possible to be involved, yet separate—to live redemptively in the common life of family and vocation (1 John 4:4; cf. Rom. 8:31-39).

B. Holiness and Human Nature

Not only do we see in Jesus a model of Christian holiness, but we see the inherent affinity of humanity and holiness. Obviously sin is not endemic to the body, for Jesus possessed a body.[3] Jesus

---

3. Docetism—that Jesus only seemed to have a material body—was early rejected by the Church as a heresy.

assumed true human nature, thereby demonstrating that human nature is not sinful per se; instead, humanity without sin is more truly human than humanity defiled and defaced by sin.

"Jesus Christ was the only perfectly mature man who ever lived," said Henry Lederer of the School of Medicine, University of Cincinnati.[4] Yet He was the only totally sinless One. Holiness, normalcy, and maturity, while not synonymous, are affinities. The holy state is the normal state and fosters maturity in every facet of the personality. Because of sin all child psychology and all adolescent psychology are abnormal psychology. It is apparent therefore that

> the desires of the body and mind toward knowledge, growth, love and procreation are not in themselves sinful. . . . "To err is human" it is said, and this is generally intended to mean, "To sin is human." The saying is true in strict reference to fallen man as a caricature of his true self. But when we see Christ, we perceive that sin is an abnormality and a distortion. It is more truly human to be holy.[5]

II. HOLINESS AND THE CROSS

While we learn from Jesus' teaching and from His example what holiness is, it is in the Cross that we find transforming power. Example alone is like a floodlight on a drowning man; he is located, and his plight revealed, but he is not thereby rescued.[6]

A. Sanctification in the Atonement

Wesley insisted that through Christ's merits alone "all believers are saved: that is, justified—saved from the guilt; sanctified —saved from the nature of sin; and glorified—taken to heaven."[7] In this he was biblical: God made Christ "our wisdom, our righteousness and sanctification and redemption" (1 Cor. 1:30, RSV).

---

4. Said in a class lecture, 1950-51, as reported by Ruth Bassett.

5. Purkiser, Taylor, and Taylor, *God, Man, and Salvation,* 267.

6. P. T. Forsyth says, "The more ethically we construe the Gospel the more we are driven upon the holiness of God. And the deeper we enter that sacred ground the more we are seized by the necessity (for the very maintenance of our spiritual life) of a real and objective atonement offered to a holy God by the equal and satisfying holiness of Christ under the conditions of sin and judgment" (*Preaching and Modern Mind,* 373).

7. *Works,* 7:313.

It was Jesus himself who declared the link between His death and our sanctification: "For their sakes I separate myself [to the Cross] that they may be separated from sin," is His meaning in His high-priestly prayer for His disciples—and for us (John 17:17-21).

That there was an *objective* transaction between the Father and Son in Christ's death that made forgiveness and reconciliation possible has never been seriously questioned by evangelicals. What has often been missed has been the moral power for personal holiness streaming from that Cross. "Pardon is the first 'end' of Christ's death, but 'to extinguish our own hell within us' is the second 'end,'" is the Wesleyan position, according to Leo George Cox.[8] And Wesley argues that a sincere Christian could hardly be comfortable with an imputed righteousness if he is still "really enslaved to the corruptions of nature." Any salvation, even from the threat of hell, must be but partial, unless "our Redeemer be . . . one that 'baptizeth with the Holy Ghost,'—the Fountain and Restorer of that to mankind, whereby they are restored to their first estate."[9]

There is abundant biblical evidence that Wesley was right. "Our old man," says Paul, "is crucified with him, that [in order that] the body of sin might be destroyed" (Rom. 6:6, KJV). The "old man," says C. K. Barrett, "is 'Adam'—or ourselves in union with Adam."[10] The "body of sin" must be interpreted by Rom. 7:14-25. It is not the physical body, but the inner sin principle that Paul is pinpointing as the underlying human problem. Therefore, the clear declaration is that not only were our *sins* nailed with Jesus on the tree, but our *sin* as well. Jesus died for *racial sin,* that our individual carnal mind might be destroyed in personal realization, as our experiential answer to the cry, "Who shall deliver [us] from the body of this death?" (v. 24, KJV).[11]

---

8. *John Wesley's Concept of Perfection* (Kansas City: Beacon Hill Press, 1964), 37, quoting Wesley's *Works,* 9:459.

9. *Works,* 7:512.

10. *The Epistle to the Romans* (New York: Harper and Brothers, Publishers, 1957), 125.

11. Other passages that clearly declare the purpose of Christ's death to be sanctification as well as justification are Rom. 8:2-4; Gal. 2:20; 5:24; 6:14; Eph. 5:25; Col. 1:22; Titus 2:14; Heb. 2:14; 10:10, 14; 13:12; 1 Pet. 1:2; 2:24; 1 John 1:7; 3:8. Of the last verse Wm. M. Greathouse says, "John means Christ came to destroy the principle of lawlessness (*anomia*—1 John 3:4) which was the devil's chief work in man" (unpublished essay, "Sanctification and the Christus Victor Motif").

B. The Vital Principle

Wiley reminds us that we must consider the Atonement "as God's method of becoming immanent in a sinful race."[12] This, of course, is the supreme objective of everything else. The expiation of our sins is a means to this end, but not the end itself. This restoration of the Divine Presence in man, in fellowship, likeness, and unity, was made possible *(a)* in the Incarnation, by which God became immanent in human nature; *(b)* in the death of Jesus as a propitiatory and expiatory sacrifice, thus removing legal and moral impediments; *(c)* in the Resurrection, by which the sacrifice was validated, and Jesus became the eternal Pioneer of the new race (Heb. 2:10, RSV); *(d)* and because of the Resurrection, in Pentecost —the reinhabitation of man by the full indwelling of God the Holy Spirit. In this the steps away from God into alienation and depravity are matched by the steps back, and the new race the Second Adam was sent to create becomes quite literally a reality. As stupendous as future glorification will be, in a sense it will be but a "mop-up" operation. The real turning point *objectively* was when Christ said, "It is finished" (John 19:30); and the real climax *subjectively* was when "they were all filled with the Holy Spirit" (Acts 2:4, NASB). The Holy Spirit within is both a foretaste and guarantee of the future glory (2 Cor. 1:22; 5:5; Eph. 1:14).

C. Theories of the Atonement

The biblical doctrine of holiness is inextricably bound up with the biblical doctrine of atonement. This is too often overlooked by holiness advocates.

The dual effects of Adam's fall are forfeiture and condemnation on the one hand, and corruption and death on the other. The counteracting effects of the Atonement by the Second Adam must be equally twofold. In answer to the first there must be an atonement providing full remission and reconciliation—that is, justification. But in answer to the second there must be cleansing from corruption and deliverance from death, including all of sin's scars—that is, sanctification and glorification. Any theory of atonement falls short that fails to see it as *extensive* (to all men) and as *intensive* (for all sin) as the effects of the Fall. Paul's primary thesis in Rom. 5:12-19 is that the Second Adam provided for a

---

12. *Christian Theology,* 2:276.

salvation that not only precisely matched but also exceeded every detriment of the Fall.

A theory of the Atonement, therefore, that leads to a mere imputation of holiness without an adequate impartation of holiness is weighed in the balances and found wanting.

The bottom-line issue concerns the nature of the Atonement's *objectivity.* By this is meant the degree or sense in which the Atonement is to be viewed as a closed transaction between the Father and the Son. An extreme stress on objectivity sees the salvation of believers as *accomplished*—totally, finally, and nonforfeitably. This is the view of objectivity underlying, for instance, the widely used pamphlet that contains (twice) the declaration that God *has* forgiven us (who are believers) all of our sins, "past, present, and future."[13] Future sins thus are not forgiven in the future, when and if we repent, for such possible repentance has no bearing on the facts. The sins are already forgiven. Such is the raw, unvarnished implication of a view of the Atonement that sees it as a finished transaction, not *providing* for certain ends but *accomplishing* them.

This grows out of the penal satisfaction theory of the Atonement (a modification of the Anselmic via John Calvin), which sees Christ's death as the exact penalty, or *payment in full,* for the sins of the elect (only), so that all the sins of the elect are precisely balanced by the substitutionary death of Christ. This assures the final outcome, since sins already punished in full can have no further power.

What this does is to make final salvation totally a matter of justification, with holiness being essentially an imputation, and only nonessentially a subjective, real work of the Spirit. Subjective sanctification is not denied by this scheme, but it is seen as a serendipity, not a requisite for eternal salvation. Salvation itself is a matter of the *declarative* grace of God, not a matter of the *operative* grace of God. But this fails to take seriously 2 Thess. 2:13, which makes salvation itself dependent on "the sanctifying work of the Spirit."

Obviously this severance of real holiness from final salvation, and the positing of *security* in justification and imputed righteousness, cannot but have in it the seeds of antinomianism on the one hand and antiholiness on the other. While sincere love for Jesus

---

13. Put out by Campus Crusade.

may prompt a desire to avoid sin and to live a holy life, it is impossible that sin should hold any terror, since there is in it no ultimate peril. Human nature being as it is, the fostering of presumption and nonchalance toward sin will be a frequent consequence.

On the other side of the coin is the antiholiness bias. Those who cling to an imputed righteousness as their security will be hostile to a denial of the validity and adequacy of such imputation. Their basis of comfort is slipped out from under them by a doctrine that insists that Christ died *not* to make our personal holiness *unnecessary* but to make it *possible,* and that sanctification will be required as one of the two halves of a whole salvation (Acts 26:18). Speaking of the "relations that bind justification and sanctification," Adolf Köberle says that the "connection between the two is actually so intimate that if one were to perish the other would be taken away."[14] But this is bad news for some people.

The biblical view of the Atonement is that Christ's death and resurrection made possible the salvation of all, but accomplished the salvation of none.[15] It is not a "closed circuit" sort of thing. The inherently ethical demands of any truly meaningful holiness include a real conditionality. A "holiness" that is an inevitable, locked-in consequence of irresistible grace is not a true holiness at all. Final salvation must be relevant to a holy relationship with Christ, involving trust and obedience that is freely chosen and continuously sustained all the way.

To suppose that this shifts the glory from God to man or creates a works salvation is utterly erroneous. God is far more glorified by a holiness that is real than a holiness that is fictitious. And continued obedience can hardly be called a works righteousness when its very possibility stems from God's initiatory and prevenient grace, and when every moment it looks to the Cross as its meritorious ground.

But it must also be the believer's faith, the believer's choice, the

---

14. *The Quest for Holiness,* trans. John C. Mattes (Minneapolis: Augsburg Publishing House, 1938), 253. For Wesley's view see *Works,* 8:68, 429. Elsewhere Wesley said, "Indeed, some have supposed, that when I began to declare, 'By grace ye are saved through faith,' I retracted what I had before maintained: 'Without holiness no man shall see the Lord.' But it is an entire mistake: These scriptures well consist with each other; the meaning of the former being plainly this,—By faith we are saved from sin, and made holy. The imagination, that faith *supersedes* holiness, is the marrow of Antinomianism" (*Works,* 7:317).

15. Excepting infants and other irresponsibles.

believer's obedience, the believer's consecration, and the believer's death to self and sin. Only if man is involved as an active participant can there be an ethically valid covenant, just as marriage requires the volition of both partners. Even though all arrangements are made by the bridegroom, and all costs borne by him, they cannot be so complete and absolute as to include the coercion of the bride's will.

It is for these reasons that some form of the Governmental Theory of the Atonement is more consonant with the biblical view of both atonement and holiness than the Penal Satisfaction Theory.[16] The notes of *propitiation* and true *substitution* are indispensable. But in addition, this theory sees the death of Christ as finding its necessity not only in the holiness of God but also in the demands of moral government. It postulates a satisfaction both to God's holiness and to moral government. It consists not of the full and precise penalty but of *a provisional substitute for penalty*— vicarious suffering acceptable by God that can be freely offered to all on condition of repentance and faith, exactly as the Word says (Rom. 2:4; 3:25-28).[17]

III. HOLINESS AND THE NEW COVENANT

"This cup is the new covenant in my blood," said Jesus when He established the Lord's Supper with His disciples (Luke 22:20; cf. 1 Cor. 11:25). Obviously He is saying that His blood will be the means for instituting the new covenant, and thus fulfill a promise outstanding for centuries.

Nothing could be more elementary to Christianity than this,

---

16. See Wiley, *Christian Theology,* 2:241-59, 273-76.

17. The moral influence theory is obviously ruled out, for it sees the death of Christ as grounded not in the holiness of God but only in the hardheartedness of men. There is in it no real propitiation or implicit expiation, but a demonstration of God's love designed to influence man to turn from sin and love God in return.

Gustaf Aulen has developed what he calls the Christus Victor theory of the Atonement. It too provides a basis for a proper New Testament doctrine of holiness, insofar as it stresses that Christ by His death and resurrection conquered Satan, sin, and death, and as Victor can impart His victory to us. However, to be whole, this motif of victory must presuppose the biblical elements of vicarious substitution, propitiation, and expiation so necessary to the idea of atonement itself, that God might be a *justifier* who is *just* (Rom. 3:26). A real forensic atonement, relating to the Father primarily and only secondarily to Satan, must be assumed before we can talk about power and deliverance.

yet the real meaning of few symbols or teachings is so commonly and almost completely missed. Many millions partake of the Communion elements with little understanding of the new covenant of which these elements speak, to say nothing of experiencing its reality and privilege.

A. The Law Internalized

This new covenant is the primary theme of the letter to the Hebrews. After establishing Christ's place as superior to angels and Moses, and His priesthood as better than the Aaronic order, and having declared the essential inwardness and spirituality of His priestly ministrations, the writer says, "But now hath he obtained a more excellent ministry, by how much also he is the mediator of a better covenant, which was established upon better promises" (Heb. 8:6, KJV). The promises are "better" in terms of substance, not reliability. The particular Old Testament enunciation of a promised better covenant cited by Hebrews is Jer. 31:31-34, the core of which is: "I will put my laws into their minds, and write them on their hearts, and I will be their God, and they shall be my people. And they shall not teach every one his fellow or every one his brother, saying, 'Know the Lord,' for all shall know me, from the least of them to the greatest. For I will be merciful toward their iniquities, and I will remember their sins no more" (Heb. 8:10-12, RSV).[18]

While justification, regeneration, and adoption are all here,[19] that which is most radically new is stated first, "I will put my laws into their minds, and write them [Septuagint says "engrave" them] on their hearts." It is in this one feature that the hope and promise of superior success lies. A covenant, the primary substance of which consisted of a change of nature, could not possibly be implemented by Moses on the basis of animal blood, but only by a better Mediator, Christ himself, with His own blood.

The Mosaic covenant was a holiness covenant also. The essential moral law, as epitomized in the Decalogue, is the same for both

---

18. Cited by the writer to the Hebrews from the Septuagint.
19. For a more extensive discussion see BBC, 10:93-100.

covenants.[20] Both covenants are marked by clearly stated conditions and promises.

Why did the first, made at Mount Sinai, fail? Because the law was written on tables of stone rather than the fleshly tables of the heart. The mind of the Israelites endorsed the Ten Commandments, but their hearts were contrary and perverse to them. The commandments ran counter to their deepest inclinations.

The new covenant has as its central genius the change, not of the commandments but of the human heart. God proposes through Christ to internalize His law, and thus fulfill His promise through Moses, "The Lord your God will circumcise your hearts . . . so that you may love him with all your heart and with all your soul, and live" (Deut. 30:6). Likewise we have the promise through Ezekiel, "I will put my Spirit in you and move you to follow my decrees and be careful to keep my laws" (Ezek. 36:27).[21]

The crucial import of all this is impossible to miss. The New Testament is all about the *new covenant,* and at the heart of the new covenant is *holiness*—a holiness not imputed, but thoroughly imparted and worked in. It is not only workable but also working. A theology without sanctification is not fully evangelical, no matter

---

20. As the Sermon on the Mount, Jesus' pronouncements concerning the great commandments, and numerous other passages abundantly show. Warning against the peril of misunderstanding the word "Christ is the end of the law," and thus falling into the trap of antinomianism, Wesley says that Christ "has adopted every point of the moral law, and grafted it into the law of love" (*Plain Account,* 100).

It is well to warn against a works-righteousness form of legalism. But rare is the preacher who can declaim against seeking to be justified by the works of the law without in the process leaving his hearers wide open to antinomianism. People can be told so often that keeping the law won't save them, that they come to feel that keeping the law doesn't matter. The confusion is compounded by the preacher's failure to distinguish between "law" as the divine prescription of basic right and wrong, and "law" as the Old Testament ceremonial and sacrificial cultus which is no longer binding. Our hearers need to understand that the opposite of legalism is not license but faith—a faith which does not dispense with the moral law, but which lays hold of Christ for power to keep it. The antinomian supposes that if law keeping, in and of itself, cannot *achieve* salvation, then law keeping can have no bearing on *retaining* salvation. It would be a healthier balance if evangelical preachers were as careful to explain antinomianism, and warn against its perils, as they are zealous to inveigh against legalism.

21. Defining the circumcision of the heart, John Wesley said, "It is that habitual disposition of soul which, in the sacred writings, is termed holiness; and which directly implies the being cleansed from sin, 'from all filthiness of flesh and spirit,' and by consequence, the being endued with those virtues which were in Christ; the being 'so renewed in the image of our mind' as to be 'perfect as our Father which is in heaven is perfect'" (*Works,* 11:367; cf. 5:203).

how zealously it waves the banner. Indeed, it is a theology still cramped by the circumscriptions of the old covenant. It believes in the new High Priest but still lives within the limitations and inadequacies of the old order.

→ B. Freed from the Law

One of the fundamental puzzles in the New Testament is the presence of two distinct lines of teaching respecting law. Read wrongly they are paradoxical, if not contradictory. Read rightly, they are complementary. On the one hand we are said to be freed from the law; on the other hand we are expected to keep it.

1. *Material Law*

The solution lies in distinguishing between material law and formal law. Material law may be defined as the principles of moral obligation that are timeless. These principles are not abrogated, or even reduced, to accommodate people who happen to claim to be "believers." Rather, Christ's death has as its objective the impartation of moral power sufficient to enable us to live comfortably and fully by these principles: "in order that the righteous requirements of the law might be fully met in us, who do not live according to the sinful nature but according to the Spirit" (Rom. 8:4).

The Mosaic law could not achieve this result because of the obstructive power of inbred sin. Christ's atonement has that very sin as its primary focus—He "condemned" this sin by His incarnation and sacrificial death. Consequently God is able to do what the Mosaic law could not do—set us "free from the law of sin and death" (v. 2). The *law of sin*, that is, the principle of indwelling sin that Paul found to be the real villain (Romans 7), combatted and immobilized the authority of God's formal law, which said, "Thou shalt" and "Thou shalt not." Therefore real righteousness was circumvented by the "dwelling in me" sin (Rom. 7:17, 20; Gk. *hē oikousa en emoi hamartia*). Real righteousness becomes possible not by lowering the standard but by removing the hindrance. This is through sanctification, and this provision is the heart of the Atonement.

That essential righteousness is expected of Christians, indeed *required*, is everywhere taught in the New Testament including Galatians, often called the "Magna Charta of Christian liberty." "Is Christ an abettor of sin?" challenges Paul, and he answers, "No, never!" (3:21, NEB). Freedom is not to be used as an "opportunity for the flesh, but through love be servants of one another" (5:13, RSV). Freedom is not license; it is rather emancipation from the inner bondage of sin and the outer bondage of Moses. But the *material* law is the same: "For the whole law is fulfilled in one word, 'You shall love your neighbor as yourself'" (v. 14, RSV). Religion without this love will self-destruct (v. 15).

Then some of the works of the flesh are listed, 15 in all, and every one is contrary to law. Instead of Christians being exempt from the righteous demands of the moral law in any of these items, the flat ultimatum is, "Those who do such things shall not inherit the kingdom of God" (v. 21, RSV). Therefore there is nothing about the salvation in Christ or any so-called freedom from law that in the least abrogates or even modifies the principle: "Do not be deceived; God is not mocked, for whatever a man sows, that he will also reap. For he who sows to his own flesh will from the flesh reap corruption; but he who sows to the Spirit will from the Spirit reap eternal life" (6:7-8, RSV).

2. *Formal Law*

Formal law may be defined as statutory law, with its sanctions and legislated authority. It thus becomes an external system for controlling human behavior. It is clear that the law from which we are liberated in Christ is the Mosaic law system. This had divine authority for the Israelites to serve as a necessary but temporary mode of control ("kept under restraint"—Gal. 3:23, RSV) until such time as the way of faith, by which the inner law could be established, was revealed. This law, Paul says, "was our custodian until Christ came" (v. 24, RSV).

The Judaizers not only wanted to perpetuate the authority and the trappings of this complex legal system for themselves but also desired to impose it on the Gentiles as a necessity for salvation. The badge of this total way of approach both to life and to God was circumcision; therefore the Gentiles, said the Judaizers, must be circumcised. This attempt to have both the grace of Christ and the law system of Moses is what prompted the Epistle to the Galatians with its hot denials and denunciations.

Furthermore, this Mosaic law system must be seen as the total network of regulations and penalties, not just the material law epitomized in the Ten Commandments. In order for that to be enforced, it had to be buttressed by elaborate details, not only of rule but also of worship, including the entire Mosaic sacrificial cultus. This was the law, for instance, that not only declared the principle of the Sabbath in the fourth commandment but also specified stoning to death as the penalty for wanton disregard. The entire system, when enforced, became a ball and chain that *chained* but could not *change*. Even Peter conceded that the system had been "a yoke" that no one had "been able to bear" (Acts 15:10).

God had originally promised Abraham a righteousness that would be by faith, to be made available by one of Abraham's descendants (Gal. 3:6-16). The Mosaic law "was added because of transgressions, till the offspring should come to whom the promise had been made" (Gal. 3:19, RSV). When Christ came, the way of law was displaced by the new way of faith.

3. *Law and Grace*

Let us think of the law principle as the method of achieving the desired behavior by external compulsion (e.g., a corps of state troopers tailing traffic). As such a method, the Mosaic law system failed to achieve inner righteousness for reasons already seen. For "if a law had been given which could make alive, then righteousness would indeed be by the law" (Gal. 3:21, RSV). A law can be enforced, but the law itself cannot create goodwill; this must come from within, created by other influences or motives. But note: By whatever mode, *righteousness* is the goal.

In sharpest possible contrast, the *grace principle* can be defined as the method of achieving the desired behavior (i.e., righteousness) by that inward change known as sanctification (cf. 2 Thess. 2:13). This change adjusts the inner man to the standard so that tension is eliminated and conformity can be enjoyed—willingly, happily, and naturally.

To thus come under the grace principle frees us from the necessity of the law principle. It is in this sense only that Christians are freed from the law.

The results of the grace principle are much more satisfactory and stable, because while law may still be needed to guide us, it will not be needed to compel us (or even threaten us), for now the moral intent of the law finds affinity within us instead of opposition. Because knowledge of legal obligations may still be deficient, outward conformity may at times be unwittingly defective; however, this is not a major problem, since it is no longer a rebellion of the heart, only an ignorance of the head.

Therefore "Christ means the end of the struggle for righteousness-by-the-Law for everyone who believes in him" (Rom. 10:4, Phillips). Christ, through the Spirit, takes over where the law leaves off, and succeeds where the law fails. But this obtains only if we "walk by the Spirit," as persons who have "crucified the flesh with its passions and desires" (Gal. 5:16, 24, RSV).

Perhaps, after all, the old Puritan Samuel Rutherford (A.D. 1600-1661) had it right:

> I have now made a new question, whether Christ be more to be loved, for giving Sanctification or for free Justification. And I hold that He is more and most to be loved for sanctification. It is in some respect greater love in Him to sanctify, than to justify; for He maketh us most like Himself in His own essential portraiture and image, in sanctifying us. . . . Let a sinner, if possible, lie in hell forever, if He make him truly holy; and let him lie there burning in love to God, rejoicing in the Holy Ghost, hanging upon Christ by faith and hope,—that is heaven in the heart and bottom of hell![22]

---

22. Letter 170, written in 1637, from *Letters of Samuel Rutherford,* ed. Andrew Bonar (Edinburgh and London: Oliphant, Anderson, and Ferrier, 1891), 320. Wesley says that the change experienced in full sanctification is "immensely greater" than the change in justification (*Plain Account,* 61 [*Works* 11:402]).

6

Pentecost and the Ministry of the Spirit

A fundamental issue, both for biblical hermeneutics and for Christian doctrine, concerns the relation of Pentecost to previous forms of religious life and experience. A systematic approach to Christian holiness requires that the question be considered at this point.

It is generally agreed that the Day of Pentecost marked a new beginning, at least in the minimal sense that it inaugurated the dispensation of the Holy Spirit. The fundamental feature of such a dispensation is that the redemptive activities of the Triune God began on the Day of Pentecost to be administrated by the Holy Spirit in a new way. But we are at once forced to raise some key questions: How radical is the newness, and what precisely is its nature? Is there total discontinuity between Pentecost and all previous redemption privileges? Was man's relationship with God formal and external only, or also subjective and experiential? Must all religious life before Pentecost be labeled not only pre-Christian but also sub-Christian? Did it universally fall short of regeneration and participation in the kingdom of Christ?

To insist on radical discontinuity is to depreciate the saving grace of God that was operative before Pentecost. On the contrary, an assumption of continuity, says Laurence W. Wood, is "the very center of the apostolic preaching."[1]

I. PRE-PENTECOST SALVATION PRIVILEGES

A. Calvary the Crux

That which was initiated by Pentecost was not a personal grace relationship to God based on atonement, faith, and obedience. Salvation experience is grounded in the Calvary-Easter event, not Pentecost. "One of the significant issues biblically," writes Willard H. Taylor, "relates to the centrality of the cross-resurrection event in biblical thought and in personal experience. The living Lord is the one with whom we must come to terms— then and now." Because of this he does not believe the biblical record supports the notion that the disciples before Pentecost were "in a sub-Christian state."[2]

Doubtless there is a certain formal difference between New Testament believers and Old Testament saints. Perhaps a greater justification exists for calling the disciples Christians than Old Testament worshipers, for the faith of the latter was not in a living Christ but in the God who delivered them from Egypt and who promised a future Savior. The faith of the disciples, however, was focused on this Savior himself, whom they identified as "the Christ, the Son of the living God" (Matt. 16:16; cf. John 6:68; 1:19-34). And since it required Pentecost to clarify their understanding of Christ's person and saving work, it can be conceded that Pentecost was necessary to make their faith fully "Christian." This, however, does not deny the reality of their discipleship before Pentecost or imply that they "became Christians" at Pentecost (see pp. 132-33).

For the saving power of the Cross is timeless, even extending to the faith saints of Hebrews 11 whose intellectual understanding

---

1. *Pentecostal Grace*, 23. The Book of Acts, he says, "reflects in the closest possible manner the connection between the history of Jesus and the history of Israel. This relationship is so closely linked that the apostles see nothing in their kerygma which is not already implicit in the ancient *credo*. Their worship, their ritual, their preaching assumes a direct relationship to the history of Israel. The essence of that relationship is that the *promise* to Abraham had its fulfillment in Jesus" (22).

2. Quoted from a letter to the author.

of God's way of salvation was vague and shadowy. It is highly significant that both Romans and Galatians point to Abraham as the grand prototype of justification by faith.[3] And while the Mosaic law, in its intricate cultic complexities, served as a schoolmaster in preparing men for Christ (Gal. 3:23), and while the blood of animals was powerless to take away sins excepting symbolically and prophetically (Heb. 10:4), many devout Hebrews nevertheless learned to love God and His law, and to "act justly and to love mercy and to walk humbly" with their God (Mic. 6:8). Their piety was not that odious self-righteousness deplored so vehemently in both Testaments but a measure of Calvary grace and some degree of divine assistance of the Holy Spirit. Since the Holy Spirit is personal, says John A. Knight, "His activity cannot be confined to a specific era." And he quotes John Fletcher, "The Old and New Testaments sufficiently prove, that the special influences of the Spirit are to be universally experienced by the faithful in every age."[4]

Paul's argument in Romans never implied the unreality or impossibility of this but was directed to the illusion that righteousness could be achieved apart from Christ by either pagan moralism or Jewish law-keeping, in and of themselves.

B. Was It Regeneration?

Was the relationship of Abraham to God, as well as that of Noah, Job, Isaiah, and Jeremiah, the expression of an inner quickening that could properly be called regeneration? Abraham was justified by faith and was called "the Friend of God" (James 2:23, KJV). God gave Saul "another heart" (1 Sam. 10:9, KJV)—though he backslid later. David described the religious life in terms of forgiveness, the joy of salvation, and profound newness. (See ECH, 1:53-60.) Isaiah experienced a cleansing of his iniquity. The continuity of grace, of human nature and need, and of the divine principles of operation, would argue that these persons experienced an inner change.

---

3. J. Kenneth Grider says, "Paul does not seem to know anything about the dispensationalism which separates the pre-Pentecost people from justification by faith, because he uses Abraham as an illustration of how one is justified" (*Entire Sanctification,* 54).

4. John A. Knight, *The Holiness Pilgrimage* (Kansas City: Beacon Hill Press of Kansas City, 1973), 69.

It would be difficult to believe that such an inner change did not constitute what Jesus spoke to Nicodemus about, a rebirth by the Spirit. It is equally difficult to suppose that the new birth is essentially different from the forgiveness of sins (and doubtless change of heart) experienced by the multitudes who repented and were baptized by John, believing on Him who was to come. While some were superficial, all could not have been. There is every reason to assume that the disciples whom Jesus gathered around himself were already changed men, though certainly not yet holy men through and through. While their understanding of the content of salvation and of the nature of the Messianic ministry was deficient, their faith was real and life-transforming.

Pertinent also is the question whether Jesus' conversation with Nicodemus was anticipatory only or immediately applicable. Was Jesus saying, "You must be born again—but you cannot be now, not until the Day of Pentecost comes"? The suggestion raises serious questions, for Jesus made the new birth absolutely indispensable for entering the kingdom of God; and if what Jesus meant by the new birth was not available before Pentecost—if all pre-Pentecost forms of religious experience were categorically different from and fell short of true regeneration—then *no one* was in the Kingdom before Pentecost. In that case Old Testament saints were disenfranchised saints, servants of God but not in the kingdom of God—a rather fantastic state of affairs.[5]

We may say, therefore, that the saving power of Christ reaches back to Adam and forward to the New Jerusalem. The redemptive

---

5. In his sermon "The Way to the Kingdom," John Wesley says, "As soon as ever God hath spoken to thy heart, 'Be of good cheer, thy sins are forgiven thee,' his kingdom comes: Thou hast 'righteousness, and peace, and joy in the Holy Ghost'" (*Works,* 5:85).

Yet some would understand Matt. 11:11 (cf. Luke 7:28) to imply that John the Baptist was not in the Kingdom—thus suggesting a sharp discontinuity between the Kingdom and Old Testament privileges. But this is by no means obvious. Compare Wesley's comments on Matt. 11:11 with his different comment on Luke 7:28. Ralph Earle says, "Evidently Christ meant that the 'least' Christian is 'greater' in privilege than John, who really belonged more to the Old Testament order" (BBC, 6:115).

Perhaps the best resolution of the difficulty is to see a distinction between the kingdom of God as a timeless entity, embracing all dispensations, and the Messianic phase of the Kingdom, which depended on Christ's advent. The Kingdom focused in Christ's person, and redemptive work became the means by which the larger kingdom of God became accessible. In relation to men, the kingdom of God *is*— since His advent—the kingdom of Christ (1 Cor. 15:24). See John Deschner, *Wesley's Christology;* also *God, Man, and Salvation,* 614-23.

downreach of God's grace cannot be confined to the dispensation of the Spirit. While Pentecost introduced a new level of privilege and a new methodology, and while the new covenant displaced the old (Heb. 8:13), neither Pentecost nor the new covenant invalidated the religious experiences of the old order. In a sense, therefore, Pentecost was the extension and expansion of salvation history. This premise underlies what we now consider.

II. THE DISPENSATIONALISM OF WESLEY AND FLETCHER

A helpful exposition of this has already been provided in the historical division of these studies. (See ECH, 2:237-40.) A reconsideration at this point is germane to the inquiry of this chapter.

"Dispensation" is a KJV translation of *oikonomia*, meaning rule or management of a household. The transliteration, *economy*, is perhaps more understandable today. A capitalist economy is a different kind of goods, labor, and monetary system than a communist economy. Therefore a *dispensation* is "a mode of dealing, an arrangement or administration of affairs."[6] This will help us understand the dispensationalism of Wesley and Fletcher. The concept, combined with their doctrine of prevenient grace, provided a rationale for God's varying requirements in different ages and with diverse categories of people.[7] John A. Knight says:

> Fletcher concluded that if Christ tasted death for every man, as the Scriptures teach, there is undoubtedly a gospel for every man. A "general gospel," then, is revealed to all men, according to the clearer or more obscure dispensation under which they live.[8]

---

6. Vine, *Expository Dictionary*, 1:320. Of course this primary meaning does not exclude the possibility of a secondary temporal meaning. Historically, the dispensation of the Holy Spirit began on the first Christian Pentecost and will continue until the Second Coming.

7. While Wesley spoke occasionally of the differences in the dispensations, it was Fletcher who refined and expanded the doctrine. This he did in his *Essay on Truth*, which Timothy Smith calls Fletcher's finest theological work. That Wesley fully endorsed Fletcher's exposition is not left in doubt. He said, "Mr. Fletcher has given us a wonderful view of the different dispensations which we are under. I believe that difficult subject was never placed in so clear a light before. It seems God has raised him up for this very thing,—
>> To vindicate eternal Providence,
>> And justify the ways of God to man" (*Works*, 13:55).

8. *Holiness Pilgrimage*, 65.

Don't believe

A. Three Dispensations

In Fletcher's schema are three dispensations: that of the Father, that of the Son, and that of the Holy Spirit. These, of course, are chronological as well as diverse economies. The dispensation of the Father prevailed to the Incarnation, then gave way (with John the Baptist mediating the transition) to the dispensation of the Son. This was succeeded by the dispensation of the Holy Spirit on the Day of Pentecost.

But while chronological, the more important note is that each dispensation is characterized by its own mode of access to God and differing degrees of available knowledge of God. Eternal salvation was possible in each dispensation, if one walked in all the light that dispensation afforded. On this basis salvation was experienced by the devout Jew under Moses, and even (at least hypothetically) by the devout heathen.

When viewed historically and chronologically, each dispensation was preparatory and promissory of the next. John A. Knight explains:

> Within each of the dispensations, there is the motif of *Fulfillment and Promise, Holiness and Hope.* That is, at every stage there is the reality of the knowledge of God in some degree; yet there is always a promise of a richer knowledge yet to come. The dispensation of the Father, for example, promises the coming of His Son for the redemption of sinners; the dispensation of the Son promises the gift of the Holy Spirit for the entire sanctification of believers; and the dispensation of the Holy Spirit promises the future return of Christ for the glorification of His saints.[9]

B. Personal As Well as Historical

"Fletcher was convinced," says Knight, "that the spiritual pilgrimage of individual men in each of the dispensations is a recapit-

---

9. Ibid., 72. Unquestionably the dispensation of the Spirit is an advanced stage in both revelation and redemptive privileges; and persons filled with the Spirit since Pentecost experience a higher level of grace than those acquainted only with the dispensation of the Son or of the Father. But this must not be misconstrued to imply that the Spirit is greater than the Son, or that a Pneumatological approach to salvation is antithetical to a Christological approach. There is no rivalry within the Trinity or jealousy when any one Person is especially honored. Never is the Son so honored as when believers become Spirit-filled, for the Spirit's mission is to clarify Christ to the soul and conform the soul to Christ.

ulation or microcosm of the way God is working in all of history."[10] The first beginning of true religion is experienced by the awakened sinner who finds himself in violation of the law of God and under God's wrath, and in whose heart arises a true fear of God and a resolution to seek to find Him and to please Him. The knowledge of Jesus Christ beings him into the dispensation of the Son, wherein he learns the way to conscious forgiveness and reconciliation. The characteristic mark of this dispensation is the new birth. Because spiritual light is progressive, God in His faithfulness will lead the honest worshiper to the knowledge of the Son, and the believer in the Son will be led to the full light and expanded spiritual privileges of the dispensation of the Holy Spirit.

However, a sincere believer who is cut off in death knowing only the dispensation of the Father would be saved, for he would be under the requirements and modes of that dispensation, epitomized by Samuel's words: "Be sure to fear the Lord and serve him faithfully with all your heart . . . Yet if you persist in doing evil, both you and your king will be swept away" (1 Sam. 12:24-25).[11]

The thesis that the dispensations are experienced in one's individual pilgrimage implies that while in the historical sense the world is under the dispensation of the Holy Spirit, some may not yet be experiencing that dispensation personally. Some may yet be under the dispensation of the Father, knowing nothing else; while others may yet be under the dispensation of the Son, having accepted Christ as Savior but not having been told that Christ desires to baptize them with the Holy Spirit. While knowing John's baptism, and even the gospel of Calvary and the Resurrection, they still live in pre-Pentecostal shadows and uncertainties, exactly as the disciples before the first Pentecost. This fact should inform the preaching of the pastor. He should know the dispensation under which his people are living, not to confirm them in it but to lead them from the lower to the higher.

The doctrine of dispensations is grounded not only in the doctrine of prevenient grace but also in the confidence that a fair and merciful God will relate himself to moral man on the level of his

---

10. Ibid., 66.

11. Wesley took the position that morality without the new birth availed nothing "to those that are under the Christian dispensation"; but he refused to state that the same principle governed God's judgment of the heathen (*Works,* 7:353; cf. 506; 8:337; Adam Clarke's commentary on Acts 10:35).

knowledge and opportunity. The common denominator in all dispensations, the single sine qua non, is sincere obedience to the full measure of light one possesses. Only on this basis can the Bible call men and women righteous and holy whose understanding of God was dim and whose ethics fell short of Christian standards.

This means also that what can be called holiness, and equally what can be called sin, is progressive, keeping step always with an individual's highest level of divine revelation. That which was innocent yesterday may be sin today. A person who could properly be called holy yesterday may not be called holy today, if his willing obedience has begun to lag behind the stage of his understanding.[12]

C. Neither Optional nor Reversible

No one can elect to stay in a lower dispensation of grace when once confronted with the possibility of a higher. This would betray a fundamental insincerity that would cancel any claim to divine approval. As Mildred Bangs Wynkoop so aptly says, "In the Bible *the lowest allowable level of obedience is the highest possible capacity for man at any given moment.*"[13] And Knight explains, "By his doctrine of dispensations, Fletcher was not saying that man can receive or obey whatever degree of knowledge he chooses."[14] The Jew, for instance, having been confronted by the Spirit with Jesus of Nazareth and rejected Him, can hardly continue to find divine acceptance in Judaism. And the entire Epistle to the Hebrews is one long warning that, having believed on Christ, they cannot now revert to Moses. By the same token a born-again Christian, having seen the Promised Land of Pentecostal privilege and power, cannot with impunity elect to settle down in the wilderness. Our response to our Kadesh-barnea is always a life-or-death response.[15]

---

12. "The true believer," says Knight, "willingly and gladly proceeds 'from faith to faith.' Those who refuse deceive themselves and are not accepted of God" (*Holiness Pilgrimage,* 76).

13. Mildred Bangs Wynkoop, *A Theology of Love* (Kansas City: Beacon Hill Press of Kansas City, 1972), 181.

14. *Holiness Pilgrimage,* 77.

15. As is most solemnly affirmed in Heb. 10:26-31.

III. PENTECOST A CHURCH EVENT

A focal thesis, therefore, is that Pentecost was not the beginning of salvation privileges; it was the empowerment of the Church for its mission. It was not for sinners but for believers. True, it signaled a new release and heightened measure of the Spirit's ministrations to unbelievers, but this was implemented by His outpouring on the Church and was to be mediated through the Church. "I will send him to you," Jesus had promised. Then, when "he comes [to you], he will convict the world" (John 16:7-8).

A. The Biblical Data

The Church focus on Pentecost is affirmed by everything Jesus said respecting this coming event (Luke 24:45-53; John 14:15-26; 15:26-27; 16:5-15; Acts 1:4-8). It was the Church that had already been commissioned to evangelize the world; Pentecost was God's promised means of qualifying and equipping the Church for this mission. "But you will receive power when the Holy Spirit comes on you; and you will be my witnesses" (Acts 1:8). Moreover, Pentecost was the fulfillment of promises made exclusively to the Church—the believing, obedient people of God. In addition, Pentecost actually happened to the Church and to the Church only: to the 120 trusting, obeying, praying disciples who were tarrying in the Upper Room.

The multitudes were arrested by the discovery of what was happening, but they were not immediate participants. On them the new power of communication was demonstrated; but they remained outsiders until they became insiders by becoming believers. This could occur only by repenting and accepting this so recently crucified Jesus of Nazareth as their Messiah and Savior, and proving their radical change by embracing the hazards of public baptism. Only then were they qualified for the same anointing of the Spirit that had come on the 120. But a faith and repentance deep enough to justify a profession of forgiveness, and a public confession in baptism, brought them into the Church. Then, as part of the Church, they were eligible for the Great Gift to the Church—the fullness of the Spirit.[16]

---

16. The final position of both Wesley and Fletcher was that the 3,000 were born again on the Day of Pentecost but were not filled or baptized with the Spirit until some time later. The story of their interaction at this point has been carefully

B. The Spirit Baptism of the Church

Pentecost, then, "is an experience of the Community of Believers and carries with it special meaning for the empowering of the Church which is only possible through a thorough cleansing of the believer by the democratized Spirit."[17] But this suggests the need for caution in designating, without qualification, Pentecost as the birthday of the Church. The New Testament lineaments of the Church as the new Israel began to be seen in the calling out[18] of the Twelve, then the Seventy, Christ's designation of them as the "little flock" (Luke 12:32); and His manifesto of the Church's foundation as the confession of His divine identity—"on this rock I will build my church" (Matt. 16:18). The essence of the Church is better defined by Matt. 18:20 than Acts 2:4; in fact, Acts 2:4 could not have occurred if the gathered fellowship had not already been in place.

The irreducible marks of the true Church were all marks of Christ's disciples before Pentecost. They had repented, been forgiven, and had been baptized.[19] They had forsaken all to follow Jesus. They were pronounced by Jesus as "the salt" and "the light" of the world (Matt. 5:13-14). They were already in Christ as living branches of the life-giving Vine (John 15:1-8). They were specifically called "clean" through Christ's word to them (v. 3). They were "not of the world" even as Christ was not of the world (17:14). They already knew some measure of the Spirit's power, for He was *with* them, even though not *in* them in the sense of the promised fullness. If all of these marks could be ascribed to a band of believers today, is there any evangelical theologian who would deny that they were indeed members of Christ, and as such members of His Church?

True, their oneness with Christ was marred by hardness of

---

traced by Timothy L. Smith in "How John Fletcher Became the Theologian of Wesleyan Perfectionism," *Wesleyan Theological Journal* 15, no. 1 (Spring 1980):68. This firm position was expounded in Fletcher's *Last Check*, in a section called "An Address to Imperfect Believers." In response, Wesley wrote Fletcher, Aug. 1, 1775, "I have now received all your papers, and here and there made some small corrections. . . . I do not perceive that you have granted too much, or that there is any difference between us." Cited by Smith from *Letters*, 6:174-75.

17. In a personal letter to the author from Willard H. Taylor.

18. *Ekklēsia*, "an assembly," from *ekkaleō*, "to summon forth." The word is used for the church 120 times in the New Testament.

19. While the primitive Church unquestionably baptized with water, the physical rite itself is not an *absolute* requirement for participation in the Body of Christ, as the Quakers and Salvation Army have demonstrated.

heart, selfish motives, unchristlikeness of spirit, and cowardice under pressure. *But that was why they needed Pentecost. And that was what prompted Jesus to pray for their sanctification.* [20]

Yet while to speak of Pentecost as the birthday of the Church is not strictly accurate, the concept nevertheless expresses an important truth. This truth is that the Church became for the first time what it was intended to be: a spiritual organism, in which the believers were bound to each other and to their living Head in a new way. It was at Pentecost that the disciples first experienced the perfect unity for which Jesus had prayed (John 17:21-23).

We may say, then, that Pentecost was the completion of the formation of the Church, not as an organization (which evolved in step with needs), but as the Body of Christ. An implication is that while today men are inducted into the Church by the new birth, it is not until they are filled with the Spirit that they know experientially the depths of their mutual bond.

Speaking of the formation of the Church at Pentecost, H. Orton Wiley says:

> As the natural body is possessed of a common life which binds the members together in a common organism; so the Holy Spirit sets the members in the spiritual body as it pleases Him, uniting them into a single organism under Christ its living Head. God did not create men as a string of isolated souls, but as an interrelated race of mutually dependent individuals; so also the purpose of Christ is not alone the salvation of the individual, but the building up of a spiritual organism of interrelated and redeemed persons. [21]

IV. PENTECOST IN ITS RADICAL NEWNESS

While the redemptive influences of the Spirit did not begin with Pentecost, and while Pentecost sustained a certain relation of continuity with salvation history, it nevertheless constituted in some respects a radical transmutation of the old order.

---

20. As Charles Carter observes, rather than Pentecost being the "birthday" of the Church, it should "be regarded as the *consecration, dedication,* or *inauguration* of the Church of Christ" (*The Person and Ministry of the Holy Spirit* [Grand Rapids: Baker Book House, 1974], 156).

21. *Christian Theology,* 2:329-30. Wiley adds, "The Holy Spirit is therefore not only the bond which unites the individual soul to Christ in a vital and holy relationship; but He is the common bond which unites the members of the body to each other, and all to their living Head. The Spirit is the life of the body, and since

A. In Contrast to Jesus

In the Upper Room Discourse, Jesus contrasts the Spirit's dispensation with His own. While the Spirit's ministry would be a continuation, or extension, of Christ's, the new modus operandi would have distinct advantages. Jesus had been with them briefly; the Spirit would abide. Jesus had been with them physically and externally; the Spirit would be with them spiritually and internally. Jesus was with the group socially; the Spirit not only would come upon them corporately but also would indwell each one personally, in the solitudes of life as well as when with the gathering.

Jesus had to communicate by the lingua franca of the day, and the communication was forever breaking down; the Spirit would illuminate their understanding from within (John 16:14). For three years Jesus had not sufficiently gotten inside of them in core reshaping; the Holy Spirit would sanctify wholly.

These are the reasons Jesus could say to them, "It is for your good that I am going away. Unless I go away, the Counselor will not come to you; but if I go, I will send him to you" (John 16:7). Many nervous evangelicals are afraid that to honor the Holy Spirit is somehow to dishonor Christ. That is not the way Jesus himself viewed the matter. He is here saying that they will actually be better off without Him (in physical presence) but with the Holy Spirit, than they would be with Him but without the Holy Spirit. When the Holy Spirit is truly honored, Christ will be too, indeed in a much larger and more glorious measure than could be true otherwise.

B. In Newness of Privilege

What are the special "breakthroughs" for Christians? Pentecost inaugurated at least four radical innovations.

His inauguration at Pentecost, has His 'See' or seat with the Church. . . . Previous to Pentecost the mild showers of the Holy Spirit descended upon Israel in drops of saving grace; but in such a manner that each gathered only for himself. This continued until the time of the Incarnation, when Christ gathered into His one Person the full stream of the Holy Spirit for us all. . . . When the channels of faith were completed and every obstacle removed, the Holy Spirit on the Day of Pentecost came rushing through the connecting channels into the heart of every believer. Formerly there was isolation, every man for himself; now it is an organic union of all the members under their one Head. This is the difference between the days before and after Pentecost." (Note: While Wiley states in *Christian Theology*, 2:329, that Pentecost is the birthday of the Church, he takes the opposite position in 3:185-86.)

1. *A New Mode of Religious Life*

To a great extent the elaborate ritual of Old Testament worship was necessitated by the feebleness of inward motivation and the absence of true spiritual-mindedness. When the inward ministrations of the Spirit are limited, the religious life must be shaped by powerful social structures that tend to establish habits, traditions, and behavior patterns. The law informed their minds concerning right and wrong, while the Mosaic cultus not only stimulated moral sensitivity and moral judgment but also fostered a profound awareness of the majesty of God and the importance of worship.

In keeping vital religion alive, the forms and regular duties had to carry immense weight to compensate for the light weight of the spiritual impulse within. The Holy Spirit's mission was to invert the required weighting of the external in relation to the internal. This change is seen significantly in a clear experience of the new birth, but how much more striking and complete it is with the fullness of the Spirit! He now makes the soul throb with the love of God and makes the invisible spiritual world real without the stimulation of color, sound, and pageantry. In the new order the most minimal forms prove sufficient to activate the joys of worship.

Jesus said to the woman at the well, "Believe me, woman, a time is coming when you will worship the Father neither on this mountain nor in Jerusalem. . . . Yet a time is coming and has now come when the true worshipers will worship the Father in spirit and truth, for they are the kind of worshipers the Father seeks" (John 4:21, 23). On the Day of Pentecost the 120 began in a new way to learn the meaning of this kind of worship, so straight from the heart and so Spirit-incited that it was acceptable with the Father no matter the location or circumstances.

The disciples had said, "Teach us to pray" (Luke 11:1), and Jesus gave them instruction about prayer and taught them a model prayer. But it was not until they were filled with the Spirit that prayer began to mean to them what it meant in the life of Jesus—a profoundly personal and real communication with God and a source of guidance and power.

The extent of the radical break with the old cultus implicit in Pentecost was not fully understood at once, even by the apostles. But the narrative in Acts shows the gradual and irreversible shift of religious life from the Temple rites to a Christian worship style, featuring singing, preaching and teaching, the Eucharist, free prayer, and the sharing through gifts of the Spirit. The apostles, not the priests, became the locus. From the Day of Pentecost this began to be seen (Acts 2:41-47).

2. *A New Universality of Access to the Divine Fullness*

It would be incorrect to say that God was ever aloof from men, or ever unavailable to the devout seeker. Yet the barrier of sinful hearts and darkened minds, of ignorance and superstition, was so thick that few rose above their environment to push their way into some degree of the knowledge of God. Enoch "walked with God" (Gen. 5:22, 24) without Bible and without church. But what it cost him we do not know. In the very nature of the case, God could reveal himself only in shadows and whispers, never clearly until in His Son. Men grasped an unseen hand by faith and worshiped a Being whom they only dimly perceived. The experience of grace began to take sharper form through the worship established by Moses, then even more clearly through the ministry of the prophets.

As for a special measure of the Spirit's tutelage and enduement, that was reserved for special agents. This was sometimes in the form of charismata, as in the case of Bezalel (Exod. 31:1-2). It was also in the form of anointing upon judges and kings; even more especially in the spiritual insight and inspiration given to the speaking and writing prophets. But when once the Incarnation bisected history, and the veil was rent in the death of Christ, and the risen Lord joined with the Father in unharnessing the Holy Spirit, suddenly the trickle became a surging stream. The breadth of its waters became as wide as humanity. There must have been a ring of exaltation when Peter "raised his voice" and declared, "This is what was spoken by the prophet Joel:

'In the last days, God says,
I will pour out my Spirit on all people.
Your sons and daughters will prophesy,
your young men will see visions,
your old men will dream dreams.
Even on my servants, both men and women,
I will pour out my Spirit in those days,
and they will prophesy'" (*Acts 2:14, 16-18*).

Access to the fullness of the Spirit would henceforth be without distinction of sex, age, or social class. The slave could have "as much of the Spirit" as an apostle. Among the 120 there were both sexes, doubtless young as well as old, educated and uneducated. Some may have been extremely poor, and some could even have been slaves, or at least bond servants. But all were equally filled and equally enabled to live victoriously and fulfill their respective callings in the days that followed.

The universal outpouring was both fact and prophecy. With the 120 it was realized experience; with the multitudes and all subsequent generations it was promised availability. For the promise was "for you and your children and for all who are far off—for all whom the Lord our God will call" (Acts 2:39). And so today the humblest believer may be mighty in the Spirit. He can stand taller and see farther than the most brilliant scholar who is without the Spirit.

3. *A New Dynamic of Religious Expansion*

The Jews could make proselytes; Christians would be able in the power of the Spirit to bring men to Jesus. The method would be preaching and teaching under supernatural enduement. Whether the speaking be public or private, skilled or unskilled, in every case the cutting edge would be the Holy Spirit.

The enduement of power (cf. Acts 1:8) is that divine activity in and through witnessing Christians which carries conviction. The Holy Spirit turns verbal communication into lightning bolts of discovery, shock, revelation, and insight. Words ineffectual in themselves become electric with impact, jolting the conscience and gripping the mind. Arrows shot sometimes at random are guided unerringly to the conscience. The proof, and first demonstration of this powerful evangelism, was in 3,000 conversions on the first day, thus fulfilling the promise of Jesus, "Greater works than these shall he . . . that believeth on me . . . do; because I go unto my Father" (John 14:12, KJV).

All contemporary emphases on church growth are exercises in futility unless participants are reminded that the components of growth—awakening, conviction, conversion, and sanctification— are events that only the Holy Spirit can effect. Without these events "growth" will be nothing but the aggregation of proximate sinners. Humanistic methods can build congregations; we can win people to ourselves through friendship; we can wrap people up in the organized church through "caring"—yet all these fall short of bringing them, in the depths of their being, face-to-face with Jesus Christat.

(C) 4. *A New Norm of Religious Experience*

It is a new norm of experience that makes the first three both possible and meaningful. The pivotal insight, the veritable arch-stone of a biblical soteriology, is that this new norm is not regeneration but the fullness of the Holy Spirit. (See ECH, 2:303-18.) The possibility of a true but initial inner change, as has been pointed out, transcends sharp dispensational lines. Because of a clearer understanding of the basis of salvation (the death and resurrection of Jesus) now being transmitted by the apostles at Pentecost and thereafter, conversions were better grounded. In this doctrinally formal sense, the converts were more completely "Christian." Even the apostles themselves, upon being filled with the Spirit, instantly had clearer views of what properly belonged to their faith. But this fact in no way invalidates the genuineness of their previous regeneration. Have not many accepted Christ in real but confused faith, whose intellectual grasp of the Cross came later?

The "promise of the Father" in the Old Testament, enunciated Christologically by John the Baptist, and reaffirmed by Jesus himself, pertained to that special baptism with or fullness of the Spirit to be experienced by God's obedient people. Both Wesley and Fletcher understood John 7:39 to mean not an absolute beginning of the Spirit's ministrations but that special advent or outpouring of the Spirit at Pentecost, a Gift to the Church of holiness and power that would make the promised "streams of living water" a reality in the lives of the believers.[22]

Furthermore, it was Pentecost that consummated the new covenant as an experiential reality. While the new covenant was inaugurated by Christ's saving deed on the Cross, and while Jesus had instituted its sacramental memorial some 50 days earlier, it was the Spirit's role to implement its promised central provision by writing God's law on the hearts and minds of the waiting disciples. As holiness was central to Sinai, so holiness is central to Pentecost. And as the first Passover marked the deliverance of the Israelites from Egypt and at the same time qualified them for entering into

---

22. See Timothy L. Smith, "How John Fletcher Became the Theologian of Wesleyan Perfectionism, 1770-1776," *Wesleyan Theological Journal* 15, no. 1 (Spring 1980): 75-76, 80.

the Sinaitic pact with God, so Christ our Passover delivers us from the Egypt of sin and qualifies us to participate fully in the Spirit's sanctifying ministry, released to the Church on the first Christian Pentecost.[23]

C. Pentecost and the Kingdom

Many attempts have been made to define the New Testament concept of the Kingdom, and to properly relate it to the Church, to Pentecost, and to eschatology. A review of the various understandings is not germane to this book. However, three observations are relevant, even fundamental.

First, a key New Testament holiness text is Matt. 6:33: "Seek first his kingdom and his righteousness." The Father's kingdom and "his righteousness" are inseparable. In its most elemental definition, the Kingdom is the rule of God, while the righteousness is that righteousness made available to man through Christ Jesus. It is a righteousness consisting not only in justification but also in sanctification. The mark of this sanctification is complete inner harmony with the uncompromised rule of God in one's life. Thus would the Kingdom be established within. Such a concept of the Kingdom is echoed by Paul: "The kingdom of God is not a matter of eating and drinking, but of righteousness, peace and joy in the Holy Spirit" (Rom. 14:17).

The emphasis, therefore, is not land but people. The Kingdom is a realm without earthly geography, but nevertheless a true entity, composed of a new race—the twice born. The spiritual nature of this Kingdom could only dimly be perceived before Christ came expressly to reveal it in His own person and open it wide for all. Other notes are sounded in the total New Testament teaching respecting the Kingdom, but its spiritual nature, and its focus in Christ, must first be seen (Luke 17:21).

Second, by implication we must say that Pentecost no more marked the genesis of the Kingdom than it did the birthday of the Church. Some have seen Pentecost as the fulfillment of Mark 9:1: "I tell you the truth, some who are standing here will not taste death before they see the kingdom of God come with power." That this relates to Pentecost at all is debatable; but if it does, the em-

---

23. Jewish tradition understood the giving of the law at Mount Sinai to constitute the first Pentecost. Cf. Clarke, Matthew Henry, BBC, and *Wesleyan Bible Commentary* on Exodus 19.

phasis would have to be on "with power."[24] Pentecost was a break-through for the Kingdom, by means of which it would now be expanding on earth with a new dynamic. It would be a stepped-up order of power, as when a 1,000-watt transmitter is stepped up to 100,000 watts. The flow was "coming" before, but this new "coming" is in a different power bracket.

Third, one may personally be in the Kingdom through the new birth and have the Kingdom within him, both in terms of its law and its King, yet fall short of entire sanctification, that full measure of inner righteousness by which the Kingdom is more perfectly defined. As Wood says:

> It is one thing to be a member of the kingdom of God through the believer's incorporation into the Church through justifying faith; it is another thing for the kingdom of God to be established with each believer in Christ through the sanctification of the Spirit.[25]

Therefore for the carnal Christian, who is yet living short of Pentecost, the prayer becomes insistently personal and acutely urgent—

> "Our Father in heaven,
> hallowed be your name,
> your kingdom come,
> your will be done
> on earth as it is in heaven" *(Matt. 6:9-10).*

---

24. Fletcher said that at Pentecost the kingdom of God "began to come with new power."

25. *Pentecostal Grace*, 39. Elsewhere (41) Wood says, "The Christian life is thus made up of two stages—the believer's being incorporated into the kingdom of Christ (justification) and the kingdom of Christ being established in the heart of the believer (sanctification)."

7

The Birth of the Spirit: Initial Sanctification

Jesus made the startling announcement to Nicodemus that before any person could "see" (enter, participate in) the kingdom of God, an event, which He called a spiritual birth, had to occur (John 3:1-8). Nicodemus had been born physically into the nation of Israel; but Israel did not constitute the Kingdom. This was a totally different entity, to be entered by a different kind of birth. It was "from above" and it was by the Spirit.

The human spirit is the locus of this birth. Because of the Fall, man's spirit is alienated from God and spiritually dormant, unable to "lay hold" of spiritual realities. The new birth is the revitalization of the spirit, so that suddenly it is alive to spiritual realities. "The natural man receiveth not the things of the Spirit of God . . . because they are spiritually discerned" (1 Cor. 2:14, KJV). Man without the new birth is an attenuated, two-dimensional creature; the new birth restores the third dimension, that of God and the invisible realm of His kingdom.

I. Prerequisites of the New Birth

A. Awakening

George Smeaton is true to Calvinism in arguing that the convicting power of the Spirit is tantamount to the conversion and assured eternal security of the elect, since He would convict of sin

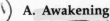

only those whom He intended to save. This explains why the first event in one's spiritual pilgrimage is believed by this school to be *regeneration.*[1]

One preacher explained the dynamics of conversion this way, "You are walking down the street, thinking of nothing in particular, when suddenly you feel a tap on your shoulder, and you turn around and see your friend. So in life. You wander down the path of life when suddenly you feel that tap. You turn around, and there stands Jesus. That is conversion." No, that is only awakening. That is hearing the "gospel call." There is no compulsion in that tap. The stopping is involuntary, and the turning around to see who it is is spontaneous. But then comes the decision, whether we will turn around and walk with Jesus, or proceed on our former way.

The awakening of the soul to its awareness of need, intensified by an aroused conscience, is a phase of prevenient grace. The agent is the Holy Spirit. The means is truth, forced upon the attention by providential events and human influences, perhaps a sermon or song or testimony, at a critical crossroad in one's life.

Without the Word, heard in sermon or read from the page, the conviction will remain hazy. It will be a vague uneasiness, a sense of dread, perhaps of impending disaster; or a restless feeling of incompleteness and nonfulfillment. The preaching of the Word will enable the Spirit to crystallize the unease into conviction of sin, and at the same time quicken hope by directing the attention from self and others to Jesus.

The more pronounced and painful the sense of guilt is in this experience of awakening, the more genuine will be the repentance, and the more the religious orientation will be favorable to holiness. A conversion based on a superficial sense of sin will be difficult to recondition toward a deep, intense desire for holiness. These variations will reflect the motifs of the evangelism by which persons have been brought to faith in Christ.

B. Repentance

John the Baptist, along with Paul, Peter, and the other apostles, all preached repentance, to say nothing of our Lord himself,

---

1. *The Doctrine of the Holy Spirit* (reprint, London: Banner of Truth Trust, 1961), 173-89.

who preached that men should repent and believe the gospel (Mark 1:15).

1. *The Battle for the Will*

The design of the Holy Spirit in awakening is to prompt repentance. Repentance is "given" by the Spirit in the sense of producing inclination and ability. But inclination struggles with disinclination—pride, lassitude, fear of man, love of sin; therefore, the issue rests with man himself. As the Lutherans teach, the sinner cannot create the hunger in his heart, but he can resist it; he cannot save himself, but he can damn himself. Adolf Köberle writes, "We cannot move God to call us, but we can stop our ear to His call when it comes to us."[2]

Because repentance is painful, involving radical reversal of direction and a totally new alignment of goals and values, there is always the temptation to receive Christ exuberantly and repent slightly. Men are prone to accept the offer of pardon without an agonizing wrestling with the moral issue involved (cf. Matt. 13:5-6, 20-21).

Here, too, much depends on the evangelistic atmosphere. Preaching that talks much about happiness but says little of holiness, that is strong on faith and soft on repentance, will encourage this "shape" of religious experience. It is very easy to direct people to Jesus as the solution of one's problems rather than as a Savior from sin. But a superficial repentance lays a flimsy foundation for ethical living later on. Curtis says that a true faith is "steeped in moral passion."[3] Any such "repentance" will be a thin facade if it is not born out of agony over one's own sins. It is axiomatic that vital holiness has its roots in vital repentance.[4]

2. *Illusory Religion or Feeble Birth?*

It is not always easy to understand the shallowness of some new converts and the ease with which they so quickly revert to the world. In some cases it is the problem of an incompletely surrendered will that lies out of sight, just beneath the receptive soil of consciousness. The first burst of joyfulness and the enthusiastic

---

2. *Quest for Holiness,* 143.

3. *Christian Faith,* 87; cf. 124.

4. The peril of so stressing *sola fide* (faith alone) as to downgrade repentance was seen very early in the Reformation, and vigorously repudiated in the Lutheran Formula of Concord (1576): "Yet we are not to imagine any such justifying faith which can exist and abide with a purpose of evil, to wit: of sinning and acting

commitment seem so promising, and the subsequent deflation and defection so disappointing.

In other cases there occurs a religious experience that falls short of a true spiritual regeneration. These persons have become religious, but the new life is a change of vocabulary, milieu, and style that is as truly in the energy of the flesh as the old life was. This is most likely to be the case when "conversion" is for the wrong reason: as when the soul responds to the caring of loving Christians and latches on to *them* rather than Christ. Or it may be when the motive is exploitive, as the young man who wanted to be saved so he could quit drinking in order to win a certain girl in the church. Or it could be like the father who said, "We have had so much sickness and so many reverses, I thought if I became a Christian things might be easier." After three years of trial, during which bills and burdens did not vanish, he did.

However, we must not discount all conversions that do not last. While we cannot press the birth metaphor too far, it is true that just as some physical babies are born weak and sickly, so are many spiritual babes. God knows the heart and will encourage and quicken any sincere approach to Jesus, even when the motives are mixed and the repentance is not as profound as it might be. In such cases a real work of grace is done, the Holy Spirit taking the person as far at this point as he is ready for.

But such a convert will be doubly vulnerable to the pull of the old life. Only careful nurturing will help him stay on his spiritual feet until the Holy Spirit can deepen his repentance and put iron in his purpose, then gently lead him on to full salvation. The holiness obligation must ever be held before such persons, not so as to discourage them—certainly not in a way that unchristianizes them—but in such manner as to both challenge and allure them.

II. Concomitants of the New Birth

The new birth, as the first work of saving grace, is an experience comprised of justification, regeneration, adoption, and initial

---

contrary to conscience." Men may "incur damnation no less by an Epicurean persuasion concerning faith than by a Pharisaic and Papistic confidence in their own works and merits." The necessity of maintaining an avoidance of sinning is also vigorously affirmed: "Moreover, we repudiate and condemn that dogma that faith in Christ is not lost, and that the Holy Spirit, even though a man sin wittingly and willingly, nevertheless dwells in him."

sanctification. These are called concomitants, in the sense that while they are definitively distinct, they cannot be separated in experience. No one is justified who is not at the same time regenerated, adopted into the family of God, and sanctified initially.

A. Justification, Regeneration, Adoption

Justification is twofold, involving both forgiveness of sins and reconciliation with God. *Regeneration* is the act of the Spirit making one spiritually alive. *Adoption* is the transfer of standing and legal relationship from the world to the family of God, and from the kingdom of darkness "into the kingdom of the Son he loves" (Col. 1:13). The Holy Spirit bears witness to our new relationship as sons—it is the Spirit himself who "testifies with our spirit that we are God's children" (Rom. 8:16). This is a divinely imparted sense of peace and assurance. It is one thing for us to "accept" Christ as our Savior; it is quite something else to know that He has accepted us.

The fourth concomitant, *initial sanctification,* requires special consideration.

B. Initial Sanctification

1. *Relative and Real Changes*

Relative changes in salvation are *justification, adoption,* and *positional sanctification.* They are relative in the sense that they are changes of relationship, not (in themselves) subjective changes in the person. *Justification* is a change of standing before the law and the Lawgiver. A discharged criminal, who is either pardoned or has done his time, is in an altered relation to society. Legally he is *right* with society. Society has no further legal ground for incarcerating him. Yet inwardly he may be unchanged. In this case the change is legal, that is, relative to the law, but not real, that is, within himself. *Adoption* also is a relative change, from one family to another; we are never sons in the way Jesus was.

Positional sanctification is that sanctity which is ours derived from our acceptance by a holy God. This is a combination of holiness that inheres in anything *devoted* to God, and of holiness because of *relation* to God. Days, places, and furnishings can be holy in this sense, as well as people. The children of Israel were a holy nation because chosen of God, and because they were His peculiar possession, even though at times they were far from being ethically holy. In this respect *all* Christians are holy, even when carnal, which explains why in the Epistles they are commonly called saints (lit., "holy ones").[5] They are positionally holy by virtue of being "in Christ."

Real changes are *regeneration, cleansing from acquired depravity* (in initial sanctification), and *entire sanctification.* They are real in the sense that they constitute inner changes in the person. In regeneration one is made alive spiritually. In entire sanctification one is (negatively) cleansed from the remains of original sin and (positively) filled with perfect love and harmonized completely with Christ.

2. Components of Initial Sanctification

Sanctification begins in the first work of grace in four respects. *(a)* There is the *positional* holiness already indicated. *(b)* There is a *commitment* to ethical holiness, involved in repentance. No one is in any sense a true Christian who has no intention of living a holy life—though admittedly his concept may be vague as to what constitutes a holy life. Then *(c)* there is initial sanctification in the sense of an *impulse to holiness,* which is of the very essence of the new life in Christ. The new spiritual life of the regenerate is in itself holy and creates a desire to be holy.

But *(d)* that which is especially peculiar to initial sanctification is a cleansing from *acquired* depravity. Acquired depravity and inherited depravity are clearly distinct. There is a cumulative deterioration of character that is continually occurring as the direct result of personal sinning. Every sin leaves its mark—in weakened will, confirmed vice, and distorted thinking. A sinner at 20 is more depraved than he was at 10, and he will be yet more depraved at 40. The fact that his depravity may not develop along bestial lines, and that through personal discipline and culture he may maintain basic respectability of character, does not cancel this. For the progressive depravity we have in mind is an inner hardness of heart and habit of godlessness. If acquired depravity were not a real phenomenon, there would be no explanation for the steep statistical decline in the likelihood of conversion as people get older.

Nothing is more amazing than the real cleansing of this layer after layer of muck and crust that is observable in true conversion.

---

5. Some 58 times; cf. 1 Cor. 1:2; 6:11.

The face softens, old habits drop off, vocabulary changes, ways of thinking are turned inside out. This is that conversion by which tough sinners become little children again (Matt. 18:3). J. Kenneth Grider says that if this "acquired bias" to sin were not cleansed in the new birth "we could not live a Christian life."[6]

Admittedly the outward change is not immediate, but the inner change is instantaneous and will very soon begin working its way outward, touching every facet of the personality and life-style. Unfortunately, this change may be partially impeded by the contrary drag of the carnal mind. But this very tension will lead to self-discovery and to an intensified desire for complete holiness. If the new Christian begins to cater to the reluctance of the carnal mind, there will be a stalemate, then fatal regression.

At any rate, theologically the term *initial sanctification* finds its primary distinctiveness in relation to *acquired* depravity, just as *entire sanctification* finds its primary distinctiveness in relation to *inherited* depravity.[7]

III. HOLISTIC YET PARTIAL

A. Holistic

Real and relative changes in the two works of grace are inseparable. In thought only, justification carries the weight of our final salvation, in the sense that a justified person will go to heaven.[8] But in experience, justification cannot *exist* apart from regeneration and initial sanctification. It cannot *continue* without the faith that obeys and the obedience that believes (Matt. 7:20-22 et al). Rejection of light will mean the death of spiritual life and the forfeiture

---

6. *Entire Sanctification,* 138; cf. his excellent treatment of the concept of acquired depravity, 137-38.

7. See Wiley, *Christian Theology,* 2:476.

8. Indeed, if death followed immediately upon the forgiveness of sins, the soul would be saved. At this point we acknowledge a biblical imputed righteousness. (The whole "package" is put to the believer's "account," somewhat as the first premium on an insurance policy instantly creates an estate for its face value. But this accounting is conditional upon maintaining the terms of the contract.)

This does not mean that imputed righteousness ever exempts the believer from being cleansed of original sin before entering heaven. It means rather that such cleansing will be accomplished by the Holy Spirit, in case of sudden death, without the usual processes. For further insight into a biblical concept of imputed righteousness see E. P. Ellyson, *Bible Holiness* (Kansas City: Beacon Hill Press of Kansas City, 1972), 63-64.

of justification. As Bonhoeffer says, *"Only he who believes is obedient; only he who is obedient believes"* (italics his).[9]

The fatal flaw in some popular forms of Calvinism is the attempt to sever relative changes from real changes (*standing* from *state; declarative* grace from *operative* grace) in such a way that the relative changes can stand alone. While justification assures one of heaven if death ensues within the hour, justification—the relative change—will, as life unfolds, be inseparable from the real changes that belong to a whole salvation, to be realized in time (see pp. 108-9).

B. Partial

Complete salvation, in one sense imputed at conversion and subject to its being imparted, is not fully realized in the first taste of saving grace. At this point the term *new birth* requires a second look. At times Wesley expanded the concept to include the totality of available changes in this life, including entire sanctification. While repudiating many misconceptions of Methodism written by a Mr. Tucker in a tract titled *A Brief History of the Principles of Methodism*, Wesley expressly endorsed Tucker's summary of the relation of the first work of grace to the second, including this:

> Sanctification, the last and highest state of perfection in this life. For then are the faithful born again in the full and perfect sense. Then is there given unto them a new and clean heart; and the struggle between the old and the new man is over.[10]

Yet at other times Wesley was careful to confine the term *new birth* to the beginning of spiritual life.[11] When he used the terms *full salvation* and *great salvation* he always was referring to the "second blessing" of entire sanctification.

It is more faithful to the birth metaphor to limit the term *new birth* to regeneration, with its concomitants, by which believing sinners are brought into the sphere of personal salvation. A "birth" is a beginning that only anticipates all that follows. By being born again and becoming children of God, we "see" the Kingdom, that is, we *enter* it (John 3:3, 5).

---

9. *The Cost of Discipleship* (New York: Macmillan Co., 1963), 69.

10. *Works,* 8:373-74. In a similar manner, E. Stanley Jones sometimes used "conversion" as including the full change of both justification and sanctification.

11. Ibid., 5:150-51; 7:205; 8:48-49; cf. ECH, 2:208-11.

Furthermore, to expand either "conversion" or "new birth" to include *full* salvation is to tend to obscure the radical difference between the first work as a *birth* and the second work of grace as a *correction* and *restoration.* The analogy for entire sanctification is not birth but circumcision (Deut. 30:6). Circumcision was related to birth (and required for *full* membership in Israel) but distinct and subsequent. Wiley warns against overloading regeneration. We "are not to infer," he says, "that because the new life is a holy life, that the simple growth and unfolding of this life will 'bring the soul to entire sanctification.'"

> Failure to discriminate here, leads inevitably to the "growth theory" of sanctification. Sanctification is an act of cleansing and unless inbred sin be removed, there can be no fullness of life, no perfection in love. In a strict sense, regeneration is not purification.[12]

It is a misunderstanding, he insists, to suppose that sanctification "is not something new, but a perfecting of that which we already possess."

> It is indeed true that there is a *substratum* which is common to both regeneration and entire sanctification, that is, a life of moral love. But regeneration is the impartation of this life of love, and entire sanctification is such a purification of the heart as to make love sole and supreme in experience. The two works are separate and distinct, and consequently the latter is something more than the mere finishing touches of the former.[13]

IV. A Birth by the Spirit

Psychologists of religion are at a loss to try to describe and explain on naturalistic or purely psychological grounds the change that occurs in the new birth. The biblical explanation is that the change is an immediate action of the Holy Spirit upon the human spirit. It involves a change in us and a presence in us.

A. An Initial Presence

The Holy Spirit becomes resident when we are regenerated. It is a birth "by the Spirit" (*ek tou pneumatos,* out of, in the sense of origin and agent). He enters the life as an active agent in revealing Christ, continuing to convict of righteousness and sin, and leading

---

12. *Christian Theology,* 2:476.
13. Ibid.

on to full holiness. There is a sense, therefore, in which it must be said that the Holy Spirit is imparted in the first crisis. "And if anyone does not have the Spirit of Christ, he does not belong to Christ," and, "those who are led by the Spirit of God are sons of God" (Rom. 8:9, 14).

B. But Not Spirit Fullness

The new birth, as the initiating experience, does not constitute in itself that privilege of grace that is normative of the dispensation of the Holy Spirit.[14] The disciples had before Pentecost all the earmarks of the new birth but were not yet filled with the Spirit. In defining the Spirit's relationship as *with* them rather than *in* them (John 14:17), Jesus implied a limited availability of the Spirit at that time.

But is the relation of the regenerate Christian to the Spirit *essentially* different in the post-Pentecost dispensation? As with the pre-Pentecost disciples, the focus of attention is on Jesus and not yet on the Holy Spirit as a person in His own right. If believers are ever to be filled with the Spirit, they must consciously choose to receive the Spirit in His sanctifying office.[15]

Furthermore, the disqualification of the world (the unregenerate) from receiving the Spirit as Comforter on the ground of their complete nonrelationship to Him, would equally apply to the unregenerate after Pentecost. It is timelessly true that the "natural man receiveth not the things of the Spirit of God" (1 Cor. 2:14, KJV). A spiritual quickening must occur before one is capable of entering into a relationship with the Spirit in His sovereignty and power.

This is confirmed by Peter's instructions to his audience on the Day of Pentecost (Acts 2:38). To do what he told them to do would be nothing short of openly confessing this Jesus, whom they had so recently crucified, as Lord and Savior, and themselves as His disci-

---

14. Acts 6:3 implies that not all believers were Spirit-filled, any more than all were men of "good report" or filled with "wisdom."

15. True, we are here in the mystery of the Trinity and in danger of Tritheism. Wiley speaks of the Spirit as "our Lord's ever-present other Self" (2:311). In this could be fulfilled His promise: "I will not leave you comfortless: I will come to you" (John 14:18). Yet the distinction cannot be utterly erased. Peter in his Pentecost sermon located the God-man in heaven (Acts 2:33-34; cf. 3:21; 7:56; 9:5; 1 Thess. 4:16; et al.). Taking the New Testament seriously will bring one to the very knife-edge of Tritheism.

ples, and experiencing the forgiveness of sins; in short, being born again. Then, and only then, would they be eligible for the special outpouring of the Spirit normative to the new economy. Moreover, only a regenerate person is capable of asking specifically for the gift of the Spirit with any degree of understanding of the true nature of his request; yet Jesus made the "gift" contingent upon such asking (Luke 11:13).

C. A Twofold Gift

A repentant, believing sinner, then, in receiving Jesus, also experiences the Spirit, though without awareness of who He is. Now, having been made alive, he is capable of deliberately *asking* for and *receiving* the Spirit, with the express desire that the Spirit himself would take charge in sanctifying and enduing power. The Gift of the Spirit, therefore, can be said to be twofold, to a real degree in the new birth, but to a deeper and more conscious degree in the baptism with the Spirit. The Person is the same, but the relationship is different. (See ECH, 2:313-15 for Daniel Steele's position.)

V. Beyond the New Birth

A. Crisis and Process

According to Hebrews, God's people are to "run with perseverance the race marked out" for them (12:1). The Christian is on a pilgrimage, and heaven is his goal. The total project may be described as a process in which there are major and minor crises. Owning a house is for most people a long-drawn-out process, which is initiated by two major crises: making a down payment including signing a contract, and some time later closing the transaction. But that is not the end, as one will be rudely reminded by the very first monthly payment on the mortgage.[16]

In the Christian life there is a usual sequence of spiritual events and experiences. They may be said to begin with awakening, conviction, and repentance, climaxing in justification as the first crucial change. Then follow growth and discovery, obstacles

---

16. This analogy is not intended to imply that we "buy" our salvation on the installment plan. It serves only to illustrate the sense in which crisis and process are compatible concepts.

and discouragements. In time there will be a painful awareness of inner sin, culminating in a renewed stage of conviction, often accompanied by wavering and temptations to despair. At this point there are likely to be attempts to remedy the spiritual need in one's own strength through intensified discipline (thus creating an echo of Romans 7). But as hunger deepens, there will develop a major crisis of confrontation with God, issuing in total surrender and the infilling with the Holy Spirit. This will be the second major change. After this will come released power and freedom, more rapid progress, new learning and advanced discoveries, increased strength, knowledge, and usefulness. But simultaneously may be peculiar temptations and trials, including some dark tunnels. There may even be minor regressions. But on the whole, the holy walk will be forward and upward, until the gates of the City swing outward, then close behind us forever.

After the second major crisis, the spiritual life will be on a higher plane, and the progress normally more rapid and consistent. "Are there any ups and downs in the sanctified life?" J. Edwin Orr was asked, to which he replied in the affirmative. "Then what is the difference between ups and downs in the sanctified life and ups and downs in presanctified life?" "One is like the ups and downs of a highway along the valley floor," Orr answered; "then we wind our way up steep grades to a plateau. The road even there has some normal dips and turns in it; but the dips and turns are on a higher level."[17]

B. The Theology of Secondness

Why two distinct works of grace? Simply stated, because there are two sin problems to be dealt with: (1) sins we commit, for which we are responsible, and for which we need to seek forgiveness; and (2) the sinful nature within, for which we are not responsible, but for which we need cleansing. There are two processes and two stages or levels of attainment. Furthermore the first (conversion) is a prerequisite for the second (sanctification). John Wesley said that he and his brother early learned that men were justified before they were sanctified, that is, entirely.[18]

---

17. *Full Surrender* (London: Marshall, Morgan, and Scott, 1957), 79.
18. *Works,* 8:300; cf. 6:43 ff.

1. *Sin in Believers*

When we speak of sin in believers we do not mean "sinning in thought, word, and deed every day." Such is a shameful caricature of the Christian life. Making allowance for known sin is ruled out (a) by the nature of repentance, as we have already seen; and also, (b) by the nature of the new regenerate life. The biblical verdict is: "No one who is born of God will continue to sin, because God's seed remains in him; he cannot go on sinning, because he has been born of God" (1 John 3:9). This is more than "able not to sin," and more than "not permitted or licensed to sin" (though both are true). It is a moral impossibility for regeneration to coexist with continued willful sinning.

But while willful sinning is excluded by the essential moral terms of the Christian life, original sin remains. The persistence of this inner *other mind* is affirmed in all the major creeds. Representative of the holiness churches is the following: "We further believe that original sin continues to exist with the new life of the regenerate, until eradicated by the baptism with the Holy Spirit."[19]

If original sin continues to "exist," we are compelled to concede the presence of a nature different in kind from the regenerate nature. As vehemently as we may object to the "two nature" theory we cannot totally escape it (see Appendix below). What we properly may object to is not the fact of this temporary state of being "double-minded" (James 1:8; 4:8, lit., *two psyches*), but the teaching that the two minds or natures must remain until death, each unaffected by the other. On the contrary, each is affected by the other, which explains the spiritual warfare within an unsanctified believer, a warfare that under the pressure of the Spirit has as its aim not supine coexistence but total conquest. The objective is to unify the soul, eliminate every recalcitrant element, and bring the totality of the psychic life under the rule of the Spirit and in harmony with Christian holiness.

Repentance and regeneration are real changes that occur in the psychological field of consciousness and volition, and are so radical in nature as to reverse the life's direction and orientation. But however significant the change that is wrought, the proneness

---

19. "Articles of Faith," *Manual, Church of the Nazarene.* The continued presence of inbred sin in the believer is stated or implied by such other holiness bodies as the Free Methodist Church of North America, The Wesleyan Church, and the Evangelical Church of North America.

to self-idolatry with which personal life began nevertheless still lurks beneath the level of full awareness and will constitute an opposing force or drag on the new direction and the new life. This is a profound disharmony in the very self, a propensity in the ego as yet unreconstructed. Harold Ockenga observes:

> Few Christians realize the presence of this corrupt nature at the time of their conversion, for they are involved in the joy of the new life of forgiveness, of the removal of guilt, and of adoption into the family of God. But finally the question will arise to plague this Christian. The first joy, peace and exultation of the regenerate experience will flee and the struggle with self will arise.[20]

"Purity of heart," said the Puritans, "is to have all the wheels of the soul turning the same direction." But in the unsanctified Christian they are not. He is like a car with the brakes dragging: Two contrary forces are creating an abnormal conflict; and while the engine is propelling forward, the brakes are holding back, with the consequent loss of power and liberty. Every struggling believer who becomes painfully aware of his remaining sinfulness of self exclaims, "That is my picture exactly!"

Since this sinfulness that plagues the Christian is essentially the same twist of nature that he brought into the world as an infant, it is unitary in nature, but with multiple manifestations. Therefore to attempt to chop off this or that carnal trait piecemeal, like removing shadows in sections, fails to reach the root of the problem, which is an unsanctified inner self. The heart needs to be purged of its perversity. The affections need to be stabilized on God. But these are but two aspects of one work, so that if one need is met, the other will be also.

The manifestations of the unsanctified ego tend to take the form of sins of the spirit: pride, jealousy and envy, bitterness, touchiness, hard-heartedness, inordinate doubting, covetousness, lukewarmness, worldly-mindedness. In turn there may be quarrelsomeness and undue interpersonal stress, stubbornness, gossip, and evil surmising. Toward God the sin may take the form of a lurking resistance to the absolute claims of divine sovereignty such as a desire to compromise and drive sharp bargains with the Lord; to hedge and angle for advantage. The tendency may be to cool off

---

20. Harold John Ockenga, *Power Through Pentecost* (Grand Rapids: William B. Eerdmans Publishing Co., 1959), 22. Cf. Wesley's description of the believer's awakening to his deeper need in *Plain Account,* 32.

in devotion, such as expressed by Robert Robinson: "Prone to wander, Lord, I feel it, / Prone to leave the God I love."

All these traits were seen in the Eleven before Pentecost (not after!), in the Corinthians,[21] in Ananias and Sapphira, Demas, Diotrophes, in the Hebrew Christians ("See to it, brothers, that none of you has a sinful, unbelieving heart that turns away from the living God"—Heb. 3:12), and in the crowd rebuked so scathingly by James: "If you harbor bitter envy and selfish ambition in your hearts, do not boast about it or deny the truth. Such 'wisdom' does not come down from heaven but is earthly, unspiritual, of the devil. For where you have envy and selfish ambition, there you find disorder and every evil practice" (James 3:14-16). We see the irreconcilable contrast when we put that passage alongside the plumb line of this one: "The wisdom that comes from heaven is first of all pure; then peace loving, considerate, submissive, full of mercy and good fruit, impartial and sincere" (v. 17).[22]

It is the carryover of original sin into the regenerate life that constitutes the need for a second work of grace. Moreover, it is the cleansing of this condition that defines the purpose and nature of entire sanctification. To deny original sin in the believer is to deny a real cleansing from it. Any "second crisis" that remains becomes a mere stage in one's spiritual pilgrimage, which can be explained quite respectably in terms of developmental psychology.

2. *The Necessity of Ethical Choice*

"Offer yourselves to God," says the Word, "as those who have been brought from death to life" (Rom. 6:13). Only those who are spiritually alive are capable of making the great consecration. If the presentation of the body urged upon believers as a "living sacrifice" is to be acceptable, it must be holy, in the sense of being free from either guilt or filthiness (Rom. 12:1).[23]

---

21. Paul did not fault the conversion of the Corinthians, but their arrested development, due to their carnal condition (1 Cor. 3:1-3). Their designation as "babes in Christ" obviously implied their new birth. Evidently Christians may be in a subnormal dual state that hinders spiritual growth. Wesley said that most believers, not yet perfected in love, "feel in themselves more or less pride, anger, self-will, a heart bent to backsliding" (*Works,* 11:423).

22. For a more detailed discussion of sin in believers see Purkiser, Taylor, and Taylor, *God, Man, and Salvation,* 473-74. Cf. Grider, *Entire Sanctification,* 105-13.

23. Animals presented as burnt offerings in the Old Testament were not presented in order to *become* free from blemish; they must be without blemish as a prerequisite.

Elsewhere the matter has been expressed this way:

> The sinner's personal sins and acquired depravity, for which he alone is responsible, must be cleared away before the deeper problem of inherited disposition can be dealt with (cf. Matt. 18:3). A restoration to spiritual life and sonship, involving the cessation of estrangement and rebellion, is logically the prerequisite for the correction of a racial fault, a fault which is not the sinner's own doing, but his heritage from Adam (Acts 2:38). The two phases of redemption available in this life, justification and entire sanctification—the pardon of personal sins and the purging of inherited sinfulness—are so momentous in themselves, and so profoundly different, that the accomplishment of both in a single religious experience would be highly improbable as a characteristic norm in the divine plan.[24]

Furthermore, while it is a mark of the carnal mind to prefer gradual processes to crises,[25] gradualness alone is not compatible with (a) the unitary nature of indwelling sin, which demands punctiliar action; (b) either the will of God that we be holy now, or the power of God to make us holy now; (c) the nature of faith, which is the conditional factor in our sanctification; (d) the hunger and thirst after righteousness experienced by a convicted believer who yearns for deliverance now; (e) the challenge and expectation of immediacy that permeates the New Testament.

Nor is either gradualness or simultaneousness with conversion compatible with the moral necessity of the believer not only seeing the remains of sin within but also pronouncing a judgment upon it. As Wesley expressed it, he must see the "ground of his heart"—its corruption and deceit. Isaiah Reid tells of a respected Sunday School superintendent who seemed a model of piety but made no profession of a "second work"; rather he claimed he "got it all at once." One prayer meeting night Pastor Reid gave a Bible reading, then suggested that they go to their knees in silent prayer, each person praying for the inner searching of the Holy Spirit. After a few moments he heard his Sunday School superintendent groaning. When he drew closer, he heard him praying, "O God, my heart! my heart!" He was shocked by the discovery of what was

---

24. Richard S. Taylor, *Life in the Spirit* (Kansas City: Beacon Hill Press of Kansas City, 1966), 85-86.

25. Believers with slight conviction of need tend to defer getting down to business with God. But honesty and sensitivity will bring them to a crisis, whether they will or no.

really within, under the surface of consistent outward Christian living.

But having once seen his need, he now could no longer be neutral or evasive. The inbred sin for which he was not responsible before would at this point become his responsibility. He must now confess, renounce, and surrender it. Thus the theological necessity of secondness includes the moral necessity of a forgiven sinner renouncing the heritage of Adam and deliberately claiming deliverance from it on the ground of Christ's sanctifying provision and the Spirit's promised power.[26]

APPENDIX: THE TWO NATURES

The whole subject of "nature" needs considerable clarification. Philosophically, just as *esse* (being) must be distinguished from *existence* (relation), so must an entity be distinguished from its nature. Nature may be defined as the attributes of particular generic being, such as the nature of a dog, of a rose, or of man. In this sense, nature cannot be severed from entity, even though distinct in thought; for nature defines dog, rose, or man in distinction from other forms of being. Canine nature is that which constitutes "doghood" in distinction from "treehood" or "rosehood." At this level entity and nature are complementary and unchangeable.

But the matter takes on new complexities and potentialities when we speak of the nature of man. There is the generic nature that, if altered, would result in something other than man. But this generic nature includes certain attributes not present in other kinds of being, such as personality, conscience, and malleability. The capacity to be complex and to change morally is endemic to human nature.[27] This fact compels us to accommodate the term *nature* to a

---

26. "The ethical nature of true holiness demands human cooperation. One of the objections given by disbelievers in a crisis experience is, 'Can ethical character be imparted by a stroke of omnipotence?' Certainly not by an arbitrary, one-sided stroke. God imparts holiness only to the degree that one is ready to receive holiness. . . . The blessings of salvation are not bestowed on non-participating recipients. . . . God demands that we *ask* if we are to receive, and that we exercise faith if we are to experience. These are conscious, deliberate acts, involving a sense of need, of deep desire, and deliberate choice and decision. Man's moral agency is thus respected in every step of vital personal redemption" (*Life in the Spirit*, 86).

27. Michael L. Peterson observes, "The classical account of natures includes not only the essential properties of substances, but also their dispositions, which are dynamic capabilities to act and react under appropriate circumstances. . . . Hence,

secondary kind of usage, by which we can speak of generic nature becoming diverse individual natures. But even more significant is the necessity of conceding that an individual or person may bear more than one nature. The classic literary example is Robert Louis Stevenson's *Dr. Jekyll and Mr. Hyde.*

The much more important theological case is Christ, who is affirmed to be one Person with two natures. To deny the capacity of a personal entity to exist with dual natures is to repudiate the entire Chalcedonian Christology. The problem of two natures in the believer is not nearly as acute as in the Christological formula, for there we have the union of two generic natures, the generic nature of the Godhead and the generic nature of man.

In the Christian, however, the situation concerns not generic natures but moral natures. The doctrine of original sin remaining in believers postulates a moral dualism in one person, consisting of two conflicting, diametrically opposite orientations in the psyche, each struggling for supremacy. The disposition to self-centeredness may very properly be called a nature. But equally may the new disposition toward Christ-centeredness be called a nature. The self finds itself torn—or at least distressed—by these contrary sets of impulse, loyalty, and affection.

It does not help to reject the term *nature* in favor of the carnal *mind* versus the *mind* of Christ. For *phronēma* is much more than a surface attitude; it is nothing less than a profound orientation that in itself is a nature. Admittedly it is paradoxical to suppose that two such profound yet opposite orientations can coexist: but is not the phenomenon of carnal Christians paradoxical? What can be conceded is that these two natures cannot be equally dominant, and that in the end one must be destroyed by the other. It is also true that the presence of this dualism cannot be a normal state of affairs and precludes a healthy spiritual life.

What must also be said is that the word *exist* in reference to original sin remaining in believers does not imply a distinct entity or psychic organism that exists *alongside* human nature. Rather it is a certain kind of proneness in individual human nature itself. This is a carryover from its unregenerate and Adamic state that consti-

---

substantialistic philosophy, properly understood, can account for real change and activity in the world; change happens to and through relatively stable objects" ("Orthodox Christianity, Wesleyanism, and Process Theology," *Wesleyan Theological Journal,* Fall 1980, 57).

tutes a moral force opposed to the change in individual nature as regenerated. The carnal nature may therefore be defined as a complex of psychic tendencies toward unbelief and self-willfulness, which in the Christian does not dominate but challenges the conscious decisions and directions.

It needs to be stressed also that we cannot speak of the carnal nature in the regenerate as we are compelled to speak of it in the unregenerate. In the latter it operates alone in full domination (apart from prevenient grace) and defines the character of the person. In this complex carnal-mindedness, the definitive term "enmity against God" is unmodified. In the Christian, however, the regenerate nature through the power of the Spirit is dominant. It is not enmity against God that defines the believer's heart—his real self—but love. The carnal nature remains only in the sense that this believer becomes aware that self does not love wholly or perfectly. It is in opposition to "Egyptian throwbacks" that, while subdued and latent, are nevertheless subtle pulls toward compromised devotion. The carnal nature in the believer therefore is only incipiently "enmity against God," for the carnal nature no longer defines the inner self in the way it once did. If this person ever again allows enmity against God to move into the center, he is backslidden or at least backsliding.[28]

---

28. Cf. Grider, *Entire Sanctification*, 107.

8

The Baptism with the
Spirit: Entire Sanctification

In the consideration of Pentecost it is impossible to ignore the centrality of what may properly be called the baptism with the Holy Spirit. The declaration of John the Baptist that Jesus would baptize with the Holy Spirit (found in all four Gospels) and Christ's own promise of the Comforter were both tied to Pentecost by Jesus himself: "In a few days you will be baptized with the Holy Spirit" (Acts 1:4-5). Furthermore, Peter later identified the Pentecost event as being baptized with the Holy Spirit, and plainly labeled it as the promised "gift" (11:16-17; see ECH, 1:123-25).

We may say therefore that on the Day of Pentecost the believing 120 were baptized with the Holy Spirit. Furthermore, this was the primary subject of Peter's sermon, as a careful reading will show. His sermon was about Christ as a means of explaining *this:* "Exalted to the right hand of God, he has received from the Father the promised Holy Spirit and has poured out what you now see and hear" (Acts 2:33). Moreover, his instructions that they be converted to Christ has *this* as its objective (vv. 38-39). Still further, *this* is identified as *the Promise* that is the special mark of the entire dispensation, not simply of its first day. Which is to say that the baptism with the Holy Spirit is the divine provision and plan for Christians throughout the entire span of the Church age.[1]

---

1. The fact that other terms denoting this experience are more commonly used in later New Testament literature would not controvert this.

A typical statement of the relation of entire sanctification to the baptism with the Spirit is: "It is wrought by the baptism with the Holy Spirit, and comprehends in one experience the cleansing of the heart from sin and the abiding indwelling

I. LANGUAGE AND TERMINOLOGY

A. Baptism Nomenclature

The more common reference has been to the "baptism *of* the Holy Spirit." This is acceptable if we mean baptism in reference to the Holy Spirit instead of a subjective genitive (the Spirit's own baptism). For strictly speaking, it is not the Spirit's baptism but Christ's. He is the one who baptizes His followers with the Spirit, according to John the Baptist (and Peter, Acts 2:33). Furthermore, in every instance (only six) the preposition used is *en*, which may mean either *in* or *with*.[2] If "in" is preferable, the idea conveyed would be a complete immersion of the believer into the presence and power and sphere of the Spirit. If "with" is preferable, in the sense of instrumentality (cf. Rev. 2:16), then the meaning is that Christ is effecting a spiritual baptism by means of the Spirit.

Other verbs descriptive (and in a sense definitive) of the event would seem to give the edge to "with." For it was an *infilling* (Acts 2:4), suggesting the pervasion of their entire being with the Spirit. It was an *outpouring* (vv. 17, 33) and a *coming upon* (8:16). These metaphors suggest the *definiteness* of the Spirit's advent, the heavenly and divine *source* of His coming, the *abundant measure* of His presence, and His *anointing* for service. In these respects Pentecost was a replica of our Lord's own baptism with the Spirit; for John testified, "I would not have known him, except that the one who sent me to baptize with water told me, 'The man on whom you see the Spirit come down and remain is he who will baptize with the Holy Spirit'" (John 1:33). There was to be a *descent* with the intent

---

presence of the Holy Spirit, empowering the believer for life and service" (*Manual, Church of the Nazarene*). The Wesleyan Church states: "Entire sanctification is effected by the Baptism of the Holy Spirit which cleanses the heart of the child of God from all inbred sin through faith in Jesus Christ." The Free Methodist statement reads: "Entire sanctification is that work of the Holy Spirit, subsequent to regeneration, by which the fully consecrated believer, upon exercise of faith in the atoning blood of Christ, is cleansed in that moment from all inward sin and empowered for service." The Evangelical Church of North America and other Wesleyan bodies have similar creedal statements.

2. Or even *by*, as in 1 Cor. 12:13 (KJV), a possible seventh reference. The meaning of baptism in relation to the Spirit here is unclear and subject to debate. (See ECH, 1:159.) As for *en*, William Douglas Chamberlain says, "The correct meaning of this preposition can be gotten only in the light of the context" (*An Exegetical Grammar of the Greek New Testament* [New York: Macmillan Co., 1960], 119). Cf. ECH, 1:106, n. 5. Cf. Grider, *Entire Sanctification*, 141.

of *abiding*—in sharp contrast to the occasional and temporary action of the Spirit in coming upon prophets and others in Old Testament times.[3]

The terms *baptize* or *baptism* themselves may refer to a literal, physical act, as in Luke 7:29—"being baptized with the baptism of John" (KJV). Or they may be metaphors of a spiritual experience, as our Lord's reference to His passion—"I have a baptism to be baptized with" (12:50, KJV). Similarly, "baptism" is essentially a metaphor in Pentecostal nomenclature. As such its exact meaning cannot be straitjacketed but must be permitted great and rich flexibility. It represents an induction into the full life of the Spirit, a cleansing by the Spirit, and a spiritual death. These paradoxical concepts become coherent in the many-faceted term *baptism*.[4]

B. Terms as Models

The British scholar Ian Ramsey[5] has called our attention to the peril of forgetting that theological terms, such as *redemption*, are not "descriptive through and through." Rather these terms convey at best a "similarity-with-a-difference." Carefulness demands qualifiers, such as *"Heavenly* Father"—and we may add, *"Christian* holiness," *"Christian* perfection," as examples. The qualifiers keep us reminded of the *difference*. For this reason he suggests that terms should be thought of as models.[6] This permits the terms to say something true without our having to "articulate" them to the last hair-splitting implication. It also permits a variety of terms, each as a model making its unique contribution to our understanding of the truth.

The "model" concept will introduce some breathing space into our use of typical holiness terms, such as *baptize, cleanse, sanctify,*

---

3. Actually the nominative "baptism with the Spirit" is a necessary accommodation of language, for only verbs are used in the six pertinent texts.

4. A very helpful analysis of different ways the Spirit is designated in the New Testament in relation to the two works of grace can be found in Leslie D. Wilcox, *Be Ye Holy* (Cincinnati: Revivalist Press, 1965), 53-65. Cf. *God, Man, and Salvation,* 405-6.

5. Nolloth Professor of the Philosophy of the Christian Religion at Oxford, and Bishop of Durham. Alden Aikens has discussed the "model" concept in a paper, "Wesleyan Theology and the Use of Models," *Wesleyan Theological Journal,* Fall 1979, 64. Ramsey's works cited include *Models and Mystery* (London: Oxford University Press, 1964), 6, and *Christian Discourse* (London: Oxford University Press, 1965), 44.

6. There is a difference between "model" and type, symbol, or metaphor, though "model" comes closest to the latter.

destroy, and eradicate. Each term says something valid and something important about the privileges of grace, but no term says it all, and the various redemptive terms used must be seen as a composite picture, not competitive strands. And no one term must be compelled to be proof against every possible objection to it.[7]

The term *baptism* also is a model. In this sense any great outpouring of the Holy Spirit, even at conversion, could be called "a baptism with (or of) the Spirit," just as we speak of "*a* baptism of suffering." Yet the New Testament never confuses this sort of baptism with *the* promised baptism with "the Holy Spirit and fire," experienced on the Day of Pentecost and subsequently. And while the birth of the Spirit could conceivably be called a baptism, the attempt to make the New Testament identify this birth with that baptism which is the peculiar privilege of this dispensation is less than exegetically convincing. Therefore unlimited flexibility is not in order. Still, even when used of this second spiritual event, "baptism" is a model in the sense that it represents a "similarity with a difference" to its empirical base idea, physical immersion.

II. FACETS OF SPIRIT FULLNESS

The above discussion may help us to appreciate more fully a legitimate breadth of view in articulating the doctrine of holiness.

This experience is also known by various terms representing its different phases, such as "Christian perfection," "perfect

---

7. In his paper, Alden Aikens documents the fact that Wesley is "the 'ring leader' of that notorious batch of 'thing thinkers.'" He uses such expressions as "remains of sin" being "taken away," all sin being "destroyed, root and branch," and so on. But Aikens insists that when such critics as E. H. Sugden read into this terminology the inference that Wesley really thought of inbred sin as a "cancer or rotten tooth," they are misunderstanding him. These are figurative expressions, which are Wesley's attempts to grapple with the reality of the condition. Aikens comments, "Sin is real and it so profoundly affects persons that to even approximate adequacy in communicating its reality, we must, in one sense do 'thing thinking'! We must use words that would suggest 'thingness' of the sin nature but realize all the while that we are using models, words indicating a 'similarity with a difference.' We are human, and for now at least anchored to an empirical world, and models enable us to come to a meaningful disclosure of spiritual realities. And we see that the grace of God is so effective in dealing with man's deep need, that when it is dealt with, it is something like a *root* being *pulled out* or an evil thing being *destroyed,* so powerful and effective is the grace of God." Laurence Wood supports this; cf. his discussion in *Pentecostal Grace,* 168; cf. also Grider, *Entire Sanctification,* 28.

love," "heart purity," "the baptism with the Holy Spirit," "the fullness of the blessing," and "Christian holiness."[8]

A. Christian Perfection

The concept of perfection as a central, basic, and indispensable note in Christian faith has never been completely absent from the Church. No term found so frequently or used so significantly in the Bible could easily be ignored.[9] In the New Testament the ideas of completion, fulfillment, and performance are predominant.[10] The various words revolve around the thought of "end" or purpose. "What is the chief *end* of man?" the catechism asks, and answers, "To glorify God . . ." The life that glorifies God is in that respect perfect, for it is fulfilling its destiny; just as the perfection of a watch must be gauged not by its case but by its performance in telling time. It may (conceivably) be perfect as a timekeeper yet the works be housed in a damaged case.

Thus Christian perfection is a matter of the heart—the inner "works" of the soul—not skill of the hands or judgment of the head. As Wesley always insisted, Christian perfection is loving God with all the heart, soul, mind, and strength, and one's neighbor as himself. Such perfection is consistent with numerous infirmities of mind and body, giving rise to mistakes in judgment and practice.[11] He also used the term as a synonym for entire sanctification, and thus interpreted Heb. 6:1—"Therefore leaving the principles of the doctrine of Christ, let us go on unto perfection" (KJV). This he understood to be a plea to move on at once to a definitely attainable level of experience. Christian perfection was not an unrealizable dream but a present privilege and duty.[12]

The baptism with the Holy Spirit ushered the early disciples into this level of performance. They now measured up to what Christ had a right to expect of them in love, sacrifice, purity of

---

8. *Manual, Church of the Nazarene.* In the doctrinal statement (Article X) the heading is not "Baptism with the Holy Spirit" but "Entire Sanctification."

9. *Telos* and its cognates appear approximately 150 times, in addition to *katartizō,* also rendered "to perfect."

10. Cf. article by Delling, *Theological Dictionary of the New Testament,* ed. Gerard Friedrich, trans. Geoffrey W. Bromiley (Grand Rapids: Wm. B. Eerdmans Publishing Co., 1972), 8:67-68.

11. *Works,* 11:394-95.

12. Ibid., 6:411-12.

motive, holy zeal, and spiritual, noncapsizable buoyancy. They exemplified "Christian perfection."

The qualifier, "Christian," is a reminder that this experience is not absolute perfection, which belongs to God only. Neither is it Adamic perfection, which included a perfection of mind and body lost in the Fall and not to be regained in this life. Neither is it angelic perfection; or for that matter, even *human* perfection, in the sense of becoming in all respects a perfect specimen of humanity—only Jesus was that. It is rather a perfection that may characterize us *now*, living as fallible and faulty human beings in a broken and marred world. But this perfection, while not defined by outward performance, *is* defined by our relation to God—a relationship of love and obedience, which in every respect is satisfactory.

In one sense, perfection must mark every stage of our pilgrimage. While the term *Christian perfection* technically is descriptive of the state of grace of those who have been baptized with the Spirit, yet it rests on perfect repentance, perfect consecration, perfect faith, and is maintained by perfect obedience. It is reasonable that this much should be expected of us, for this much, by divine grace, is within the reach of every person. Jesus "became the source of eternal salvation for all who obey him" (Heb. 5:9). But now we are using the other meaning of *teleios*, "complete." Our repentance, consecration, and obedience are to be *complete*. Why not?

B. Perfect Love

This term expresses the essential content of Christian perfection. It is a perfection or completeness of love. When it is once seen that Matt. 5:48, "Be perfect, therefore, as your heavenly Father is perfect," is in the context of a discussion about the Father's love, we will stop making foolish alibis, and we will cease being embarrassed by this verse. It is not a command to be as perfect as God is in every respect, but in one thing only—to be complete and universal in our love, as God is. Our love is not perfect unless it includes the enemy as well as the friend, for only then is it godlike. But the term *perfect love* is also a model, in the sense that the "second blessing" (another model) can be described this way, without claiming that the term is exhaustive of the second blessing, or that it can be forced to carry more weight than it is intended to. When we try to articulate the term too far, we run into problems, as will be seen in the next chapter.

Power forms to be mard

T

*Acts
1:8*

C. Enduement of Power

It is Jesus himself who associates the gift of power with the baptism with the Holy Spirit—"But you will receive power when the Holy Spirit comes on you" (Acts 1:8; cf. Luke 24:49). The adversative conjunction "but" draws a sharp contrast between the kind of power they were to receive and the dreams of political power in the disciples' minds, implied in their question, "Lord, are you at this time going to restore the kingdom to Israel?" (v. 6). Jesus' answer was that even if such a visible restoration of Israel might ultimately be in God's plan, that was not germane to their immediate need, or to the baptism He had just been promising. The mission of the Holy Spirit would be to establish the kingdom of Christ's rule in the hearts of men, one by one, and to endow Christ's disciples with the spiritual power necessary to be His instruments in accomplishing this.

The purpose of the power, therefore, is to equip them for their function as Christ's witnesses—"and you will be my witnesses." The primary sense of *martus*, "witness," as used here, is verbal communication. The mission of the Church is to bear witness to the life, death, and resurrection of Jesus, not only in respect to the bare historical facts but also in the interpretation of their meaning for salvation. The Christian religion is a speaking religion; it is to be propagated not by the sword but by word of mouth.

The promised power is related to this task in a twofold way. First, it is *the moral power to do it,* as demonstrated by Peter before the multitude. He now has words of incisive truth and stinging rebuke in the place of cowardly words of denial. Second, it is *the supernatural impact of the words* upon the hearers. Such impact is explainable not by any eloquence or persuasiveness in the words themselves but solely by the action of the Holy Spirit in and through them. This is that indispensable anointing that "makes preaching preaching" and that elevates even stumbling words of humble testimony to unexpected levels of influence.

In the Early Church *martus* also came to mean *martyr,* one who witnessed to Christ if necessary by the giving of life itself.[13] According to Paul, martyrdom without love was at least a hypothetical possibility (1 Cor. 13:3). But what he had seen in the first

---

13. The process by which *martus* came to mean "martyr" is traced by H. Strathmann in *Theological Dictionary of the New Testament,* 4:504.

martyr Stephen was light-years removed from this. It was the incredible power to face death with the glory of God on one's face, perfect poise in the heart, and a prayer on the lips for the forgiveness of one's murderers. It is more than probable that the demonstration of such power proved to be God's time bomb in the tortured soul of young Saul.

Stephen illustrates a further implication. Effective witnessing is not only a matter of speaking and dying, but of living. It wasn't "dying grace" Stephen received at the last, but the end product of living grace. Far greater than the power of miracles seen on Pentecost was the power of transformed men and women. The true power of Pentecost was (and is) demonstrated in the power to be holy in the midst of defilement, to endure hardship not only courageously but triumphantly, and to rejoice because of being "counted worthy of suffering disgrace for the Name" (Acts 5:41; cf. Eph. 5:18-21).

While it is true that the "apostles performed many miraculous signs and wonders" (Acts 5:12), there is no evidence that this was normative among the 120, or that miracle power was ever identified as an evidence of having been baptized with the Holy Spirit. For the hallmark of the new dispensation was not charismata (such power had been given before Pentecost—Matt. 10:1) but power for holy living and effective witnessing.[14]

D. Heart Purity   *Cleansing*

Purity is a state of freedom from forbidden or obnoxious and alien elements. Purity of heart therefore must be a state of heart free from sin. Since Jesus locates the root of sin (another model) in the heart, it is obvious that if men are to enjoy the blessedness of a pure heart, by which they will "see God" (Matt. 5:8), their hearts must be purified by grace. Here too we must beware of being trapped by too narrow definitions.[15] The term *heart* is a model (in

---

14. The emphasis on power in the Keswick and Moody type of teaching on the baptism with the Holy Spirit is not wrong, unless it is at the expense of heart cleansing. See *Why God Used D. L. Moody,* by R. A. Torrey (reprinted 1973 by the Department of Evangelism, Asbury Theological Seminary, Wilmore, Ky.).

15. It is significant that Jesus locates this inner defilement in the heart in contrast to the stomach. When He denied the defiling power of what went into the stomach and passed out of the body, He was showing the great moral gulf between the body as a biological organism and the inner man who thinks and chooses. He

some languages "liver" serves this function) that represents the inner man in moral relations. The accent may variably be on intent, the thought life, the conscience, or the deepest, controlling affections. The "heart" is not a constituent element of human nature, but a descriptive word referring to the real inner quality of the self-life.

Heart purity, therefore, is an inner state satisfactory to God. But if so, the "heart" must have been *cleansed* of guiltiness, filthiness, and the bent to self-sovereignty. Actions are observable, words are audible, but the real motives and intentions are hidden in the heart. Peter's claim, therefore, that in the baptism with the Holy Spirit their hearts were purified becomes highly significant (Acts 15:9), and "heart purity" can be seen as a model that helps us to understand the state resulting from the baptism with the Holy Spirit.[16] It can mean nothing less than the removal of inbred sin.

The Book of Acts fairly teems with evidences in the lives of the apostles and all who experienced this baptism, of purified motives and cleansed affections. Each one could be said to have a "one-track mind for God." The old rivalry, self-seeking, and "self-protectivitis" were gone. This is why the Great Commission was being fulfilled. They were "eager to do what is good" because they knew by experience the purpose of Christ "to purify for himself a people that are his very own" (Titus 2:14). They had been purified

---

is saying, "The problem of defilement is not *there*, it is *here*." And He switched from the precise empirical word *stomach,* which meant the digestive organ, to *heart*— which did not mean the blood-pumping organ. He thus used "heart" as a model of the spirit, and in so doing went from literal language to figurative.

16. Some have limited the purifying of the heart in Peter's testimony (Acts 15:8-9) to the forgiveness of sins, or the "purifying" of expiation, on the ground that the term is an aorist participle and therefore means "having purified their hearts by faith." Careful handling of the many aorist participles in Acts is indispensable to sound exegesis—and should be more consistently done. But in this case the temporal precedence does not apply because the kingpin word *giving* ("giving the Holy Spirit to them") is also aorist participle. To press the tense in this case therefore would result in: "God, who knows the heart, showed that He accepted them, *having given* them the Holy Spirit, and made no distinction between us and them, *having purified* their hearts by faith." So the purifying and the giving of the Holy Spirit remain simultaneous. The purifying is the answer to the descriptive promise of John the Baptist of a baptism typified by purifying fire. The symbol of fire rested upon each of them on the great Day of Pentecost, which Peter saw as the prototype of this blessing. As far as the forgiveness of sins is concerned, the supposition that the disciples were not forgiven until the Day of Pentecost would be very hard to support in the face of the plethora of contrary evidence.

from that residue of resistance to the Lordship of Christ, which is the plague of Christians yet double-minded.

The relation of purity to power, and the relation of both to the baptism with the Holy Spirit, is graphically expressed by Juji Nakada, cofounder with Charles Cowman of the Oriental Missionary Society. He writes:

> I did not get inner satisfaction though I sought after the "Baptism in the Holy Ghost" very earnestly. While I was seeking after this I found that my motive was questionable. I sought it simply because I wanted to become a wonderful evangelist. The "empowering for service" had a good sound to me. Through the Scripture I slowly learned what I needed mostly was not *power,* but *purity.* I found my heart was not pure in the sight of God. . . . When I began to seek after Holiness many people opposed me, telling me that "as long as we live in this world we cannot be free from the evil nature." But I thought that if God cannot change our disposition, wherein does Christianity differ from other religions? Even Buddhism teaches us to *suppress* the old nature. What I was seeking after was not another way of *suppression,* but to get free from Sin, the *carnality* which is enmity against God. . . . When I fully surrendered to Him He definitely answered my prayer and "baptised me in the Holy Ghost."[17]

E. Entire Sanctification

As a model this term contributes to our overall understanding of our privileges in Christ. It suggests that there is a side of sanctification that can be completed, just as there is a side that remains progressive. There is a state of grace at which we may arrive, in a definite experience, of which we may be sure, and to which we may humbly bear witness. There is always the peril that the conscience may be lulled into an illusion of piety by a permanent stance of longing, yearning, and even a kind of seeking. Such persons revel in aspiration, but when someone claims to have realized the experience, they become highly nervous. People too often set-

---

17. *OMS Outreach* (Greenwood, Ind.), June 1979. In relating power to purity J. Paul Taylor trenchantly observes, "Simon Magus would have to completely die to Simon Magus before it would be safe for him to have the gift of power. The unholy man would try to manage the power to further his own ends; the holy man is managed by the power to secure God's ends. The Holy Spirit comes in His fullness to use us and not to be used by us" (*Holiness, the Finished Foundation,* 108). The entire chapter is an excellent discussion of the relation of power to purity and of its relation to love.

tle for the virtuous feeling of a sentimental hungering after holiness as a substitute for the experience.

1. Beyond Initial Sanctification

Furthermore, the term *entire sanctification* implies a previous state of partial sanctification, which, as we have already seen, is exactly what initial sanctification is. Real but partial holiness is implied by Paul's exhortation to the Corinthians: "Since we have these promises, dear friends, let us purify ourselves from everything that contaminates body and spirit, perfecting holiness out of reverence for God" (2 Cor. 7:1). It is implied by the designation of the Corinthians as being "in Christ," yet carnal—unspiritual (1 Cor. 3:1-3). It is implied by Paul's earnest wish for the Thessalonian believers, that they be sanctified "through and through" (1 Thess. 5:23; "wholly," KJV). A "through and through" sanctification can hardly be called less than "entire." And Paul appends the assurance that the God who calls them to this "is faithful and he will do it."

2. Our Lord's Prayer

But Paul was not the first to desire the entire sanctification of disciples. The Spirit was simply directing Paul to pattern after his Lord, who had prayed for *them* and *us* that they and we might be "truly sanctified" (John 17:19; cf. 17-20). Their previous *partial* sanctification is attested by Jesus' declaration that they were "not of the world, even as I am not of it" (v. 16). He had earlier stated, "You are already clean," and "I am the vine; you are the branches" (15:3, 5). There are many like evidences.[18]

Was our Lord's petition a vain prayer? Was it ever answered? If so, when and where? Surely an open-minded reading of the Scripture brings one to the obvious answer—Pentecost. For one thing, the juxtaposition of this high-priestly prayer with His discourse on the coming of the Holy Spirit, the Comforter, who would do so much for them, could scarcely be accidental or insignificant. It would be hard to suppose that there was no connection between what Jesus was promising respecting the Holy Spirit and what He

---

18. An earlier British writer, Rudolf Steir, says of the disciples' partial sanctification: "In fact, so far as they are already pure through the word given to them (15:3) and Christ lives in them through their world-renouncing faith, they are already sanctified in the sense of 1 Cor. 6:11—but that is not enough for the *hagiason* yet in reserve, which must be explained according to 2 Cor. 7:1; Acts 26:18; and 20:32" (*The Words of the Lord Jesus* [Edinburgh: T. and T. Clark, 1863], 486).

was now praying respecting their sanctification. But beyond this, the change in them when they were filled with the Holy Spirit matched perfectly what the prayer itself had predicted as its answer.

"To sanctify" (*hagiazō*, to make holy) is a rock-ribbed word meaning, essentially, to separate to God or to a holy task, and inferentially, to separate from sin. In the case of the disciples, the primal sin from which they needed to be separated so glaringly was the sin of self-seeking, manifest in hard-heartedness, cowardice, bickering, and unbelief. Without such a separation from this evil side of themselves, the mission would have collapsed and the Church withered to a feeble sect of Judaism—if it had survived at all. But fortunately (for us as well as for them) this kind of cleansing is precisely what happened to them on the Day of Pentecost. It is scarcely possible, therefore, to separate entire sanctification from the baptism with the Holy Spirit. Furthermore, our entire sanctification today is as dependent upon the immediate, personal, and radical action of the Spirit as it was in their case. This is an inner dynamic, so truly of the essence of a real experience of entire sanctification, that questions of pre-Pentecost and post-Pentecost distinctions become irrelevant (2 Thess. 2:13).

3. *Consecration and Purification*

At times "to sanctify" is equivalent to "to consecrate" as, for instance, in Christ's use of the same term to designate what He was voluntarily doing to make their sanctification possible. While Jesus was sanctifying himself, He was asking the *Father* to sanctify *them.* God's sanctifying is a purging *unto* perfect consecration in response to our surrender *for* purging unto the consecrated life. *Perfect* consecration is hardly possible until our honest decision to consecrate is answered by perfect divine purification. "Perfect consecration would be complete and absolute holiness. No purity would be wanting to the motive, no elevation to the character, of one who should be devoted to the Lord his God, with 'all his heart, and all his soul, and all his mind, and all his strength.'"[19]

Our consecration therefore must be authenticated by self-purging on our part as far as we know and are able (2 Cor. 7:1; James 4:8; 1 John 3:1); but beyond that it must be perfected by the sanctifying work of the Holy Spirit (2 Thess. 2:13; 1 Pet. 1:2).

---

19. *Great Texts of the Bible,* ed. James Hastings (Grand Rapids: Wm. B. Eerdmans Publishing Co., n.d.), 12:294-95.

It follows almost without saying that if you set apart a person or a thing to the service of an absolutely holy God, anything that defiles that person or thing renders it unfit for God's use, and hence, though the first meaning of the word is separation, it speedily "acquires," as Archbishop Trench . . . points out, "a moral significance;" thus the thought of purification is added to the fundamental idea of separation. If I want to separate a cup to God's service, and that cup is polluted, I must not only set it apart for God's use, I must separate it from the pollution that is in it. . . . If I am to be separated to God, and sanctified for God's service, it is not enough that I should be set apart without any reference to my intrinsic character. The character itself must be purified from the defilement which makes it unfit to be used in a holy service . . . (2 Tim. 2:21). Thus we see that the deeper thought of the moral and spiritual renovation follows close upon the first great meaning of separation, and in fact springs out of it.[20]

4. *Entire—Both Qualified and Unqualified*

The minimal sense of "entire," then, as indicative of that sanctification that is available now, must be complete purging from the carnal mind in order that our subsequent life of consecration will be acceptable, untarnished, and uncompromised by inner discrepancy. But this minimal sense must also include as much as Paul does—the entire person. "May your whole spirit, soul and body be kept blameless at the coming of our Lord Jesus Christ." Or as Weymouth puts it: "May God Himself, who gives peace, make you entirely holy; and may your spirits, souls and bodies be preserved complete and be found blameless at the Coming of our Lord Jesus Christ." By implication this includes entire surrender, entire trust, entire availability, entire obedience. But it extends only to *blamelessness,* which means freedom from real cause for condemnation. It is not entire faultlessness, or entire understanding, or entire maturity, or entire skill in the things of God. Nor is it entire Christlikeness in terms of outward personality or culture. Yet further refinements and alterations are needed, which means that in the broadest sense of the term, the sanctifying process goes on.

---

20. Ibid., 301. The tendency therefore of some to equate consecration and sanctification "straight across the board" is both incorrect and dangerous, for it reduces sanctification to an act of the believer without giving due recognition of sanctification as an act of God in and upon the believer. Cf. preface of RSV (1952), viii.

9

Experiencing Heart Holiness

The command to be "filled with the Spirit" (Eph. 5:18), while implying a continuous Spirit-filled life, also implies a beginning. "Almost all Christians want to be *full* of the Spirit," observes A. W. Tozer. "Only a few want to be *filled* with the Spirit."[1] Here is the very human tendency to desire results without meeting conditions and facing crises. But there must be a point in time when the Spirit is received in His fullness; when, in other words, the "baptism with the Spirit" is experienced.

I. CONDITIONS TO BE MET

That the Spirit's sanctifying infilling is a gift to be received in simple faith is a basic New Testament emphasis. It would be a grave error, however, to assume that because the blessing is a gift there are no human conditions to be met. The biblical instructions to "offer yourselves to God" (Rom. 6:13), to "offer your bodies" (12:1), to "purify ourselves from everything that contaminates" (2 Cor. 7:1), and to "purify your hearts, you double-minded" (James 4:8; cf. 1 John 3:3), are all admonitions directed to believers, and all are related to the matter of our sanctification. Therefore it is a mistake to suppose that there is no methodology in the New Testament.

---

1. *Keys to the Deeper Life* (Grand Rapids: Zondervan Publishing House, 1957), 26.

Even the disciples were given precise instructions by the Lord: They were to "stay in the city" until they had been "clothed with power from on high" (Luke 24:49). Precise instructions also were given by Peter on the Day of Pentecost by which the inquirers could qualify themselves for the same promised Holy Spirit (Acts 2:38).

However, the Book of Acts does not suggest that the 10-day waiting period before Pentecost is the norm for post-Pentecost times. The Spirit infilling at Samaria, of Cornelius and his friends, and of the Ephesian disciples was associated with instruction, prayer, and laying on of hands. The result seemed simple and direct. The Holy Spirit was already outpoured dispensationally; now His personal, individual fullness was always available. Yet the spiritual readiness essential for the blessing to be received can be reasonably assumed. There could also have been a longer time involved and greater spiritual struggles than were recorded. Even the readiness of Cornelius had a background of earlier prayer, almsgiving, and obedience. He was in an attitude of faith, and the "heart-knowing" God *(kardiagnostēs)* responded by giving him the sanctifying gift of the Spirit.[2]

It is significant that when competent spiritual guides have attempted to prepare specific instruction, the lists have been remarkably similar, whether the guide has been Keswickian or Wesleyan. A. W. Tozer's instructions are: *(a)* Surrender (Rom. 12:1-2). *(b)* Ask (Luke 11:13). *(c)* Obey (Acts 5:32). *(d)* Believe (Gal. 3:2).[3] Harold Ockenga lists the following steps: *(a)* Confession of being in a carnal state. *(b)* Consecration. *(c)* Prayer. *(d)* Faith. *(e)* Obedience.[4] J. A. Wood, in his classic, *Perfect Love*, summarizes the preparatory steps toward faith by the following questions:

1. Do I clearly see my *inbred sin,* and consequent need of holiness?
2. Am I *willing, anxious,* and *resolved* to obtain it?

---

2. See ECH, 1:123-25. For further discussion of the spiritual preparedness of Cornelius see Grider, *Entire Sanctification,* 48-52.

3. *Keys to the Deeper Life,* 22-24. There is also a striking similarity in the actual experiences of finding "the blessing" between Calvinists and Arminians; cf. V. Raymond Edman, *They Found the Secret* (Grand Rapids: Zondervan Publishing House, 1968).

4. *Power Through Pentecost,* 22-24.

3. Am I willing to give up all to God—self, family, property, reputation, time, talents, everything—to be his, used for him, trusted with him, and never withheld or taken from him?
4. Do I believe?[5]

A. Repentance in Believers

The insistence of Wesley on a deep repentance in the believer if faith is to take hold is essentially sound (though the suitability of the word *repentance* in this case could be challenged). This repentance, he says, is "widely different" from that which leads to conversion, for it "implies no guilt, no sense of condemnation, no consciousness of the wrath of God." Rather it is a profound conviction of need.

> It is properly a conviction, wrought by the Holy Ghost, of the *sin* which still *remains* in our heart; of . . . *the carnal mind,* which "does still *remain,*" (as our Church speaks,) "even in them that are regenerate;" although it does no longer *reign;* it has not now dominion over them. It is a conviction of our proneness to evil, of an heart bent to backsliding, of the still continuing tendency of the flesh to lust against the spirit *[sic].* . . . It is a conviction of the tendency of our heart to self-will, to Atheism, or idolatry; and, above all, to unbelief, whereby, in a thousand ways, and under a thousand pretences, we are ever departing, more or less, from the living God.[6]

Not that we are sanctified by this "repentance," especially not if it stalemates into mere self-castigation. The deflation of self is healthy only if it leads to that faith which casts itself on the mercy and grace of God for purity as completely as it did for forgiveness.

B. The Primacy of Prayer

With the possible exception of the Ephesians (Acts 19:1-6), every instance of Spirit baptism or reinfilling recorded in Acts was

---

5. Rev. and enl. ed. (Chicago: Christian Witness Co., 1880), 98. Eldon Fuhrman suggests the following steps: *Awareness*—of need; *Acknowledgment*—of the need; *Asking*—for the blessing; *Abandonment*—of all remaining self-willfulness; *Appropriation*—by faith; *Affirmation*—in open testimony. From unpublished classroom notes, Wesley Biblical Seminary.

6. *Works,* 6:50. What Wesley describes may be called "repentance" in the sense that it is a grief over the discovered presence of sin, inbred if not actual, and a renunciation of it through confession and consecration. Grider, however, believes that "penitence" would be the better word, and that "repentance" should be reserved for what sinners do in becoming converted. Cf. *Repentance unto Life* (Kansas City: Beacon Hill Press of Kansas City, 1965), 78.

associated with prayer. This is in harmony with Christ's assurance that the Father would give the Holy Spirit to "those who ask him" (Luke 11:13). No asking, no receiving. The necessity of prayer implies several basic principles. It is an acknowledgment that holiness is the work of God in the soul; if God does not act, we will never be holy. Further, it is a recognition of the gift/grace nature of the Spirit's fullness. Here is an experience and a relationship that cannot be achieved, merited, or earned. It can be obtained only by coming to its source, the Triune God.

Furthermore, prayer implies the necessity of human initiative. It is not enough for the believer to be languidly receptive, to be willing to be filled if and when God chooses—in the meanwhile doing nothing. This is a high and precious Gift that is available only to those who want it enough to ask for it, specifically, sincerely, and if need be, persistently.

C. Intensity of Desire

The promise of fullness and the pronouncement of blessedness must concern not only sinners who "hunger and thirst" (Matt. 5:6) after the righteousness of justification but also upon believers who hunger and thirst after the inner rectitude of holiness. This is in the nature of the case, since regeneration in itself imparts a love for holiness and sets up an inner tension with remaining sinfulness, which gradually becomes acutely distressing. If the Christian pursues the goal of a closer walk with God, and a greater degree of personal victory, he will come to abhor the corruption within. He will ultimately reach a state of holy desperation of soul that simply refuses to go on without cleansing. This very intensity of desire will compel earnest and determined seeking.

Only such intensity of desire will overcome that sluggishness that tends to make one drift and procrastinate. It will dispel that fear of man that shrinks from ridicule from holiness objectors, or that paralyzing pride that fights the humiliation of open seeking and would seek to protect religious standing and profession. Furthermore, only this deep longing and purpose will overcome theological prejudice, push past stalling "intellectual" questions, and stop one from hiding behind false professors.

It is to be feared that too often the necessary desire is dissipated by compromise and worldliness. The consequence is either complete backsliding, or at best a settling down to a feeble spiritual existence, stunted in growth and wizened in spirit. To avoid such a miserable caricature of the Christian religion, the new convert should be urged early to cultivate a sensitivity to the pull of the Spirit toward ever new vistas of truth and privilege.

D. Consecration

This is the decisive presentation of self to God for sacrifice or service, according to Rom. 12:1-2.

1. *A Devotement*

Consecration is an act, done in studied deliberateness, in full awareness of the implications, and without reservation. It is definite, decisive, and final. It includes submission to God's deployment as well as employment. It is a commitment to unlimited obedience—to the point of being "obedient to death, even death on a cross" (Phil. 2:5-8). It is a surrender to God of all claims to one's life. It means "putting on the altar" our present and future circumstances—marital, economic, ecclesiastical, and social—with total commitment to be holy no matter what the issue or at whatever cost or pain.

Moreover, consecration accepts the full demands of thorough stewardship—not my ownership but God's, not my glory but His, not my advantage but the Church's advancement, not to "use" God but to be used by Him. It is impossible for a consecrated person to be carrying on a running battle with God over such stewardship issues as tithing.

Furthermore, consecration is active as well as passive. It is not only "Thy will be done" *in* me and *to* me, but *by* me and *through* me. To this end the consecrated person will be *actively* engaged in seeking the mind of God, *actively* engaged in developing his abilities for greater usefulness, and *actively* engaged *now* in reaching out to the lost. He will not be an indolent bystander who allows others to do the praying and sacrificing, and working.

2. *A Concentration*

Consecration, moreover, demands by its very nature *concentration.* The holy person may have many and varied interests, but they focus in the supreme interest—Christ. All other interests are not only secondary but also dispensable. Activities that make no contribution to the glory of God will be quietly laid aside. Since no person can do everything that might be both legitimate and fascinating, or that he might be capable of doing, he will concentrate on the main things. And his spiritual sense, illumined by the Spirit, will tell him unerringly what the main things are. A consecrated person has his priorities in order and keeps them that way (Matt. 6:33).

Consecration in respect to business implies the priority of persons over profits. It implies the priority of spiritual values over material values. Therefore it makes a large place for prayer, the Word of God, the house of God, and the work of God. Such a consecrated Christian is content with the consequences even if it means making less money and stopping at a lower rung of the ladder. Such trifling "sacrifices" disturb him not at all.

3. A Death

Consecration remains superficial if it does not reach the jugular of the self nature. Traditionally, both Wesleyan and Keswickian writers have made much of the concept of self-crucifixion. In part this is based on the understanding that when Paul testified, "I am crucified with Christ" (Gal. 2:20, KJV), he meant more than a positional identification with the Cross, by which Paul was a beneficiary. He meant also a subjective reality, by which he personally experienced a crucifixion. This interpretation is confirmed by what follows: "It is no longer I who live, but Christ who lives in me" (RSV).

When did Paul "die"? Did not those three days in Damascus, before Ananias came, involve him in a real death to self? On the road to Damascus he surrendered to Jesus as the Messiah, and said, "What shall I do, Lord?" (Acts 22:10). Now, alone, he faces up to what open avowal of Christ will mean. He has been the Sanhedrin's prize hope, its "golden boy." Every possible honor and position of power—excepting the priesthood—is open to him. As he contemplates the cost he sees all his personal ambitions, all of his dreams as a zealous young Jew, his prestige and influence in the Jewish nation, everything he has valued, suddenly shattered. That is, if he goes forward instead of drawing back. Perhaps he will say, "Jesus, I now acknowledge You as Messiah, and I promise no longer to persecute Your followers. But I will just quietly withdraw and insulate myself in a cocoon of secret faith." But he chooses to "die." He learns the meaning of Jesus' words: "Unless a kernel of wheat falls to the ground and dies, it remains only a single seed. But if it dies, it produces many seeds" (John 12:24; cf. Phil. 3:4-10; Acts 20:24).

It is reported that when George Mueller of Bristol was once asked what the secret of his great usefulness was, he replied, "If God has been able to use me it is because there came a day, as a young Christian, when I died. I died to George Mueller—to his preferences and plans. I died to the world, with its praise or blame. I died to everything but the will of God."

Graphically Clarence W. Hall traces the "death route" of Samuel Logan Brengle. Brengle was appalled at the big "I" he discovered in himself. He said:

> I saw the humility of Jesus, and my pride; the meekness of Jesus, and my temper; the lowliness of Jesus, and my ambition; the purity of Jesus, and my unclean heart; the faithfulness of Jesus, and the deceitfulness of my heart; the unselfishness of Jesus, and my selfishness; the trust and faith of Jesus, and my doubts and unbelief; the holiness of Jesus, and my unholiness. I got my eyes off everybody but Jesus and myself, and I came to loathe myself.[7]

The struggle focused on Brengle's ambition to be a great preacher. "Let us look closely at this inner battle," writes Hall the biographer. "Note the subtle arguments of the 'I,' and see how the Spirit progressively breaks them down." Hall continues:

> It would be as a great preacher, Brengle tells himself, that he could best reflect glory on God; and is not the glorifying of God the chief end of man? The Light flashes, showing him that God can best be glorified through the winning of souls.
>
> Granted, Brengle agrees; the more souls saved the more glory for God. Hence, to save many, he must have a large, influential ministry. But again the Light flashes and, seeing "I" still smeared all over his aspirations, Brengle capitulates: "Lord, if Thou wilt only sanctify me, I will take the meanest little appointment there is."
>
> So far, good. Yet he still has something left of the "I." The thought comes that, even though his following shall be small, he can still be eloquent, a powerful orator, building up his small section of the Kingdom of God through the sheer force of his rhetoric and the cadences of his voice. Yet again, however, the Light flashes; and now we see the final gesture that empties his hands, as he casts away the last segment of the "I." Listen: "Lord, I wanted to be an eloquent preacher, but if by stammering and stuttering I can bring greater glory to Thee than by eloquence, then let me stammer and stutter!"[8]

7. *Samuel Logan Brengle: Portrait of a Prophet* (New York: National Headquarters, the Salvation Army, 1933), 55.

8. Ibid., 56-57.

And so his cherished dream is finally "on the altar." Throughout his great ministry he *did* preach with eloquence; but the touch of God's fire was on it because Brengle had died to it.

Harold Ockenga surmises that during the pre-Pentecost days of prayer, a lot of getting right, confessing, and consecrating were going on among the disciples. He selects Peter as a possible example. On Thursday, Ockenga suggests, Peter's mind was distracted by thoughts of his fishing business and his family complications. He could not pray "under them, or over them, or around them, for they occupied the centre of his attention. Finally, in despair, he consecrated his nets, his interests in the fishing industry to the Lord, and then he could pray again." Friday the Lord dealt with him about his mother-in-law; he had to pray through on her. On Saturday he struggled with the thought of leaving his beautifully situated home overlooking the blue Galilee. "Finally, he prayed through that: consecrated his home, agreed to take his wife with him, whether in poverty or abundance, to labour with an eye single to the glory of God." On Sunday it was his personal ambition to be "chief" that had to die. On Monday Peter confessed "his own irritation and hard feelings toward James and John for wanting to be seated on the right and the left of the Lord in His kingdom; he confessed his denials, his shortcomings, his unworthiness and his need of the cleansing and empowerment of the Holy Spirit. Other apostles did the same. There was a great melting . . ." And so on through the week.[9] When the Day of Pentecost finally came, they were not only "all together in one place" physically, but spiritually. They were ready.

II. THE CATALYST OF FAITH

A. The Place of Faith

In various ways the Bible makes receiving the Spirit in His sanctifying power dependent upon our faith (Acts 15:8-9; 26:18;

---

9. *Power Through Pentecost,* 32-33. Many suppose that in pumping a manual organ they are filling the bellows with air, when in fact the pumping is *emptying* the bellows. A vacuum is needed. Then simply depressing the keys allows the air from God's great outdoors to do its work. Begging the Spirit to fill us is missing the mark. Our task is to prepare a place for Him. This means that we do not so much pray ourselves *full* as pray ourselves *empty.* Faith is depressing the keys and receiving the Spirit in His sweet offices of sanctifying, strengthening, reinforcing, illuminating, and indwelling.

Gal. 3:2, 14; Rom. 5:2, NASB; Eph. 3:17; 1 Thess. 3:10 with 5:23-24). Jesus commonly asserted the necessity of faith for both physical and spiritual blessings. "According to your faith will it be done to you" (Matt. 9:29) is a fundamental principle. Jesus challenged the distraught father to believe without seeing "miraculous signs and wonders" (John 4:48-50), and commended the centurion for being willing to rest solely on His simple word (Matt. 8:5-10).

When Peter declared to the assembly in Jerusalem that "their hearts" were "purified . . . by faith" (Acts 15:8-9), he was affirming a purification not dependent on the works of the Mosaic law (as represented by circumcision). It was, rather, purification available now in response to simple faith—a faith that laid hold of the power of the Spirit for this immediate objective. By implication, Peter's testimony means that just as justification is provided by grace as a gift and therefore to be appropriated by simple faith, so precisely is sanctification obtainable through faith—not by means of works, discipline, time, or growth.

Faith, whether justifying faith or sanctifying faith, is a particular kind of attitude toward God. It is an attitude (1) of belief that God has spoken, supremely and finally in His Son, but also in His written Word, the Bible; and that this Book is still God's Word, by means of which we know His will. But faith is also (2) an attitude of complete confidence in God's integrity—His faithfulness to make good His Word. For this reason unbelief is a sin, the sin of slander; and such unbelief makes pleasing God impossible (Heb. 11:6). The human race fell away from God through doubting His Word. There is no way back without believing His Word. Christian faith, therefore, is believing what God says in His Word *about* Christ, the Cross, the Holy Spirit, and about holiness; and what He has *promised* respecting us. It is with such faith that we come to God in humility asking for entire sanctification.

Yet the Bible does not teach that our faith alone accomplishes the sanctifying. Our sanctification is also ascribed to the Word (John 17:17; Acts 20:32); to the blood of Christ (John 17:19; Eph. 5:25; Heb. 13:12; Titus 2:14); and more directly to the Holy Spirit (2 Thess. 2:13; 1 Pet. 1:2). Theologians have at times named the will of the Father as the *originating* cause of our sanctification, the blood of Christ as the *procuring* cause, the Word of God as the *instrumental* cause, and the Holy Spirit as the *efficient* cause. Faith then becomes the *conditional* cause—the voluntary response of trust that makes realization of the provisions and actions of the Triune God in our hearts possible. Faith is the condition in the sense that the Word, the Blood, and the Spirit will avail nothing if we do not believe.

B. The Enigma of Faith

The exact relationship of faith to the experience—especially to the "witness of the Spirit"—is elusive. John Wesley insisted that we were sanctified when we believed, yet he stopped short of instructing Christians to claim the blessing without any assurance.[10] In a letter to a friend he made the astonishing statement: "That every man may believe if he will I earnestly maintain, and yet that he can believe when he will I totally deny." This makes sense only if he meant that the will to believe must be enabled by the Spirit who alone knows *when* the person is ready. But Wesley wisely added, "But there will always be something in the matter which we cannot well comprehend or explain."[11]

One's understanding of faith's dynamics will be determined to some extent by his concept of the nature of the work for which faith is to be exercised. If entire sanctification is viewed simply as a relationship, then exercise of faith becomes a confidence that God accepts our self-presentation—a relatively easy assumption. But if entire sanctification is perceived (as Wesley perceived it) to be a real subjective change wrought instantaneously by the Spirit—a spiritual "circumcision"—then the working of faith becomes more difficult to grasp. For in this case faith is in no sense the real agent of power; that agent is the Spirit. Faith is rather the attitude and action that receives the Spirit for the performance of this inner change. But the complexity deepens, for here too there is a parting of the ways:

a. If the work of sanctification is understood to be a change in the inner being, that is, the nature, below the field of consciousness, then there is a basis for boldly claiming the blessing solely on the authority of the divine promises and the divine faithfulness: "I believe God does what I ask, and my feeling in the matter is irrele-

---

10. *Works,* 6:52.

11. *Letters of John Wesley,* 6:287. Quoted by John Leland Peters, *Christian Perfection and American Methodism* (New York: Abingdon Press, 1956), 113. See also Melvin Easterday Dieter, *The Holiness Revival of the Nineteenth Century* (Metuchen, N.J.: Scarecrow Press, 1980), 30.

vant." Charles G. Finney seems to express this view when he says, "To receive the Holy Spirit is to take Him for our *Parakletos,* our comforter, guide, instructor."[12] Again: There are no "circumstances in which men are ever placed where they may not enter into rest at once by anchoring down in naked faith upon the promises of God."[13]

b. If, on the other hand, entire sanctification is perceived to be a change that of necessity and invariably includes the field of consciousness, it follows that the attempt to believe will be no more than an attitude of expectancy, until the consciousness is flooded with assurance. One approach stresses the inductive knowledge derived from trust in God's Word; the other stresses the knowledge of experience, or feeling.

1. *The Faith of Expectancy*

Peter says that both the 120 at Pentecost and the household of Cornelius were purified "by faith." When and how did they exercise faith? Of what sort was it? In both cases it was primarily the faith of obedience, which issued in the faith of expectancy and receptivity. In neither case was there any clear mental vision of what to expect. It would have been psychologically impossible for them to have *claimed* the fullness of the Spirit, for they would have had no idea what it was they were claiming. With them the faith of assurance could only coincide with the dramatic, unmistakable inrush of conscious experience. Jesus had commanded the disciples to "tarry until," and they *tarried until.* But it was a tarrying in faith—of sure confidence that the promise of Jesus would be fulfilled. Cornelius, also, exemplifies this faith of expectancy. He obeyed the angel in sending for Peter, then listened in full confidence that God would meet his need through Peter's words. The faith of expectancy must at the same time be the faith of obedience.

Wesley's teaching on faith would appear to support the faith of expectancy, in spite of his stress on "now." In answering the question "But what is that faith whereby we are sanctified;—saved from sin, and perfected in love?" Wesley elaborates the following fourfold summary:

---

12. Timothy L. Smith, *The Promise of the Spirit: Charles G. Finney on Christian Holiness* (Minneapolis: Bethany Fellowship, 1980), 188.

13. Ibid., 209.

a. "It is a divine evidence and conviction . . . that God hath promised it in the Holy Scripture."

b. "It is a divine evidence and conviction . . . that what God hath promised He is able to perform."

c. "It is . . . a divine evidence and a conviction that He is able and willing to do it now."

d. "To this confidence . . . there needs to be added one thing more,—a divine evidence and a conviction that He doeth it. In that hour it is done."

He insists that "there is an inseparable connection between these three points,—expect it *by faith,* expect it *as you are,* and expect it *now*" (italics his). But he does not surrender the word "expect," even with his "now." He does not say, "Claim it now."[14]

2. *The Faith That Appropriates*

This is that deliberate asking for the fullness of the Spirit that issues in accepting the blessing solely on the ground of the divine promise. James Oliver Buswell, Jr., tells of James M. Gray who as a young minister supposed that to be filled with the Spirit was to have a great emotional experience. When he became convinced that simple faith was the key, he "prayed that God would fill him with the Spirit," then "simply believed that God would honor His promise," and went on "without special emotion." But soon his associates began to notice a difference in him. They said, "You are a new man. . . . There is a spiritual power in your ministry which was not there before."[15]

There is a certain logic operating here that can, if one is not careful, actually depreciate the value of a direct witness of the Spirit. It is the inference that true faith in one witness does not demand a second. If faith rests squarely and firmly on the Word of God, it is content with that. The Word becomes the witness. This is indeed solid ground to build on. Yet the real trust is not in the Word

---

14. *Works,* 6:52-54. Yet he comes closer to the faith of appropriation in his sermon "On Patience," ibid., 492. Repeating the four approaches of faith, he words the fourth as follows: "Believe, Fourthly, that He is not only able, but willing to do it *now!* Not when you come to die; not at any distant time; not to-morrow, but *to-day.* He will then enable you to believe, *it is done,* according to his word." The will to believe must have the Spirit's enablement, an enablement that in itself turns faith into assurance.

15. *A Systematic Theology of the Christian Religion* (Grand Rapids: Zondervan Publishing House, 1963), 2:214-15. It should be acknowledged that Buswell's view, even though helpful at this one point, is not Wesleyan.

as an independent power—that would be bibliolatry—but in the God of the Word. Our faith is in the promises only because it is confident of the Promiser. This recognizes that the Bible cannot be detached from the action of the Spirit, who alone can authenticate the promises. Only He can turn the letter into the life of experiential reality. To stress, therefore, the method of resting on the promises, apart from feeling, is safe only if our "appropriating faith" is a sure confidence that God will and does make the promises good, because He is that kind of a God.

In actual experience, the mode often seems to be a quickening by the Spirit of a particular promise that then becomes the bridge to assurance. This was Brengle's experience. When he had truly "died out" and had prayed himself empty, yet was disappointed that nothing "happened," he was reminded of 1 John 1:9—"If we confess our sins, he is faithful and just to forgive us our sins, and to cleanse us from all unrighteousness" (KJV). Hall describes what happened:

> The words break across his heart like a sky rocket, illuminating the fact that since God is "faithful and just" his promised blessing must now be received by simple faith in those attributes of God's character. Instantly the Grace and faithfulness of God dawn upon him, and as he drops his head in his arms and murmurs confidently, "Lord, I believe that!", a great sense of peace flows over his soul.
>
> Is this the Blessing? He need not put the question twice. Like a great, wordless, all-enveloping "YES!" he gets the answer from every chamber of his body and soul.[16]

While this inner peace swelled into torrents of blessing and two days later became a mighty baptism of love, Brengle was sanctified when the Spirit enabled him to believe the promise. But the power of the promise to effect release was really in Brengle's sudden vision of the absolutely trustworthy faithfulness of God behind the promise. Resting in *that* brought soul rest.

3. The "Altar Theology"

This faith-in-the-Word approach was developed as a clearly articulated system in the mid-1800s, chiefly by Phoebe Palmer (hence sometimes called the Palmerite Method). In spite of some opposition, her teachings permeated the holiness movement until

---

16. *Brengle: Portrait of a Prophet*, 57. Some might question the relevance of this verse to the second work of grace. But if the sovereign Spirit thus applied it in Brengle's case, who can find fault?

to close communion

they virtually became standard. Many thousands, of all denominations, preachers and laymen, were helped into full assurance by following her instructions. Since Jesus is our altar, she affirmed, and "the altar sanctifies the gift" (cf. Matt. 23:19), our part is to make sure that we are on the altar, and accept the fact that therefore Christ is faithful to sanctify. From this standpoint, failure to believe is unbelief, which is sin. Therefore a definite *step* of faith becomes morally obligatory. In effect, this struck a new note of urgency. "If you delay presenting the sacrifice from any cause whatsoever, you make food for repentance. God demands present holiness."[17]

In addition to building on the principle of Christ as our altar, there were four basic components in Mrs. Palmer's teachings. Together these marked the holiness movement with what, in effect, was a new methodology.

a. The obligation to be entirely holy *now.* To wait, even in an attitude of expectancy, to be made holy at some future time, is unscriptural.

b. The obligation to make a complete consecration *now.* If Christ is our "altar," our part is to place the sacrifice on this altar at once. Without this conscious and thorough presentation there can be no sanctification.

c. The primacy of the Word of God. The Bible is God's living Word *now,* by which He commits himself to do certain things in and for the believer who meets the scriptural conditions. It is unthinkable for this Word not to be fulfilled, if the conditions are met.

d. The obligatory nature of faith. Failure to believe that God *now* does what He promises is sin because it is a denial of His Word. This faith rests in the promise, and the divine integrity back of the promise, not in any kind of feeling.[18] Yet such faith will bring

---

17. *Phoebe Palmer, Faith and Its Effects: Or Fragments from My Portfolio* (New York: Privately printed at 200 Mulberry St., 1854), 104. Quoted by Dieter, *Holiness Revival,* 32.

18. Mrs. Palmer would have denied as a caricature the formula: "Believe that you have it and you have it." Her position was rather, according to John L. Peters, an emphasis "on such a full and complete consecration that faith would be simply the next and necessary step" (*Christian Perfection,* 112). For a fair and balanced exposition of Mrs. Palmer's teaching, and survey of its extensive influence, see Peters, 109-13; Dieter, *Holiness Revival,* 26-32; Timothy L. Smith, *Revivalism and Social Reform* (New York: Abingdon Press, 1957), 116-28; and Delbert R. Rose, *A Theology of Christian Experience* (Minneapolis: Bethany Fellowship, 1965), 31-45.

feeling, just as faith in the doctor's word that there is no cancer will bring to the patient a feeling of relief and joy. To remain anxious is to demonstrate unbelief in the doctor's word. While such lingering anxiety may be justified in dealing with a human physician because of his fallibility, it is not justified when dealing with Christ.

On biblical grounds, one cannot fault this emphasis on immediacy. Entire sanctification is both the privilege and duty of every Christian the moment he sees the scriptural provision. "Knowledge," Mrs. Palmer insisted, "is conviction."[19] Neither can the emphasis on the Word of God as the true ground of assurance be challenged.

However, the weak link in the chain of Mrs. Palmer's argument is in drawing too close a parallel between the ceremonial principle of altar sanctification and the New Testament teaching. "Whatever touches . . . the altar . . . will be holy" (Exod. 29:37) means that any offering placed on the altar shares in the sanctity of the altar. The altar (one might say) "claims" it for God. It becomes hallowed, and any misuse is a desecration. But this is holiness by association, not by purging. It is positional, and hence imputed.

When Jesus made reference to this (Matt. 23:19) in rebuking the scribes and Pharisees, He was confirming the principle of hallowedness by presentation within the context of Old Testament ceremonialism. To extend this as a descriptive of the New Testament mode of sanctification is highly questionable because it opens the door to (1) the equating of sanctification with consecration (see p. 166, n. 20), (2) implying a merely positional holiness, and thus (3) an imputed holiness. There was no substantive change in the "holiness" of being on the altar, only *relational change.* Yet certainly Wesley, and presumably Mrs. Palmer, understood entire sanctification to be true holiness, not just hallowedness.

A biblical case can be made for perceiving Jesus as the Christian's altar, thus magnifying the importance and appropriateness of a specific presentation in consecration. But it is a non sequitur to conclude that the sanctification effected by Christ is on the same basis as, and no more than, the sanctification effected by the Old

---

19. *The Way of Holiness,* ed. and abr. Alathea Coleman Jones (Wilmore, Ky.: Christian Outreach, Asbury Theological Seminary, 1981), 11. For a helpful discussion of the sometimes puzzling dynamics of faith see Grider, *Entire Sanctification,* 116-18.

Testament altar. Christ is our "altar," not in a ceremonial sense but in a spiritual and metaphorical sense. He is not a functional sacred object, but a Person who in both faithfulness and freedom responds to our consecration and faith by the gift of His sanctifying Spirit.

In one respect our offering to God is holy simply by virtue of its being made. If made in good faith, the offering is God's, and any "taking off the altar" or misuse is a breach of contract and therefore sin. But the essence of authentic Wesleyanism, and the touchstone of New Testament soteriology, is that holiness is more than hallowedness. In response to the offering is the divine fire. Holiness is not an automatic consequence of relation, but the product of the purging energy of the Holy Spirit. Only then is the promise fulfilled, "He will baptize you with the Holy Spirit and with fire" (Matt. 3:11; Luke 3:16; cf. Mark 1:8).

Faith, then, gets back to the principle that it consists not only in our claiming Christ as our Sanctifier but also in the certainty that He will *accomplish* this work in us by His Spirit, and *make it real to us.*

III. Evidences of Spirit Fullness

A. The Witness of the Spirit

The witness of the Spirit to our entire sanctification is a divinely imparted inner assurance that the work is done. This assurance may take the form of a flood of ecstasy, a sense of cleanness, a profound inner peace, or an outpouring of love—or a combination of these. In any case the distress is gone, the struggling is over, the doubts are settled, and the mind is at rest. One cannot dictate to God the form in which the assurance comes. It is often missed, perhaps for years, by false conceptions of what to expect. One should never set another person's experience before one's mind as a model to which God must conform.

A. W. Tozer says, "The only witness He gives is a subjective one, known to the individual alone. The Spirit announces Himself to the deep-in spirit of the man." But this witness is indispensable. Tozer insists that no believer was "ever filled with the Holy Spirit *who did not know he had been filled.* Neither was anyone filled *who did not know when he was filled. And no one was ever filled gradually"* (italics his).[20]

B. Is Tongues the Evidence?

Any insistence on tongues or any other physical manifestation as an evidence of the infilling of the Spirit is a dead-end street that cannot but siphon off authentic power and stultify spiritual growth. Acquiring the modern so-called gift of tongues is relatively easy for some kinds of temperament. The acceptance of this as proof of a deep and valid experience in the Holy Spirit is a delusion that tends to short-circuit the deeper hunger for holiness.[21]

Speaking in divinely given languages, besides being symbolic, was an arresting and evangelizing tool on the Day of Pentecost. At Caesarea and Ephesus it was a proof to the skeptical Jews that the Holy Spirit was equally available to Gentiles. But the supposition that this or any other gift was uniformly indispensable to the baptism with the Spirit, or an evidence of a deep state of grace, was expressly and vigorously repudiated in Paul's discussion of the gifts in 1 Corinthians 12—14.[22]

C. The Evidence of Change

The distinction Wesley made between the witness of the Spirit and the indirect witness, that is, the witness of our own spirit by which we know we are different, is valid. We thus have a dual witness, one being confirmed by the other. The need for the second witness lies in the ease with which a seeker can prematurely interpret an emotional experience as the witness of the Spirit. He needs to be able to see a change in himself, a change corresponding to the

---

20. *Keys to the Deeper Life,* 30-31.

21. Michael Harper, an internationally known leader in the charismatic movement, said in an interview in *New Covenant,* Feb. 1981: "A few years ago I really thought that if only all Christians became charismatics, the church would take off. I see more clearly now that what we need most are lives of obedience under the lordship of Christ. . . . I would like to see the renewal replace the word 'wholeness' with the word 'holiness.' There's a world of difference between the two. . . . What the Bible does speak about, page after page, is holiness. . . . Yet people leave aside holiness, as it's commanded and promised, to pursue this wholeness. . . . I think a lot of people in the charismatic renewal are not crucified with Christ." Here is an admission from within the charismatic movement that "gifts," in and of themselves, do not evidence a deep state of grace.

22. For further discussion of the "Gifts of the Spirit" see pp. 196-99.

needs that prompted him to seek heart holiness in the first place. One cannot seek intelligently without a conviction of need. How can he rest in a "blessing" unless in the days that follow there is the glad discovery that thé needs have been met, or that something of the promised "power" is now his? It is really the indirect witness that Sherwood E. Wirt is describing in the following testimony:

> But when I informed him that I was abdicating the throne of my life (my Christian life, that is); when I said that my ego had been deposed and driven into exile; when I asked him to crucify me, he accepted my statement and fulfilled my request.
>
> In his own time and at his own pleasure he sent a divine solvent into this troubled heart. It was like the warmth of the sun burning off the layers of fog.
>
> I don't know just how the love came in, but I know that all the bitterness I held against others—including those near to me—disappeared.
>
> Resentment—hostility—hurt feelings—you name it.
>
> They all dissolved. Evaporated.
>
> Went.[23]

He knew he had been filled with the Holy Spirit by the change he saw in himself.

Love, with its associated fruits, is declared to be the universal and indispensable evidence of the Spirit (Rom. 5:5; 1 Corinthians 13; Gal. 5:22). A "deep, settled peace" combined with a marked expansion and intensity of love is the most common experience. The spirit sees itself to be free from malice or ill will, sees the heart to be cleansed of pride and self-willfulness, and sees these inner differences manifesting themselves in a dispositional change. There is a new relaxation and quietness of spirit, a more victorious acceptance of God's providences, and a new capacity to handle annoyances and disappointments—even sorrows. One finds a more spontaneous bent to look to Jesus in every circumstance (Heb. 12:1-2).

But there is also a new freedom in witnessing, a new holy (not brassy) boldness, a new aggressiveness in the things of God. The

---

23. *Afterglow—The Excitement of Being Filled with the Spirit* (Grand Rapids: Zondervan Publishing House, 1975), 19.

Missionary Raymond Browning reported to George Coulter (general superintendent emeritus, Church of the Nazarene): "When a national gets sanctified, I have observed

1. A new consistency in conduct;
2. A new self-forgetfulness;
3. A new zeal in service."

fire burns. This does not necessarily mean eloquence or public speaking gifts. It does mean a tongue at least as free to talk about Christ as the weather.

In answering the question, "By what 'fruit of the Spirit,' may we 'know that we are of God,' even in the highest sense?" Wesley said:

> By love, joy, peace, always abiding; by invariable long suffering, patience, resignation; by gentleness, triumphing over all provocation; by goodness, mildness, sweetness, tenderness of spirit; by fidelity, simplicity, godly sincerity; by meekness, calmness, evenness of spirit; by temperance, not only in food and sleep, but in all things natural and spiritual.[24]

Furthermore, Wesley discredited the profession of some because these evidences were lacking. Some of the deficiencies he cites are:

> Some are wanting in gentleness. They resist evil, instead of turning the other cheek. They do not receive reproach with gentleness; no, nor even reproof. Nay, they are not able to bear contradiction, without the appearance, at least, of resentment. If they are reproved or contradicted, though mildly, they do not take it well; they behave with more distance and reserve than they did before. If they are reproved or contradicted harshly, they answer it with harshness; with a loud voice, or with an angry tone.

After several paragraphs of such indictments, Wesley concludes, "You have not what I call perfection; if others will call it so, they may. However, hold fast what you have, and earnestly pray for what you have not."[25]

It is apparent that to Wesley the quality of the spirit is the real touchstone. There may yet be numerous cultural deficiencies and

---

24. *Plain Account,* 89. His statement elsewhere that one should not rest in any supposed fruit without the direct witness of the Spirit is directed to sinners seeking the assurance of adoption (*Works,* 5:133-34). His belief that a direct witness was also normative for the second work of grace was more in the nature of an inference (cf. *Plain Account,* 86-87).

25. Ibid., 92. Dennis Kinlaw recalls preaching on 1 Corinthians 13 to a group of missionaries. One day at the dinner table a veteran missionary said, "Now, Dennis, you are not going to tell me, are you, that you think we can live up to that chapter?" He answered, "Yes, I am. Here it is in the Word of God; and the scripture says if we have everything else and do not have love, we have failed in everything. So if it is essential to please God and to do His will, there must be a way through the grace of God that a person can come to this" (sermon, Radiant Cassettes, Vancleve, Ky., Jan. 1981).

personality quirks that are not immediately corrected because they are not expressions of a sinful self-centeredness.

It is equally apparent to Wesley that no religious experience can be identified as Christian perfection or entire sanctification if it does not produce a change in the disposition. While not everything is altered that may yet need to be altered, nor every personal problem solved, the change that does occur is radical, deep, and (other things being equal) lasting.

SUMMARY

The last several chapters have attempted to expound the doctrine of holiness as an available privilege in Christ. Every effort has been made to grapple honestly with the sometimes complex doctrinal issues. The discussion has failed unless these chapters have helped the reader become acutely aware that holiness cannot remain simply an abstract or academic subject of inquiry. Even a correct intellectual grasp will elude the person who attempts to examine holiness as a detached observer, as one might study insects. For these matters concern persons in their inner lives, in their deepest relationships, and in their eternal destiny.

The reality of holiness can only be experienced; it cannot be known by verbal dissection alone. No matter how correct and biblical our exposition may be, if readers do not seek and obtain the experience for themselves, doctrinal exactness will avail nothing. It is equally true that if readers are aided by these chapters in their personal quest for holiness, and guided into satisfying and "testifiable" reality, the work will have accomplished an incalculably important mission—even if eternity should reveal flaws in expression or positions taken. For it is not infallibility "without which no man shall see the Lord," but holiness (Heb. 12:14, KJV).

10

The Life of Holiness

The crisis experiences leading to holiness of heart have as their objective the life of holiness. This is a life of spiritual vitality, exemplary behavior, and soul-winning impact. When Paul urged the Philippians to continue to "work out [their] own salvation with fear and trembling" (Phil. 2:12-13, KJV), he was reminding them that what God had done and was even then doing in them through grace must be translated into the practicalities of everyday living.

Sanctified people must act like it. Furthermore, the responsibility for seeing to this is squarely theirs. While the grace within is sufficient to enable one to accomplish this, it is not an automatic cause-and-effect mechanism. If experience is to be validated by ethics, if faith is to be translated into daily consistency and Christlikeness, there must be the acceptance of responsibility, and deliberate systematic attention must be given to this task.[1]

I. A SPIRIT-FILLED LIFE

Personal effort apart from the Holy Spirit will quickly bog down into fleshly humanism. Pride will glory in whatever attrac-

---

1. "We believe that there is a marked distinction between a pure heart and a mature character. The former is obtained in an instant, the result of entire sanctification; the latter is the result of growth in grace.

"We believe that the grace of entire sanctification includes the impulse to grow in grace. However, this impulse must be consciously nurtured, and careful attention given to the requisites and processes of spiritual development and improvement in Christlikeness of character and personality. Without such purposeful endeavor one's witness may be impaired and the grace itself frustrated and ultimately lost" (*Manual, Church of the Nazarene*).

tiveness self-discipline manages to achieve, and this will satisfy shallow souls who are building on the sand in the first place. But those who have higher aims will be overwhelmed with despair. As responsible as the believer is, the Spirit is his Resource on which he is absolutely dependent. This is the Spirit who strengthens inwardly as a divine dynamo (Eph. 3:16-19). The "life of holiness" therefore is an idle dream unless first of all it is a Spirit-filled life (5:18-21).

A. The Spirit and the Self

1. *The Concept of Fullness*

The two words most commonly used in expressing Spirit fullness are *pimplēmi* (or *plēthō*) and *plērēs (plēroō* and *plērōma)*. They suggest completion, full of, wholly occupied with, completely under the influence of. To be filled with the Spirit may be said *(a)* to find our personal fulfillment in Him, *(b)* to be pervaded by His presence, and *(c)* to be completely under His influence.

Three striking pairs of analogies make this fullness graphic. Luke 4:1 has Jesus "full of the Holy Spirit," while 5:12 speaks of a man "full of leprosy" (KJV). As he was given over to leprosy, saturated with it, mastered by it, so was Jesus given over to the Spirit, "saturated" with Him, mastered by Him. Again: As the disciples were said to be "filled with the Holy Spirit" in Acts 2:4, so was it said in verse 2 that the sound of wind "filled the whole house."[2] As the sound of wind pervaded and dominated every part of the house, so the Holy Spirit pervades and dominates body, soul, and spirit—upstairs and downstairs. He permeates the appetites and habits, the aspirations and goals, the values and affections, the manward life as well as the godward life.

Again: Wine fullness is contrasted with Spirit fullness (Eph. 5:18).[3] Humanity suffers the great void, the emptiness within, producing perpetual restlessness, longing, and searching. Getting drunk with wine is symbolic of the world's way of filling that void. Fulfillment and satisfaction are sought in things, drugs, sensual pleasure, applause, and power. This is the flesh way. Paul is saying, "Don't ape the world, but find your fulfillment—fill that void—by

---

2. Admittedly it is aorist indicative of *plēroō* in verse 2 and aorist indicative passive of *pimplēmi* in verse 4, yet the essential sense is the same.

3. *Methuskō,* to make drunk, implies wine fullness. For a helpful comment on Spirit fullness as a way of life see BBC, 9:235.

letting the Spirit continuously fill you." *For it is the lack of Him that created the void in the first place.*

While there are similarities between leprosy fullness, wind fullness, and wine fullness with Spirit fullness, the dissimilarities are even greater. On the physical level are impersonal forces that impose themselves and destroy. Especially is this true in wine fullness. When one surrenders to alcohol one is submitting to a chemical tyrant that subverts the will and the judgment and reduces the personhood to pulp. When surrendering to the Spirit, we are inviting in a Person as a Friend and Helper who never debases our personhood and never subjugates our will into impotence, but energizes and reinforces our will. No person was ever made better by wine fullness, always worse. No person was ever made worse by the Spirit, always better. Wine enslaves; the Spirit liberates. No one is ever more free or ever more truly himself than when enabled and directed by the Spirit.

2. *A Relationship, Not a Merging*

While the biblical concept of "fullness" stresses the Spirit's control, Jesus' doctrine of the Paraclete (John 14—16) saves us from any notion of automation. Strictly, *paraklētos* signifies one called alongside to help. The term has been variously translated as Spokesman, Advocate, Counselor, Strengthener, but never as Operator. Jesus describes the relationship of the Spirit to the disciples as a Teacher and Guide, relationships that are free and interpersonal, not monolithic impositions of force. The Spirit will dwell *in* them, but as a Friend and Helper, not as a puppeteer. The "complete control" of the Spirit remains an *invited* control. Our subjection continues to be voluntary, even though complete and unqualified.

What is being said is that the Spirit does not cancel the self or swallow up the human self into the divine self. This is the error of mysticism, which Wesley so roundly rejected. Being controlled by the Spirit does not mean He alone acts, and the self becomes either a puppet or a nonentity. On the contrary the self acts, thinks, chooses, but with the aid of the Spirit who is continually there.

How persons can be inhabited by another person, who remains in touch yet distinct, is a great mystery. That this happens in a horrible, enslaving way in demon possession is clear from the Scripture and to everyone who has once seen it. If demons can be allowed in with their power to wreck, it is surely reasonable to believe that the Spirit can indwell with His ability to repair and ennoble.[4]

3. Spirit and Brain

If we think in strictly scientific terms, we confront what seems to be pure physicality, with the brain as an intricate computer. Sound mind becomes almost the equivalent of a healthy brain; damage the brain and the functioning of the mind is impaired. Surgery on the brain can alter behavior and even, to some degree, the disposition. In some cases drugs can improve brain functioning, resulting in better memory and thinking capacity. Does all this mean that, after all, human behavior is only a matter of chemistry, electricity, and perhaps psychosurgery?

Such a conclusion is unwarranted. Not only does the brain's condition affect behavior, but chosen behavior can harmfully affect the brain. Furthermore, healthy brains do not guarantee good people; mental sharpness is no antidote to selfishness. To trust in neurobiology and genetic engineering to solve our social problems is a vain and credulous faith. That promise is humanism's siren song, luring the race to destruction. For the sin that drugs and scapel cannot dislodge will exploit for evil every advance in genetic control, as it has man's other scientific achievements. Therefore Christians need not fear that science will create saints and that drugs will displace our need for the Holy Spirit.

We are not mere products of chemistry. While many activities are automatic reflexes, and powerful subvolitional impulses arise to induce action at the level of consciousness, there is happening all the time a kind of response that is not being determined for us but is being selected from multiple possibilities. A *self* is directing

---

4. It is difficult to grasp the fact that one Holy Spirit can be equally available to millions of persons. Even more staggering is the confidence that we possess the Spirit as a whole person, not simply a fraction of Him. If we were dealing only with a divine influence, streaming from the Godhead as light streams from the sun, we could easily picture-think ourselves to be at one point of this stream. But the mystery is in the possibility of having the presence of a distinct person, with whom I may have an *I-Thou* relationship without diminishing the equal privilege of other believers. Obviously the infinite God, who himself is not subject to the space-time order of existence, but who created it, can bring himself into intimate relationship with it, omnipresence becoming localized. But the fact is little more astonishing than the reception by a TV tube of the entire picture, even though only one picture is being transmitted in all directions, and is being shared by thousands of receivers. A simple common sense view would suppose that each receiver would be able to pull in only a fragment of the picture!

the "playback" or directive mechanism of the brain, so that my hunger pangs can be satisfied now or put off until lunchtime; I can read this book or write a letter; I can "count sheep" or get up and walk around. The higher the development of an integrated self, the greater is the range of control (as is demonstrated by modern biofeedback techniques).[5]

The Holy Spirit prods and reinforces this control process. How He does this we do not know. We do not understand the point of contact betwen the spiritual and the physical, or the modus operandi of the Spirit's action. That the Spirit *does* influence the self is too universally reported in the Scriptures and believed by the Church to permit debate. We can assume that the brain is the primary instrument of communication. If so, He acts on the brain either mediately or immediately. If mediately, His direct contact is with the human spirit, which then activates the brain cells as its instrument of response. If immediately, His action is on the brain cells themselves, creating thoughts and impulses that the spirit endorses or resists.

On the basis of anthropological monism the Spirit's action could only be directly on the brain cells and would of necessity be irresistible. If there is no distinct, independent agent to receive or reject, we cannot escape the implied determinism. The only difference between this and Skinner's behavioristic determinism would be that instead of all the stimuli being solely natural, some would be supernatural. But regardless of the origin of the stimuli, the activated brain cells would account for the whole of personal activity and there would be no ground whatsoever for postulating personal responsibility for conduct. In such a case "sin" and "holiness" would be mere names for produced effects on robots, and hence devoid of ethical value. If we insist on acknowledging a person, an agent, or a self that can cooperate with the impression on the brain cells or reject them, we are back to dualistic assumptions.[6]

---

5. Unfortunately many people live largely on the autonomic level, more as animals than as human beings. They are almost totally controlled by impulse, appetite, mood, suggestion, stimuli, and vagrant thoughts. The self is carried aimlessly along on the tide of the biological and sociological signals within and without. Such persons are passive subjects, not active agents. But if normally intelligent, they are nevertheless accountable, for the drift toward dwarfed personhood is the result of their failure to choose otherwise.

6. What is commonly overlooked, especially by those who stumble over the mind-body problem in the traditional doctrine of man, is that the *fact* of the Spirit's

4. *Ways the Holy Spirit Leads and Teaches*

When once the Spirit has been given the rights of full occupancy, and a daily habit of honoring Him has been established, He will make His presence known and felt. He will awaken the mind, create new desires for knowledge, shame laziness and lethargy, and foster a frame of mind that is tractable and teachable. Resistance here will stymie the whole process and destroy the relationship of "fullness."

The Spirit keeps stirring the self toward that "thus mindedness" Paul wrote about (cf. Phil. 3:15, KJV), which is eagerly "reaching forth unto those things which are before" (v. 13, KJV). This creates an alertness and awareness that turns every event into a lesson and every situation into a classroom. The soul in touch and in tune with the Spirit is forever being edified from the Word (most of all), from other people's testimonies, and even from poor sermons. The Spirit helps the entire being to organize such input into working capital for growth and usefulness. Christians on the wave-length of the Spirit *see* their own faults, *see* needs around them, *sense* the urge to speak or be still, and *grasp* truth with spiritual insight. They are tinglingly alive. Such persons learn to recognize the impressions of the Spirit and distinguish them from fanatical notions. The Holy Spirit prods, shames, reminds, arouses, illumines. To walk "in the Spirit" (Gal. 5:25, KJV) is to "keep in step with the Spirit" in all of this.

The one most important proviso is that the Spirit will never lead or teach contrary to the Bible. He will never elevate a Christian to a level of special private knowledge that transcends and supercedes the Scripture. He will never endorse a course of action that the sanctified person would condemn in others.

---

affective power is itself a proof that an immaterial entity can move a material entity. "The fundamental problem of dualism is the feasibility of one sort of substance acting on another sort of substance," writes D. Gareth Jones in *Our Fragile Brains* (Downers Grove, Ill.: InterVarsity Press, 1981), 261. But matter was created by the God who is essentially nonmatter. Every miracle, including the Virgin Birth and the Resurrection, is a demonstration of the power of pure spirit to affect matter. Therefore, while the phenomenon may be a mystery, it cannot be a problem to an evangelical Christian. And the interactionism of spirit and body is no more difficult to conceive than the interactionism of Holy Spirit and person.

A strong development in modern terms of traditional interactionism is *The Human Mystery*, by John C. Eccles (Berlin: Springer International, 1979). Two studies by neuroscientists that attempt to preserve personhood and responsibility on a holistic approach are MacKay, *Brains, Machines, and Persons*, and Jones, *Our Fragile Brains*. Neither one quite succeeds in dispensing with dualistic assumptions.

Neither will the Spirit tolerate a disposition to despise human authorities and teachers whom God has called and ordained. "If the whole body were an eye, where were the hearing?" asks Paul (1 Cor. 12:17, KJV). What the Spirit *will* do is give us discernment in evaluating teachers and their doctrines.

5. *The Spirit's Refining Influences*

The Spirit who in the beginning brooded on the waters, bringing order out of the void (Gen. 1:2), will brood over the human personality. He will alter our value systems, show us what is important, and make us aware of the chaotic areas of life. He will create a desire for self-improvement, for Jesus' sake.

The Holy Spirit will manifest an interest in *every* facet of life. If we *listen*, He will develop in us a sense of propriety. Loudness, immodesty, crudeness, and otherwise disorganized and haphazard life-styles He will rebuke and shame. "Slovenliness," said Oswald Chambers, "is an insult to the Holy Ghost." But when He gently shows us some area that needs correction, we must obey.

6. *Sins Against the Spirit*

The most serious of sins against the Spirit is direct disobedience. This not only disqualifies us from continuing to entertain the Spirit (Acts 5:32), but will ultimately lead to the "sin unto death" (1 John 5:16, KJV). The two forms of disobedience to which we are most vulnerable are *(a) quenching* the Spirit (1 Thess. 5:19), and *(b) grieving* the Spirit (Eph. 4:30).

The first means literally, "Do not put out the Spirit's fire." Public worship should be marked by the warmth of freedom in the Spirit. This freedom should not be destroyed by cold, dead formalism. Revival fires should be fed, not quenched by criticism and belittling. Private prayer should be energized by hot burden and concern. This fire must never be put out by the chill of mere self-interest. "The Spirit's movements can be quenched by a ceremonialism that substitutes human wisdom and ingenuity for the mind of Christ and human rituals for the will of God," says W. O. Klopfenstein.[7]

Quenching the Spirit is one way to *grieve,* or displease, the Spirit. Other ways are the sins warned against in the preceding

---

7. *Wesleyan Bible Commentary,* ed. Chas. W. Carter (Grand Rapids: William B. Eerdmans Publishing Co., 1965), 5:541. See Wesley's list of ways the Spirit may be grieved, *Works,* 11:424.

verses: carelessness with the truth, smoldering anger, laziness, "unwholesome talk" (vv. 25-29). Off-color stories, crude vulgarisms, and joking about sacred things should be avoided like the plague. They are sure ways of smudging the soul and bringing one's spiritual life into eclipse.

One very common way of grieving the Spirit is to fail to be "kind one to another, tenderhearted" (v. 32, KJV). When we are edgy and fretful, or permit a negative frame of mind, we are "out of the Spirit." It doesn't take many sharp words to grieve Him.

The Spirit also can be grieved by ignoring either His promptings or His checkings. He prompts prayer, a special monetary gift, a letter to someone in need, or a personal testimony. When we feel a distinct urge to do these things, failing to obey is a sin both against the Spirit and the person (or persons) who needs our help.[8] In like manner, we experience the Spirit's touch of restraint, an inner caution: Don't say it; don't go here; don't buy it. If we override these checks, we may even face calamity; at least we will probably experience embarrassment and regret.

The Holy Spirit lets us know when He is grieved. We find ourselves in darkness and deep distress. Communion is broken. If we confess in humility and contrition, He will restore us. But it is a serious thing to trifle with the Spirit—ever. He is the *Holy* Spirit and will not tolerate anything that dishonors Christ. He is sensitive to resistance and the beginnings of a reversion to self-willfulness.

Sanctified people rarely backslide and certainly never fall into shameful forms of sin without first going through a period of grieving the Spirit. In every possible way the faithful Spirit will flash warnings. This will include arousing the conscience, stirring up guilt feelings, warning through Scripture and sermon, and bringing every *inner* pressure to bear to prevent disaster (see p. 216). Final decision is nevertheless still ours, as truly as with Adam and Eve. If we persistently grieve the Spirit, we commit spiritual suicide, for it is by Him that we "were sealed for the day of redemption" (Eph. 4:30). "To grieve Him," says Charles W. Carter, "is to break that seal and thus lose the hope and promised benefits of ultimate redemption."[9]

---

8. We must not assume, however, that every urge is of the Spirit. We must "test the spirits" (1 John 4:1). See Richard S. Taylor, *Life in the Spirit,* 125-26.

9. *Wesleyan Bible Commentary,* 5:417.

B. The Spirit and Christ

1. *A Christ-centered Religion*

Life "in the Spirit" is not a super religion that is a step higher than "being in Christ." What Francis Schaeffer calls a super-spirituality has appeared in recent years, which seems to suppose that to be filled with the Spirit is to graduate from Christ. On the contrary, the Spirit's mission is to direct attention to Christ and bind us to Him. Jesus explained, "He will bring glory to me by taking from what is mine and making it known to you" (John 16:14). Christians who truly honor the Spirit will be made most aware of Christ and will make Christ central in their devotion and theology. For while Paul could speak of the action of the Spirit as "the Spirit himself" (Rom. 8:16), he also paradoxically could speak of this person being equally "the Spirit of God" and "the Spirit of Christ" (v. 9), and immediately follow with, "if Christ is in you" (v. 10; cf. Col. 1:27).

2. *Conformity to Christ*

Our divine destiny is to be *like* Christ as well as to belong to Him, in order that He might be "the firstborn among many brothers" (Rom. 8:29). Because Jesus "who makes men holy" and "those who are made holy are of the same family," He is "not ashamed to call them brothers" (Heb. 2:11).

Here is a unity based not only on justification but also upon sanctification, a veritable kinship of family likeness. But such conformity is supremely the work of the Holy Spirit (2 Thess. 2:13; 1 Pet. 1:2).[10] This the Spirit does essentially in the second work of grace. But He does not stop with this. He disciplines and fashions us into a recognizable, visible likeness.

Where "the Spirit of the Lord is, there is freedom" (2 Cor. 3:17)—freedom to be "transformed into his likeness with ever-increasing glory, which comes from the Lord, who is the Spirit" (v. 18). A deep life in the Spirit will be reflected in the face—"The God whom you serve writes His name on your face" is the old adage. An evangelist asked a Christian one time how she was spiritually. When he got the glum reply, "Saved and sanctified!" the evangelist asked, "Where's the shine?" In contrast, others are so radiant in their holiness, so gentle and kind, that sinners cannot but think of

---

10. See *Wesleyan Bible Commentary* on Rom. 15:16.

Jesus. They have never seen Him but intuitively recognize Him in the Christlike Christian.

C. The Gifts of the Spirit

The word *charis* has a variety of meanings in the New Testament, the most important, of course, being "grace"—that shining word of our holy religion. We are ever reminded that "it is by grace" that we "have been saved" (Eph. 2:5, 8). But a variation of *charis* is *charisma,* meaning "gift."

1. *Service Gifts*

While the Spirit himself is God's Gift, the Spirit also bestows gifts upon Christians. These are special powers or abilities for the performance of functions needful to the life of the Church and to its ministry of evangelism. They are called "service gifts." In the early, post-Pentecost surge of the Church many such gifts were given as divine confirmations of the truth of the gospel (Heb. 2:4)

Insofar as gifts constitute a permanent feature of the Spirit's mode of working in this dispensation, we should think of them as special abilities to match particular responsibilities and tasks. They may coincide with natural talents, but they cannot be defined solely as natural talents. They belong to the Church, and their purpose is to build up the Church both in edification and evangelism. There is about them the distinct mark of the supernatural. Together they constitute "the manifestation of the Spirit" (1 Cor. 12:7). The most familiar list is:

"the message of wisdom"

"the message of knowledge"

"faith"

"gifts of healing" (Greek is plural, *healings*)

"miraculous powers"

"prophecy"

"the ability to distinguish between spirits"

"the ability to speak in different kinds of tongues" (or, *languages*)

"the interpretation of tongues" (or, *languages*) (1 Cor. 12:8-10)

Often overlooked are two unglamorous gifts that Paul adds to the

list in this same discussion: "gifts [*charismata*, plural of *charisma*] of
. . . helps, administrations" (v. 28, NASB).[11]

2. *Elementary Principles*

While a full study of the "gift" question cannot be attempted
here, a brief summary of principles is in order. *(a)* While greatly
diverse in nature and function, the gifts have a common source,
"the same Spirit" (12:4, 8-9, 11). If so, they will all be in harmony
with holiness and will all honor Christ. Any supposed "gift" that
does not enhance the Christian witness and does not promote the
holiness of the Church is not from the *Holy* Spirit but from some
other spirit, and therefore it is not authentic. *(b)* These are not
available at the whim of the believer but are bestowed by the Spirit
according to His will (cf. Heb. 2:4). *(c)* Their diversity and broad
distribution is explained in terms of the body metaphor. The
Church is an organism, like a body, with many different functions;
therefore the abilities must be as numerous and diverse as the
functions. *(d)* If there is any sense at all in which a believer may
have a preference, let him desire the greater gifts—and these are
not the most spectacular, or those the Corinthians valued so highly.
(e) The gift most desirable for the rank and file, which can profitably be used by the most number of people and for maximum
edification, is *prophecy*, which is the ability to speak a message
from God. *(f)* The gifts are not given for private enjoyment, but for
the "common good" (1 Cor. 12:7). *(g)* The whole matter is secondary and not to preoccupy the attention of the Church. There is
something else so much greater that if taken seriously the gift gal-
axy will lose its fascination. "I show you a supremely excellent
way," says Paul (v. 31, A. T. Robertson).

This leads to what might be called a further principle *(h):* Paul,
while not disparaging the gifts, plainly plays down their relative
importance and by clear implication bursts the evidence bubble—
that the possession of gifts proves superior spirituality. They do
not. Gifted Christians may yet be carnal, and spiritual Christians
may have few gifts—at least not showy ones.

3. *Relevance for Today*

In the last few years a new gift consciousness has exploded on
the Church scene. Carnal Christians are always more fascinated by

---

11. A less familiar but equally important list is in Rom. 12:6-8: prophesying,
serving, teaching, encouraging, contributing, leadership, showing mercy.

the showy than the holy. The spectacular is congenial to them. Not that there has been a lack of true spiritual hunger for reality. But it is easier to settle for the sensational and the miraculous than attain true reality at the holiness-of-heart level.

The contemporary interest has been sparked by neo-Pentecostalism on the one hand, and the body life concept on the other. The body life concept is an insight "whose time has come," provided it is kept in perspective. Its value is in shifting the reliance away from mere human organization to spiritually vital activity that honors the Holy Spirit. Some churches have thus become organisms of the Spirit. Not only has the concept created a new spiritual tone, but Mr. Average Christian has discovered his vital role, for he has learned that the Holy Spirit desires to work through him too. Such a discovery fosters spiritual growth and fresh excitement. It reaffirms one's intuitive sense that if the Holy Spirit is not running affairs and if He is not present in some degree of supernatural authority and power, the church soon becomes formalized and fossilized.

However, when the emphasis is lopsidedly on the gifts to the neglect of the graces, and when the atmosphere degenerates into a feverish chase after signs and wonders, and when religious fireworks distract attention from the prior need of holiness, then the end result will be death. Spiritual pride is engendered rather than humility. This is especially the peril where the body life concept is in control of charismatics.

Any movement that centers its promotion on tongues and healing, or that encourages seeking gifts as badges of spiritual power, is running directly counter to the mood of Paul in First Corinthians. Christians who have been encouraged to chase after miracle workers will be easy marks for false Christs and false prophets who in the last days will exploit the sensational and spectacular in order to deceive (Matt. 24:24; 2 Thess. 2:9; Rev. 13:13). It is still true that destiny at the Judgment will hinge on holiness, not the ability to say, "Lord, Lord, did we not prophesy in your name, and in your name drive out demons and perform many miracles?" (Matt. 7:22).

All the evidence suggests that the more spectacular kinds of miracles after Pentecost marked the ministry of only a very few and did not characterize the ordinary Spirit-filled believer. Even this kind of manifestation seemed to begin to wane before the apostolic age came to an end. While the Spirit still distributes His gifts, He will major on those already designated in the Bible as the most important. Miracles will occur, but not in ways to foster racketeering exploitation by charlatans, or to titillate a carnal lust for religious excitement.[12]

II. A LIFE OF LOVE

To say that the life of holiness is a Spirit-filled life is also to say that it is a life of love, for one cannot be had without the other. The previous discussion of the gifts of the Spirit led straight to the "most excellent way" (1 Cor. 12:31)—the way of love, described so eloquently by the inspired apostle in the well-known 1 Corinthians 13. Volumes have been written seeking to mine the gold of this remarkable chapter. But no amount of knowledge *about* love will compensate for its lack. Here, too, the key is the Holy Spirit.

A. The Gift Nature of Love

Love also is a gift, indeed the supreme gift. Beside it all other gifts pale into insignificance, and without it they become empty sound and fury, signifying nothing (1 Cor. 13:1-3). This also is the universal gift of the Spirit (Rom. 5:5), thus it alone is the evidence of the Spirit's fullness. Almost invariably the testimony of those baptized with the Spirit is that they obtain a new and overwhelming baptism of love. Commissioner Samuel Brengle testifies that the morning following his entire sanctification:

---

12. While the idea of developing one's gift is compatible with Paul's discussion in Romans 12, it does not altogether fit the precise wording of his related discussion in 1 Corinthians 12. In Romans the emphasis is on *functions,* and more or less permanent callings or assignments to fulfill our particular function. For instance, if one's gift is teaching, "let him teach"; and likewise, if it is "leadership, let him govern diligently." The passage is really an admonition to "do with our might what our hand finds to do." We are to accept our role and fill it cheerfully and efficiently. This implies cultivating the necessary skills required as well as exercising the Spirit's special degree of enabling. The Corinthian passage, however, sounds as if the gifts were not permanent endowments that could be carried about and displayed at will (cf. Heb. 2:4). It is not a gift of "wisdom" that elevates some above others, but a *word of wisdom* given on the occasion of special need, a *word of knowledge* when insight or information is needed; a gift of *faith* when special achieving faith is needed; a gift of *miraculous power,* as when Paul struck Elymas with blindness (he couldn't always exercise such power). For further helpful discussions of the gift question see W. T. Purkiser, *The Gifts of the Spirit;* Wesley L. Duewel, *The Holy Spirit and Tongues.*

> I walked out over Boston Commons before breakfast, weeping for joy and praising God. Oh, how I loved! In that hour I knew Jesus, and I loved Him till it seemed my heart would break with love. I was filled with love for all His creatures. I heard the little sparrows chattering; I loved them. I saw a little worm wriggling across my path; I stepped over it; I didn't want to hurt any living thing. I loved the dogs, I loved the horses, I loved the little urchins on the street, I loved the strangers who hurried past me, I loved the heathen—I loved the whole world![13]

Clarence W. Hall asks, "Was it a mere vision, a momentary exultation, that a calmer moment would disillusion? Ten, twenty, thirty, forty years and more would pass, and yet he would give that same fadeless testimony."[14]

It is true that there is a volitional element in love. It is what we are commanded to *do*—to "love the Lord your God with all your heart and with all your soul and with all your mind and with all your strength," and "your neighbor as yourself" (Mark 12:30-31). But for sinful man, God's commands not only imply His enablings but require them as well. It is as impossible for the natural man to fulfill these commandments in his own strength as it is to "add to his stature one cubit" simply by "taking thought" (Luke 12:25, KJV).

B. Facets of Love

In his book *The Four Loves,* C. S. Lewis discusses *eros,* the love of man and woman; *affection,* which should prevail in families; and *friendship,* a love between friends. All of these are gifts of common grace to the human race. But all are to some degree marred by sin and find their true perfection and preservation only when sanctified by the divine dimension—*Christian love* (which Lewis calls *charity*). Only Christians know this love, and only wholly sanctified Christians experience its joys and power as the master motive of life. William R. Cannon of Emory University interprets Wesley's doctrine of sanctification as "the inward purifying grace begun at justification and bringing man to entire holiness of life by reducing all his motives to the single motive of love."[15]

---

13. *Brengle: Portrait of a Prophet,* 59.
14. Ibid.
15. *The Journal of Religion* 42, no. 3 (July 1962), 227.

1. *Human Love*

The nature of love is such that all four kinds or levels of love have common characteristics. There is in love—always—an element of tenderness and compassion. Hardness of heart and love are mutually contradictory. Also, love absorbs us, controls us, dominates our thoughts. The object of our affection is frequently and naturally in our minds. (No normal youth will deny this!) Furthermore, love's natural desire is to be with the one or ones we love. Finally, we are concerned unselfishly about their welfare and happiness. We desire to help them, not hurt them. True love is never sadistic. "Love worketh no ill to his neighbour," says Paul (Rom. 13:10, KJV). All of this is true of a mother's love for her child, a friend's love for his friend, and equally of our love for God. We think of Him often, want to be with Him, and are intensely concerned about the honor of His name and the advancement of His kingdom.

2. *Grace Love*

Christian love acts like this, too, but has in it the plus of grace. It is not so dependent on reciprocity but can love when the love is not returned. Neither is it dependent on inherent attractiveness in its object; rather by God's grace the Christian can feel a warm tenderness and compassion toward those who are personally unattractive and unlovable, even those who are enemies.

Furthermore, such a love is not confined to our own kin or color or race but is capable of outgoing concern toward all men, simply as human beings created in God's image and for whom Christ died. God loves them, and through the indwelling Spirit we are participating in His flow of love. It could be said that God is loving them through us, and we are aware of the glow of it. Neither is this love limited to proximity but may be genuinely felt toward countless numbers whom we have not seen. Obviously such love is totally supernatural. It is not achieved by self-effort but created by grace.

3. *Love's Redemptive Impulse*

Our love, if truly Christian, will be godlike in its redemptive orientation. We too will see the multitudes, as did Jesus, not only as hungry people but also as sheep having no shepherd, who need to be taught many things (Mark 6:34). Our chief concerns will be moral and spiritual issues and the eternal welfare of human souls. It is in the nature of love to desire the best for its object; Christian love will see this best as salvation through Christ and will be incapable of resting in any lesser goals. Its sights are never just temporal, never just physical, but also and most profoundly spiritual and eternal. It is superior, therefore, to the love of the natural man, because it sees the whole man and the whole need. C. E. B. Cranfield comments: "Love means the refusal to see, think of, or deal with, one's neighbor except in the light of what Christ has done for him, as the brother for whom Christ died"[16] (cf. Rom. 14:15; 1 Cor. 8:11).

4. *The Triangle of Christian Love*

This kind of love toward man is never found—indeed it is impossible—except as it is the rebound of a prior devotion to God. Love for one's neighbor is the second commandment, not the first. Our love is primarily directed neither selfward nor neighbor-ward but Godward. Our love for God both purifies and controls love for self and for others. God does not intend that our relationships be merely two-way but three-way, with God the controlling center. When we love people through our love for God, then we see them as God sees them, and our love for them is shaped by our love for God. Only then is it holy and safe. We will love them not as we please, but as God pleases, and in perfect harmony with His laws.

This imparts to our love not only a deeper intensity, but a different quality. The moment we leave God out and start loving people "straight across," so to speak, our love drops to a different and vastly lower range. Self-pleasing becomes the dominant and controlling factor, which then becomes people-pleasing. The love that remains will tend to become selfish and exploitive. This is true even with parental love, no matter now sacrificial and sincere such love may be. This divine element is most vital to the child's welfare. One day a young woman came to Joseph Sizoo, a pastor in New York City, seeking counsel. When asked why she had come, she replied that "she had at home a 17-week-old baby. She didn't want that little one to miss something she had missed, and she believed it was God."[17]

5. *The Safeguard of the Home*

If holiness is to be lived anywhere, it must be in the home. If it does not work there, it will be a facade and a sham everywhere

---

16. *Theological Word Book of the Bible,* ed. Alan Richardson (New York: Macmillan Co., 1951), 136.

17. *Preaching Unashamed* (New York: Abingdon-Cokesbury Press, 1949), 41.

else. Only that love which is the product of the indwelling Spirit, which the prism of life breaks into its spectrum of joy, peace, patience, kindness, goodness, faithfulness, gentleness, and self-control, will cement the home into an unbreakable unity and adequately counter the disrupting forces of our day.

For one thing, the romantic love that men and women "fall" into and out of so easily is too fragile and temperamental. It withers before the irritations and misunderstandings of everyday life. Some stress and tension will be the lot of every household. Christian love would rather be holy than happy and desires to honor God at all costs. Above every earthly goal, it wants to help the spouse and the children to heaven and is thus capable of absorbing hurts and making adjustments to a degree any other kind of love is not. Such love is the "bond of perfectness" in the home as well as in the character (Col. 3:14, KJV).

And this difference will make better parents, for their whole outlook will be anchored in a different kind of motivation. They will not be driven by vanity and pride, or personal pleasure and whim, or by fear of the neighbors and the PTA or a poor grade card. Instead they will be motivated primarily and most profoundly by an all-mastering sense of responsibility toward Almighty God and to the immortal souls that God has put in their care. This will give parents the strength to say no when it would be much easier to say yes, and to impose punishment at times when the way of least resistance would be to ignore the offense. It will help them to be courageously firm and yet loving, all the while singing, "A charge to keep I have."

6. *The Service Motive*

Only a fervent love for God and people will keep us going in our service responsibilities when all other incentives fail. There are many motivations that stir people to action. A guilty conscience drives some to "work their fingers to the bone," while the love of praise and position energizes others. Pride keeps some doing their duty, and still others strive to chalk up "points" with God. But sooner or later the telltale tarnish of unworthy motives will show. The work will become galling and tedious and unrewarding. When the excitement of some special project is absent, the Lord's work will be done without heart. Only love keeps the glow and turns drudgery into delight.

When a missionary spoke to a peddler about God, the quick

reply was "This is my god," as he jingled the money in his pocket. When his great bundle was tied up and with much effort heaved to his back, the missionary asked, "Isn't that a heavy load?" The man shot back, "I don't mind it; and if you loved your God as much as I love mine, you wouldn't mind carrying big loads either." Suddenly the missionary understood the poverty of his ministry over the years. The night was spent in prayer until he was baptized with the Spirit—and with love. A revival broke out and spread to surrounding mission stations.

C. Love Perfect yet Limited

1. *Marks of Perfect Love*

When can love be said to be perfect? The answer is not whether or not it is *agapeic* love (the love of supreme preference), for that may be evil as well as good (cf. John 3:19; 2 Tim. 4:10; 1 John 2:15). To be perfect as *Christian* love the *agapē* love must have certain indispensable marks.

(a) It meets the standards of the great commandments. (b) Its objective source is the Holy Spirit (Rom. 5:5). (c) Its subjective source—or "quality control"—is "a pure heart and a good conscience and a sincere faith" (1 Tim. 1:5). (d) It is practical, even sacrificial in its expression (1 John 3:17). (e) It is a communion with God that excludes the fear of the Judgment (4:17-18). (f) It is free from its opposites—hatred, bitterness, resentments, injustice, wrong dealing, an unforgiving spirit (Gal. 5:13-26). The love of carnal Christians either blows hot and cold, or is lukewarm, or is mixed with emotions and attitudes contrary to love. It is this very condition that becomes to them a painful discovery and makes them keenly aware of their need of "something more."

Finally, (g)—to risk repetition—it is dynamic, which is to say, strong enough to be the driving force of one's life. Secondary motives are submerged in the master passion. When our service becomes dilatory and our Christian work boring, and when we have to be paid well to do our job half well, something is wrong. When we are more responsive to gimmicks and winning than the cause itself, our love is lukewarm and is no longer perfect. Practiced smiles, contrived testimonies, and sharp personalities are poor substitutes for radiant faces, artless praises, and sincere service for the Lord.

2. *Limitations of Perfect Love*

The most obvious limitations are imposed by our finiteness.[18] Not having all the facts on which to act, our love is sometimes expressed unwisely, even blunderingly. Unless our love is balanced by the gift of discernment, we might, because of our very love, be gullible and overly trusting.

Our love also is limited in expression by our meager resources and energies. We cannot do all that needs to be done or that we would like to do. The gap between the resources and the need is often so great that we are haunted by a feeling of inadequacy and failure. Those who love little have no problem with stress over the missed opportunities, but with the caring person the gap is a constant torment.

At some point loving Christians must come to terms with the fact that health, time, and money are simply not enough to go around. We are single, not multiple, and can be in only one place at a time. There is a sense in which the statement is true that "two duties do not conflict," and at times we must simply commit to God the people who need us whom we can't quite reach. Yet we must avoid becoming so accepting of our limitations that we lose the "stretch" necessary to spiritual health. We must not settle down to a comfortable kind of life that shirks the pain of loving.

D. A Growing Love

1. *Maturing the Fruit of the Spirit*

None of the marks of perfect love mentioned above is incompatible with the concept of a growing love. Love in its eight-foldness (Gal. 5:22-23) is first experienced as joy and peace in conversion. Then more gradually (but increasingly) under the molding and sanctifying ministration of the Spirit, it becomes patience, kindness, and goodness (benevolence).

Slowest to ripen are the forms of love manifest as faithfulness, gentleness, and self-control, which relate to our private view of ourselves and of our little world. A Spirit-filled Christian is not unfaithful in major obligations but is sometimes slow to learn the importance of faithfulness in small matters. These might include promptness in appointments, carefulness with confidences, de-

---

18. No one has more graphically stated the limitations of love than Wesley. Cf. *Works*, 11:397, 415, 417.

pendability in fulfilling commitments, and regularity in family and personal devotions.

Gentleness (KJV, "meekness") is in some ways the crowning virtue, most like Christ who said that we were to learn of Him who was "meek and lowly in heart" (Matt. 11:29, KJV; cf. 5:5; 21:5; 1 Pet. 3:4; 1 Thess. 2:7; 2 Tim. 2:24). Domestic turmoil and church divisions more often stem from a want of meekness than from any other cause. Toward God, meekness is "that temper of spirit in which we accept His dealings with us as good, and therefore without disputing or resisting," says Vine.[19]

Many who are submissive to God have trouble becoming sufficiently meek in interpersonal relationships. There is confusion in sorting out problems of self-esteem, proper roles (such as masculine and feminine, proprietary and subordinate), and proper self-assertion. The Holy Spirit will teach that strength of poise and that assurance of self-worth that can be unflappable when roles seem threatened. This becomes increasingly a matter of perspective (what does it matter?), quietness in the Lord (it is His work!), and loving understanding of why others are giving us a bad time. It is only the meekness of vibrant and tender love that can be squelched without squelching back. Here is a form of love that needs much growth in many of us. "Thou wilt keep him in perfect peace, whose mind is stayed on thee: because he trusteth in thee" (Isa. 26:3, KJV). This includes those times when we are misunderstood, sat upon, and walked on. The supreme test of maturity is the ability to accept criticism with poise and profit by it.

And what can we say of temperance? The Holy Spirit will prompt self-control. He will insist on extending its areas of practice to our expenditures, moods, talking, recreations and hobbies, and yes, our eating. A non-Christian doctor said to a Christian worker: "You are too fat. If you would lose weight, you would gain credibility."

2. *The Need for Wisdom*

Paul prayed for the Philippians "that your love may abound more and more in knowledge and depth of insight, so that you may be able to discern what is best" (Phil. 1:9-10). Apologizing for the antics of a well-meaning preacher, the superintendent said kindly, "That dear brother has more religion and less sense than

---

19. *Expository Dictionary,* 3:55.

anyone I have ever known." This is not an unusual dichotomy. Love imparts goodwill but not good judgment. It does not of itself create information or know-how.

It was not enough for the deacons to be full of the Holy Spirit; they must also be full of wisdom (Acts 6:3). One does not necessarily assure the other. Paul therefore was anxious for the love of the Philippians to grow, not simply in emotional exuberance, but in quality control. It needed to grow along the lines of knowledge and depth of insight. If we are to live a life of love helpfully, we must learn to be understanding as well as caring. This takes love disciplined by intelligence.

Only by such intelligent love will we be able to discern what is best in any given situation. There is a modicum of truth in "situation ethics." The detailed application of divine law *is* to some extent to be determined by the particularities of the concrete case. The *error* of situation ethics as advocated by Joseph Fletcher and others in the contemporary mood is the premise that love is the only law needed. It affirms that all men are capable of seeing in any given situation the loving thing to do and then doing it. This flies in the face of the hard realities of sinful human nature. Only a grace-love, experienced by the regenerate person, and enthroned within the Spirit-filled believer, is adequate to create the disposition and the compassion to perceive the most loving thing. But even such love will miss it if not trained by the Spirit in the basic ground rules of God's will and in ethical judgment (Heb. 5:14).

3. *Manner Is Important*

Not only must our love grow in wisdom, but it must be supported by general personal culture. A loving heart may be hidden by a crude, brusque manner. Uncultivated, unrefined people often offend with outlandish (even indecent) appearance, loudness, and boisterousness. Raucous, uncontrolled laughter in public places, the habit of interrupting the person who is speaking, and continuous and obnoxious self-reference are abrasive to others. Opinionated people who are quick to set others right or who make scenes about petty details in the presence of others are social undesirables. God may see a heart of gold, but what comes across is not love but boorishness. It is the duty of the Christian to cultivate tact, politeness, and good manners for Jesus' sake.

Nowhere is this more important than in the home, where so often it is not lack of love that is at the bottom of irritations but lack of tact and gentle consideration. Thoughtlessness is the culprit. Spirit-filled persons above all must demonstrate their Spirit fullness by letting the Holy Spirit teach them quietness and gentleness. And there must be the cultivation of that love which is truly compassionate, not just for starving millions across the sea, but for sensitive, very human persons under the same roof.

Love has in it the disposition to feel for the other person—to be alert to his feelings, to protect him, to avoid embarrassing him needlessly before others. In short, it is *to be kind.* But in the hurry and bustle of today's complicated, busy life we so often forget and wound needlessly and unintentionally. Spouses should prayerfully study their mates to understand why they react as they do to certain situations. They should learn to accommodate *them,* rather than be forever demanding that they be accommodated. This kind of home religion is holy religion and imparts credibility to our profession of perfect love.

III. A Righteous Life

Paul said that the kingdom of God is "not a matter of eating and drinking, but of righteousness, peace and joy in the Holy Spirit" (Rom. 14:17). The "eating and drinking" summarize all the various minor matters of practice he is discussing in chapters 14 and 15. They are cultic, dietary, cultural, and personal. They are not to be elevated to a definitive place in religion, but must be kept in the category of personal opinion and variable practice (cf. 14:5).

But not so with basic righteousness. It is even more elementary than peace and joy, for the latter are illusory without it. Even eating and drinking can become issues of ethical Christian living, if taken out of the cultic context and evaluated in terms of temperance, health, and example and influence. "It is better not to eat meat or drink wine or to do anything else that will cause your brother to fall" (14:21). So the eating and drinking, discounted at one level, may yet be vital at the righteousness level. *It is especially so at the love level,* for it is love that is willing to see the possible ethical implications of one's personal freedom and act accordingly.

A. The Ethical Demand

The ethical standard that is to mark holy living is summarized in many passages, but no more comprehensively than in chapters

12 and 13 of Romans.[20] The primary purpose of the summary of the commandments, "Do not commit adultery," "Do not murder," "Do not steal," "Do not covet," and "whatever other commandment there may be" (Rom. 13:9-10), is to show their agreement with love. Because these forbidden activities are hurtful to their victims, and love is a disposition to protect from such hurt, love will have no problem with these laws. Christian love is not liberation *from* them, but liberation *within* them. Love will want to fulfill all duty toward the neighbor and avoid all detriment. Any professed love, therefore, that tends to set aside law, and trespass what is right and fair and legal, is phony.

Professors and exponents of holiness, above all, should be absolutely blameless in ethical practices. This includes relations with the opposite sex, which should be above reproach. The contemporary freedom between the sexes can be healthy, but it can also be a booby trap. There is a fine line between a wholesome camaraderie among friends which is beautiful and pure, and careless license that can with astonishing subtlety and rapidity suck people down the drain of moral collapse. Christians who would avoid overt sin must rigorously guard their affections.

In business, too, there is no place for shadiness. One axiom that governs the holiness person in all his business relationships is: *People are more important than profits.* Whether we are buyers, sellers, or managers, we should be able after a transaction to witness for the Lord or invite to church, without creating a stench and a reproach. Holiness keeps its word, pays its bills, and gives good measure. It makes things we sell or install come up to our claims. It works an honest hour. It is straightforward and aboveboard, without trickiness or duplicity.

B. The Training of the Conscience

1. *The Ethical Gap*

In spite of the fact that holiness in theory and in personal attitude makes no allowance for shabby ethics, it is nevertheless unfortunately true that sometimes the ethical sense is slow in catching up with spiritual experience. An example is the newly sanctified young man testifying of his experience to his friend be-

---

20. A very short epitome, in general terms, is: The grace of God teaches us "to say 'No' to ungodliness and worldly passions, and to live self-controlled, upright and godly lives in this present age" (Titus 2:12).

side him—while driving 90 miles an hour! Almost anyone can trot out examples of such inconsistencies that he has observed. Tragically, they are noticed also by neighbors, business partners, and especially youth, often with devastating consequences.

Why this gap? If a strong motivation to live right is not present, then the heart is not truly holy. But among the sanctified the gap occurs through ignorance, and sometimes through intellectual limitations. Some practices have been so much a part of life so long that no thought has been given to them. The discovery that some people think them wrong comes as a shock.

This can be true of language, dress, driving habits, Sunday observance, honoring promises, punctuality, handling money—dozens of areas. Furthermore, even with intelligent people, not many unconverted persons are in the habit of thinking through the fine points of ethical situations, such as tax filing, expense accounts, reporting figures, explaining actions, recounting events. Added to this sometimes is the complicating factor of limited capacity for doing such intelligent thinking. Holiness does not necessarily raise the IQ.

2. *Closing the Gap*

It is the duty of the Church to set ethical standards and raise ethical issues, if for no other reason than to discharge its teaching responsibility. It is the duty of preachers to preach not infrequently and very plainly about honesty, purity, fair play, and exemplary conduct. No new converts should remain unaware of these ethical issues.

The philosophy back of this is very simple: Whether we are dealing with children, teenagers, or new church members, we must be willing to raise issues, for only by so doing can we teach ethical thinking. Wrong practices must be talked about, and right practices explained. Wholly sanctified Christians are eager for such instruction and quick to adjust their life-style. Carnal Christians will quibble and fuss, but often their very obstreperousness can be used by the Spirit to put them under conviction.

But the Spirit-filled Christian has a duty too. He should not only listen to instruction but study the Scriptures to find the life-style that exemplifies holiness. Then he must learn to apply the scriptural principles to the everyday rough and tumble of the 20th century. *He must train himself to think in ethical terms.* If he does not, he will remain a stumbling block to others.

The motivation for this will deepen when this Christian sees the havoc that will accrue in the lives of others as a result of his failure. He may make heaven, while those he has influenced by his inconsistency may be lost. One churchman was held in high esteem by a newly converted teenage boy until one night in a social gathering he heard his hero regale the laughing group with a string of off-color stories. In disappointment he said to the hostess, "That's the kind of story I used to tell before I was converted." He was so shaken that he lost spiritual balance and dropped out of church.

We are being watched!

3. *The Relation of Conscience to Love and Faith*

The biblical teaching is that perfect love will prompt great conscientiousness. Lack of such sensitivity disproves any claim one might make to perfect love. The corollary is that saving faith is canceled when the conscience is tampered with. In 1 Tim. 1:19 faith is shipwrecked by thrusting away a good conscience (cf. RSV, NEB). Of a good conscience Wesley says, "It goes away unwillingly. It always says, 'Do not hurt me.' And they who retain this, do not make shipwreck of their faith." Then he adds solemnly, "These therefore were once true believers. Yet they fell not only foully but finally."[21]

Paul points to two examples, Hymenaeus and Alexander. They evidently believed that the conscience and saving faith were unrelated; that faith could be retained without a good conscience. It is striking that what some people today call orthodoxy Paul called blasphemy.

C. Holiness and Social Issues

A holy heart is predisposed to be on God's side of every moral issue, and to implement, as far as he is able, what is perceived to be God's will. An evangelical Christian believes that God's mind on questions of conduct and human welfare is to be found in the Scriptures; therefore he seeks conformity to this authority. Involvement in popular social causes will be prompted by profound moral concern and a spirit of obedience, not simply by the excitement of attaching ourselves to whatever happens to be the "in" thing at the moment. During the last century and a half the causes

---

21. *Explanatory Notes upon the New Testament.*

of slavery, women's rights, temperance, civil rights, and others have each held center stage in the limelight of public attention for varying periods of time. More currently to the forefront are the issues of abortion, homosexuality, euthanasia, poverty, welfare, minorities, capitalism, separation of church and state, and war.

Where the Bible speaks with clarity, the sanctified believer aligns himself accordingly. However, it is not to be expected that holy people will always see eye to eye about all of these issues; for while some are clear-cut, as are abortion and homosexuality, others are very complex and multifaceted. Equally good men may differ both as to what is the truly biblical position and as to methods and means for bringing about change. The disposition of the sanctified person will be to keep uppermost in mind the honor of Christ, the welfare of the church and the home, the sanctity of human life and of human personality, and the eternal salvation of souls. These will be the fixed landmarks from which he will take his bearings and determine his directions.[22]

---

22. For a more detailed discussion of holiness and ethics see Richard S. Taylor, *Life in the Spirit,* 169-203; Purkiser, Taylor, and Taylor, *God, Man and Salvation,* 527-59.

11

The Holy Warfare

Holiness of heart conditions one to view life through a biblical lens. Life is seen from the standpoint of Calvary and from the standpoint of eternity. This means a radically new orientation. Value judgments, priorities, personal interests, and goals are the opposite of those prevailing in society generally, or even among nominal Christians. One has a new view of the realities of the human situation.

We are involved in a holy warfare. It is a real war, not a chocolate-soldier make-believe. From this war there is no rest and no discharge until God himself transposes us from the field of battle to the throne of victory.

The holy person, whose eyes have been cleansed and thoroughly opened, sees all this with sharp clarity. He is not living in a fool's paradise. For this reason he does not expect perfect happiness in this world. Indeed his motivations have been elevated above that goal, so that he is no longer consumed with the objective of happiness. His prime concern is with being holy before God and being effective in this holy warfare. He is willing to be available anytime, to serve anywhere, and if need be to be expendable. Considerations of prestige and position and honor have lost their power.

God's holy person may and should be joyful, but in the Spirit (Rom. 14:17; 15:13; Gal. 5:22). He is elated because he has found life's answer, both for himself and for others. He is at peace with his own conscience and with his God. But he is not at peace with the enemy. He cannot rest comfortably in a world of rapine and violence, bloodshed and debauchery, hunger and disease. Therefore he will suffer in ways others do not, even other Christians. He will not be able to escape his sense of responsibility and involvement.

This will go on as long as the sanctified believer is surrounded by lost souls and the enveloping desecration of sin. What breaks God's heart will break his. True holiness will put this kind of iron into one's spiritual blood. Christians not conditioned to accept the holy warfare as a way of life will go AWOL. They will find some quiet cove or glade far from the front lines where they can live comfortably, undisturbed, in the contentment and security of their bovine pursuits.

The natural man dreams of idyllic existence. The holy person has surrendered the dream and is willing to "endure hardness, as a good soldier of Jesus Christ" (2 Tim. 2:3, KJV). Many of God's people may appear to live in relative quietness and security, but even so they will be engaged in the holy warfare through prayer, giving, and Christian labors, using all their available energies and resources.

I. WITHIN THE SELF

The *civil* war is over. Nevertheless many aspects of the warfare against the common enemy will continue to involve and sometimes agitate the self.

A. Holiness and Sinning

1. *The Possibility of Sin*

Wesley insisted that the lowest level of saving grace was sufficient to give victory over sin.[1] By this he meant the commission of known sin according to his narrower definition, "a voluntary transgression of a known law."[2] But he recognized that inner sins of the spirit, such as pride, anger, and envy, plague those not yet perfect in love. At any stage there could be a gradual reversion to sinning through neglect and carelessness.[3]

This potential danger of carelessness is present even after entire sanctification. The fires of holiness must be fed by prayer and

---

1. *Works,* 6:15 et al.
2. Ibid., 11:396.
3. Ibid., 7:341 et al.

Bible reading, by attending to the means of grace, by a habit of watchfulness, and by constant sensitivity to the Spirit. If these conditions for victory and growth begin to be neglected through succumbing to the practical pressures of a busy life, the flame will go out. To change the figure: The fortifications will be undermined and the citadel of the soul thus become vulnerable.

There is never a state of grace in this life where sin becomes an impossibility. "I write this to you so that you will not sin," said John. Then he added, "But if anybody does sin, we have one who speaks to the Father in our defense" (1 John 2:1). The *if* of possibility is always there. But our Advocate is the same as for anyone else; He is the atoning Sacrifice for our sin too. C. W. Ruth once quoted to the author 1 John 1:9 ("If we confess our sins, he is faithful and just to forgive us our sins, and to cleanse us from all unrighteousness" [KJV]), then exclaimed, "That's for us, too, isn't it? Doesn't the 'we' include us?"

The question of sin is peculiarly acute for the entirely sanctified because they, above all, fear and hate sin. They are sensitive to shades of evil that might to others seem inconsequential. Conscience is doubly sensitive and easily wounded. It is proper for holiness people, when aware that the Spirit has been grieved, to face the failure in all seriousness and label it sin. If their poise does not match the occasion, if impatience gets the upper hand, if thoughtless gossip brings an inner rebuke, if they override the check of the Spirit, if they disobey the impression to witness, they should never harden their hearts or practice the ignoble art of rationalizing and excusing themselves. They should at once apologize if the situation calls for apology, and at once confess to God and ask forgiveness.

2. *The Effect of Sin After Sanctification*

Does sin immediately cancel salvation or merely break fellowship with God? Also, can one lose his entire sanctification without losing his justification? These are common questions that have troubled many people. Holiness teachers have been divided in their answers. J. B. Chapman, for example, believed that one could lose perfect love and normal victory without being completely backslidden. Others have vehemently argued that sin is always spiritually fatal—all the way. The advice concerning restoration has also been diverse. Some say that full recovery can be experienced at once, others insist that there must again be two crises of grace.

Where good and able men have disagreed, dogmatism seems unbecoming. However, dogmatism can be avoided by pointing out that there is no simple yes or no answer. Of course, sin, "when it is full-grown, gives birth to death" (James 1:15). Even a single sin, unrepented of and unforgiven, can cost one his salvation. And serious, overt sins are rather strong evidence of a backslidden state.

But such sins are not likely to occur without an inner partial backsliding first, during which time there is some stirring of grace. The Spirit has not withdrawn but is battling to arrest the drift (see p. 194). During this period there may be sins of regression, of neglect, or the beginnings of ill will and self-will. Perhaps there will be the germination of resentment and bitterness toward someone, even God. Obviously this is the state of a sick Christian. He can scarcely testify to the "fullness of the blessing." But in his heart of hearts he knows he is still a child of God, for he continues to have a prayer life, even if feeble, and to carry out religious duties. But he is a defeated Christian!

How long one can struggle in this condition without the complete loss of even justifying grace is uncertain. It *is* certain that it must be temporary. The battle will have to be resolved one way or the other. If such a badly bent Christian will call a halt and take time to pray clear through, there is no reason why his recovery cannot be total, all the way to normal Spirit fullness.

Especially is this true if the spiritual shadow is not caused by a period of regression but only one isolated, out-of-character failure, which he at once sees and "puts under the Blood." A strained wrist does not have to be broken in order to be mended. A climber who slips back a few steps does not have to descend to the foot of the mountain for a new start. Yet if the defection has become open backsliding and reversion to sinning and has lasted over a period of time, it is more reasonable to postulate the necessity of doing "the first works" over—both repentance and consecration. Even so it is impossible to be reclaimed at all unless the return is to the *full measure of light.*[4]

Also in order to understand the complete picture we must take

---

4. But how does such resanctifying relate to inherited sinfulness? It does not, in the same sense as the first experience. The depravity that needs to be cleansed is self-generated—but equally virulent.

into account the fine line between real sin in God's sight and innocent human failure. Conscientious but supersensitive Christians
may be suffering guilt feelings needlessly. If the adversary cannot
lull to sleep, he will crack the whip of continuous accusation. Clear
thinking is needed here. There is no virtue in forever confessing
sins that are not sins; although, of course, this fault is preferable to
never confessing sins that are.

B. The Struggle with Temptation

1. *The Advantages of the Sanctified*

It is a mistake to say that temptation with the entirely sanctified "is on the outside, never on the inside." All temptation involves desire of some kind or a struggle of some degree that is *in* us
(James 1:14).[5] Our thoughts and emotions are involved. It is *our*
resolution that is being attacked, not someone else's. Yet the saying
may be a figurative way of expressing a certain truth. Entirely
sanctified Christians have detected a before-and-after difference,
though it is often almost indefinable.

For one thing, there is some difference in the *kind* of temptation that may torment. The prevailing winds of temptation are
more likely to be in interpersonal relations, trials over circumstances, and even the acute awareness of our own limitations; less
from the allure of worldly values and pleasures. Some things that
once seemed important have lost their attractiveness, therefore
they no longer constitute avenues of temptation. They belong to
the past.

Also there is detected a strong difference in one's response to
temptation. The very aliveness of spiritual commitment, the intensity of our love for Christ, the desire to please God in the secret
recesses of our being, the jealousy for His honor and good name
and the welfare of the Church, the abhorrence of letting others
down, the perspective of heaven and eternity that always shapes
our thinking—all of these are powerful motivations to resist temptation. Pleasing God has displaced pleasing self as one's constantly
perceived supreme value. Breach of trust is seen as a heinous thing.

---

5. The word *epithumia* means strong desire and should not here be translated
"lust," as if a temptable desire were necessarily an evil desire. See Richard S. Taylor,
Life in the Spirit, 204-17.

2. *Avenues of Temptation*

There are primarily three avenues of temptation: the appetites, illness, and the natural propensities of the self.

a. The appetites are always clamorous, therefore must be kept under tight reign. Paul said, "I beat my body and make it my slave so that after I have preached to others, I myself will not be disqualified for the prize" (1 Cor. 9:27).

Sanctified people, like others, will be more or less aware of *sex urges*. In part, this is due to a normal, God-created biological subvolitional activity, which will challenge every resource of grace. But in part also it is the profound and mysterious magnetism between male and female, which in its uniquely human dimension is spiritual and intellectual as well as biological. It is an empathetic feel for the opposite sex, of admiration and compatibility, which up to a point can make for wholesome, beautiful, and innocent relations.

For holy people the temptation will not normally develop directly via the passion route, but by way of warm affection and appreciation. Perhaps affinity is the word. But affinity is dynamite. In it is explosive and destructive potential. Therefore to remain holy, God's people need to guard their affections and watch against sticky attachments and compromising situations. They will not stupidly play with fire. And they will be doubly careful to avoid mental fantasies they have no intention of pursuing in real life.

b. Physical weakness makes us more vulnerable to temptation, but in this case the temptations are more likely to be in the realm of the spirit. Great pain or great fatigue tends to cloud the mind. Life gets out of perspective. Reality becomes distorted and the soul is prey to false impressions and imaginations, maybe even hallucinations. Rash actions or words may result.

We have no right to burn the candle at both ends until gradual disorientation sets in. Occasionally circumstances beyond our control force us into such a black hole, in which case we can only keep crying to God in our spirit for His upholding. But let us be sure the circumstances are really beyond our control rather than of our own making. The zeal that is self-destructive is not a Spirit-prompted zeal.

c. The natural propensities of the self become avenues for temptation. There are in all of us the instincts for self-expression and for community. There is in the normal self a combativeness against obstacles, a desire to achieve, desires for knowledge and for the acquirement of personal skills. Acquisitiveness, or the desire to possess, seems to be native to the self also. It is natural to want *my* spouse, *my* home, *my* job; books or tools and bric-a-brac that I can call my own.

Also the self spontaneously desires and craves love. Without it the self withers and shrinks and twists into grotesque shapes. There is something in the self that needs recognition and acceptance. It wants to belong. In a TV talk show the subject was "What I Fear Most." Learned educators and business people talked of war and the various perils of modern man. One man was silent until pressed, when he said quietly, "The thing I fear most is not being loved." All of which is a way of saying that God has built into the human psyche great, cavernous needs that must be met if the self is going to be healthy; and the greatest of these is love. Holiness does not remove these needs but conditions the soul to find their satisfaction within the will of God.

In wholly sanctified persons, also, the self spontaneously reacts negatively to some things, positively to others. They react negatively to vandalism, littering, cruelty, injustice, wanton disregard of law. They may, for instance, feel disgust and irritation against a driver who jeopardizes human lives by foolish recklessness.

Then there is the very personal, intimate area of natural preferences that are as present in the holy as in the unholy. We prefer success to failure, praise to blame, being understood to being misunderstood, health to illness, pleasure to pain, freedom of movement to being bound (Acts 26:29), comfortable circumstances to pinching poverty.

We could add others, such as preferring to be married than single, or staying with loved ones to going to strange lands, eating familiar food to eating unfamiliar food.[6] In these ways and dozens of others of a similar nature, the self is still very much alive, in the sanctified as well as the unsanctified. Holiness doesn't mean that we have to *like* everything that comes to us or that we are called on to do. We may be able through grace to rejoice in our minor sacri-

---

6. It is not racism to have a natural preference for one's own kind, for the simple reason that with them we have more in common. However, the saved are "one's own kind" at a deeper, more fundamental level, regardless of nationality, color, or race. Therefore grace can transcend the natural (and innocent) preference for cultural and racial affinities, by creating a new kind of affinity.

fices for Jesus' sake, and even to rejoice in our sufferings; but it is through grace we rejoice, not through nature. In his spiritual maturity Paul could testify, "I have learned to be content whatever the circumstances" (Phil. 4:11).

And of course we cannot omit the great crises of life. We may be in pain and wish God would heal us and restore us to normal living. But perhaps He is saying to us what He said to Paul, "My grace is sufficient for you" (2 Cor. 12:9). Or worse yet, a loved one may be in pain and we know God could heal if He would. We wonder why He does not. And perhaps the worst comes, and death claims our loved one. Holy people hurt as truly as others and weep honest tears of grief. Being holy does not mean that we will enjoy the blows of life.[7]

But every one of these items of preference or avoidance, of like or dislike, becomes an avenue of temptation. The temptation may be to doubt God's care, or become mistrustful of people, or lose faith in ourselves, or submit to feelings of discouragement and then depression.

Or, we may be tempted to avoid certain unpleasant experiences by manipulating providence ourselves, or perhaps by running away from distasteful duties. The pastor who has no yen for "no" votes is tempted to soft-pedal unpopular issues. He likes this community and this house and does not want to move—all perfectly natural (not carnal) desires, but dangerous. These are the realities of the self-life that must be kept on the altar day after day, year after year, if there is not to be a reversion to self-enthronement.

C. Overcoming the Enemy

The holy warfare would be simpler if only self and environment were involved. But "our struggle is not against flesh and blood, but against the rulers, against the authorities, against the powers of this dark world and against the spiritual forces of evil in the heavenly realms" (Eph. 6:12). The purpose of the "shield of faith" is to "extinguish all the flaming arrows of the evil one" (v. 16). This is the same "evil one" from which Jesus prayed that the disciples would be protected (John 17:15). This is the one whom

---

7. Even Paul prayed three times for the removal of his thorn. He was able to rejoice in it only when he came to see it as a means of glorifying God.

Paul had in mind when he warned, "Do not give the devil a foot-hold" (Eph. 4:27). He taught that we must learn to do spiritual battle in order to "stand against the devil's schemes" (6:11; cf. 1 John 5:19).[8]

To deny the adversary is unbiblical; to ignore him is folly. Two extremes are equally wrong: (1) to act as if he doesn't exist, or (2) to become so obsessed with a devil complex as to live in fear. The New Testament counsel of Paul, James, and Peter is to be intelligently aware of the nature of our enemy and know how to handle him. We "are not unaware of his schemes," says Paul (2 Cor. 2:11); but that is the problem—most of us *are* all too unaware.

1. *Satan's Modes of Attack*

It seems clear that Satan has access to our thought life and can thus influence our train of thought. He understands full well the power of suggestion. He prompts thoughts of self-pity, and exaggerates the injustices we may have suffered. He seeks to keep our minds glued to our hurts so that we cannot divert our attention to practical duties. He will encourage brooding until our problem is ballooned far out of proportion to reality.

Satan will accuse God to us and equally accuse other people to us, seeking in every way to drive wedges of suspicion and mistrust. He will create feelings of strong compulsion that we must do this or that immediately. He engenders a driving spirit that breeds fanaticism and fosters mental breakdown. Normal desires he will seek to fan into a fever. All of this can be the impingement of demonic or satanic power on our mental processes. "Ananias," Peter asked, "how is it that Satan has so filled your heart that you have lied to the Holy Spirit . . . ?" (Acts 5:3).

The peril of all perils is in not knowing the source of such thoughts. If we know "who's talking," we will know how to respond. But of course Satan never announces himself by saying,

---

8. Most instances of "devil" in the New Testament (KJV) are translations of *daimonion* and should be translated *demon*. Demons are many, probably fallen angels; they comprise the kingdom of evil. When the New Testament intends a reference to the archdemon, Satan, the words *diabolos* and *satan, satanas* are usually used. "Satan is not simply the personification of evil influences in the heart, for he tempted Christ, in whose heart an evil thought could never have arisen (John 14:30; 2 Cor. 5:21; Heb. 4:15); moreover his personality is asserted in both the O.T. and the N.T., especially in the latter, whereas if the O.T. language was intended to be figurative, the N.T. would have made this evident" (Vine, *Expository Dictionary*, 3:320).

"This is the devil speaking." We must discern what is going on. The danger is in supposing that it is our own reason leading us along in a logical train of thought. When we assume this, we will follow the train of thought into the wrong attitudes and unwise actions. James admonishes, "Resist the devil, and he will flee from you" (James 4:7). But how can we resist one whom we do not recognize?[9]

But Satan attacks us not only in our thought life but also in our bodies. Jesus went around "doing good and healing all who were under the power of the devil" (Acts 10:38). Much psychosomatic illness, otherwise inexplicable, is of satanic origin. Even Spirit-filled people can be subject to demonic oppression on their spirits, which is dangerous to the soul if not recognized and resisted. They also can have peculiar physical symptoms designed to unfit them for the Lord's work and even eliminate them from their God-called form or field of labor.

2. *Our Mode of Battle*

Fundamentally, of course, our *faith* is our shield. We must believe in the sufficiency and power of the blood of Christ, and in the fact that in the absolute sense Satan is a defeated foe. Even in his roaring he is chained (as illustrated in *Pilgrim's Progress*). He cannot get *at* us beyond God's permission, and he cannot get *in* us without our permission. Our yielding must always be to God in Christ, never to strange influences or questionable religious leaders.

The manipulation of the human mind and will into passive receptivity (such as with transcendental meditation) is a satanic maneuver. Our minds should be actively directed by our sanctified will. Disobedience to Christ at any point, no matter how small, will provide a crack for satanic deception. Any disobedience will dull our spiritual senses so that we will be less likely to recognize the demonic nature of the suggestions that come to our minds. Our safety is in purity, trust, obedience, and living in the Word.

Also, we must understand the power of our weapons—the Blood, the Word, and prayer. As the old saying goes, "Satan flees when he sees the weakest saint upon his knees." Believe it! Like-

---

9. The reality of this warfare, and the cunning of the enemy, as well as some of his methods, would become more graphic to us through the reading of C. S. Lewis' *Screwtape Letters*. An exceptionally helpful discussion of our confrontation with Satan is by Marion H. Nelson, M.D., *Why Christians Crack Up*, rev. ed. (Chicago: Moody Press, 1967), 145-60.

wise Satan cowers before the Cross and is powerless to resist the Word.

Together with this is the importance of seeing the authority we have as Spirit-filled people. Christ has given us this authority and we must fearlessly exercise it. Satan can be rebuked in a situation and be commanded to leave. We must learn what it means to *resist.* When it is done in prayer, in purity of heart, in the name of Jesus, and on the authority of the Blood and the Word, Satan is powerless. To unspiritual minds this may seem extreme, but it is not incredible to those who have actually engaged Satan in combat and have seen him cower before spiritual authority.

It is tragically true that many churches have been disintegrated by strange powers, and many Christian workers have gone to pieces physically and emotionally without adequate clinical cause. Many potential victories have been lost by default, simply because God's people were "unaware of his schemes" and did not know how to engage in this phase of the holy warfare.

II. PRESSING FOR MATURITY

It is one thing to enjoy by faith the blessing of heart holiness, it is quite another to become established therein. It is still another to reach a level of maturity essential for maximum happiness and usefulness. Ideally, Spirit-filled Christians should be able to forget themselves and be occupied with others. Certainly they are no longer self-centered in a carnal sense. But if growth is to occur according to 2 Pet. 3:18, some deliberate attention must be given to the process, especially in the early Canaan-land years.[10]

A. Becoming a Disciplined Person

Even a truly sanctified person may drag into the holy life many vestiges of the past habits that, while not sinful in themselves or even evidences of carnality, are nevertheless obstacles to efficiency and growth. Years after graduation from seminary, a stu-

---

10. Even John Wesley conceded that "it is an exceeding common thing for persons to lose it [the blessing of perfect love] more than once, before they are established therein" (*Plain Account,* 94). To aid his Methodists in avoiding this he wrote his famous "Advices to the Sanctified," which every person who would take seriously 2 Pet. 3:18 should read frequently (*Plain Account,* 95-105). *Note:* By "enthusiasm" Wesley meant fanaticism.

dent wrote, "I've come to the conclusion that most of my questions on the subject [of holiness] are not intellectual, but confusion as a result of trying to live a holy life with careless ethics. Rebellion has never been my problem—just plain carelessness—but the results have been just as costly."

Another, a professional high school counselor who had struggled for 25 years to become established in an experience of heart holiness, took up the study of what is sometimes called responsibility therapy. When he began to apply it to himself in everyday ways, he discovered that he had stumbled on to the key for maintaining victory. For one thing, he began taking the responsibility for a solid prayer life, including getting up early enough in the morning to assure it. His life was revolutionized, and with it the extension of his influence.

Discipline is the governor that keeps the wheels of life from flying apart. If there is no application to the task of being orderly, disorderliness will be the consequence by default. We must organize our time to see to it that there is a place for prayer and Bible reading. Otherwise time will get away from us, God and our souls will get leftovers and fragments, and spiritual vitality will drain away. We must organize our work, or it will crush us. We must organize our expenditures. They should be governed by intelligent awareness of our stewardship as consecrated persons. If we do not, haphazard, impulse spending will play havoc both with our solvency and our witness.

The high-water mark of being a disciplined person is perhaps twofold: (a) the ability to say no to ourselves; and (b) the capacity to do *what* we ought to do *when* we ought to do it, regardless of feelings. The supposition that because we are sanctified, self-effort in becoming such a disciplined person is not necessary is a gross misconception.

B. Learning to Cope

One might almost say that in spiritual progress there are three levels of grace: converting grace, cleansing grace, and coping grace. The last is the ability to handle the "nuts and bolts" of everyday life as a Christian. High claims are made for the grace of cleansing in creating proper inward conditions for learning to cope. These claims are justified. If the experience of entire sanctification made no difference in handling the common irritations and frustrations of life, it would be of questionable value. The fundamental difference, of course, is that the excessive egoism of the self has been removed. Much of life's irritations arise from people getting in *our* way, cluttering *our* lives, and shattering *our* plans. Or it may be by someone doing or saying things that subtly convey a reflection on *our* judgment or behavior. A sick ego is forever rising to its defense.

The first requisite, therefore, in learning to cope is to make sure that self is kept "nailed to the Cross." When there is freedom from a divided mind, from the heaviness of a hungry heart, from the strain of carnal ambition, and freedom from envy, greed, malice, and hostility, there will be not only released love toward God and man but also a release from tension. Outwardly, there will be increasingly evident—

A more relaxed manner
A happier disposition
A humbler spirit
Greater interest in others
A new capacity to empathize

Such a person has stopped trying to impress and no longer feels the need to be trying to be something he is not. Furthermore he has the humility that is oil on troubled waters. A soft answer *does* turn away wrath (Prov. 15:1, KJV). He can now learn from his blunders and even his stinging humiliations, for only "by letting oneself be humbled does one learn from experience."[11]

1. *Coping with Life's Obligations*

Heart holiness does not create an instant skill in coping with either the nitty-gritty or the major crises. It will assure a fixed resolve to be true to God and to keep a right spirit (2 Tim. 1:7), and it will constitute a submissiveness to the Holy Spirit as our Teacher. But it will not immediately prevent some painful experiences of acute emotional stress and frustration.

There is a human side of effective living and serving, as well as a grace side. Some things must be learned, and everyday coping is one of them. The ability to handle life without breaking rests on a proper combination of several factors: (*a*) sufficient energy for our tasks; (*b*) a load commensurate with our knowledge, skills, and capacity; and (*c*) a degree of control over events and circumstances. When any of these factors goes awry, pressure builds and per-

---

11. Helmut Gollwitzer, *The Demands of Freedom* (New York: Harper and Row, Publishers, 1965), 71.

formance declines. Take, for instance, the matter of energy level. Most people are trying to do too much on too little energy. When E. Stanley Jones suffered a complete physical collapse as a young missionary, he was forced to concede that he was not a superman but required eight hours sleep each night. He wisely adjusted his life-style accordingly—which had much to do with his continued productivity to his death at 83.

Also basic are the requisite skills. Poise in handling conflicts and difficult situations comes from natural ability plus education and training, combined with the wisdom of experience. If we have worked our way through this kind of a situation before, we can more easily cope with it now. If it is a new experience, we may feel overwhelmed. Fortunately, the Holy Spirit can buoy us when our vessel of personal resources is about to go under. Even so, many truly sanctified persons have failed more than once in church jobs (maybe saying or doing unwise things in the process) before their abilities finally caught up with their eagerness.

There is no way of carrying our share of the loads of life without at times finding ourselves "in over our heads." This will be true for the young pastor, the wife and mother, the bread-earning father, the adolescent teen, the conscientious church worker, the professional and business person. Yet it is our duty to do what we can to improve our coping ability because our witness is at stake. This will involve an honest and realistic appraisal of our energy needs, our abilities *and* limitations, plus our situational resources. Along with this we need a humble willingness to structure our undertakings within these boundaries. In other words, pace ourselves.

2. Coping with the Unexpected

Even when we have learned to cope with our jobs and routine duties, we must still reckon with the unexpected. How do we react when our little world crashes in on us by a sudden turn of events? It may be a death, or an accident, or a fire. Perhaps our vacation is planned, and at the last moment a child becomes seriously ill, or the house is burglarized, or someone runs into the car, or the boss says, "We have an emergency, and I must ask you to defer your trip." Or it may be your guests have already arrived, and the power goes off with the roast in the oven.

To be victorious in such circumstances it is necessary to be in firm grasp of Rom. 8:28, even for little things. If we see ourselves simply as victims of cruel fate, we may fret and complain. If we are in touch and in tune with God with a faith that really believes God to be in control, we can learn to accept the unexpected as an unscripted *opportunity*.

Here again, if we are centered around *our* plans, we will resent the interruption; but if we are centered in allowing our lives to be momentarily shaped by God's providence, we can literally "rejoice in the Lord always" (Phil. 4:4). One mark of a Spirit-filled life is the ability to give "thanks to God the Father for [lit., "above" or "concerning"] everything, in the name of our Lord Jesus Christ" (Eph. 5:20). This is possible if we view happenings from above them instead of from beneath them. From the standpoint of eternity the Christian in his most calamitous circumstances has always infinitely more to praise about than to be glum about.

This does not mean that our spontaneous emotional reactions are always ideal. The promise is, "Thou wilt keep him in perfect peace, whose mind is stayed on thee: because he trusteth in thee" (Isa. 26:3, KJV). This will be literally fulfilled if we are always meeting conditions. But when our first reaction is one of hurt or shock or dismay or even a degree of irritation, we must then *choose* to act responsibly, regardless of our feelings.

It requires the perspective of maturity to be able to see the supposed calamity in its larger relation. When a young wife was struggling with the problem of water seeping into their basement apartment because of the rain-sodden ground, she exclaimed to her mother petulantly, "Mother, we prayed that God would stop the rain! Why did He allow this awful trouble?" Quietly the mother, who knew life better, said, "Dear, this is not trouble; this is just inconvenience."

The learning is more likely to occur if it is buttressed by (a) that genuinely *submissive* spirit that belongs to holiness; (b) the practice of the *presence* of God, as advocated by Brother Lawrence;[12] and (c) the habit of *seeing God* in everything (2 Cor. 12:7).[13]

---

12. *The Practice of the Presence of God*, published by Peter Pauper Press, New York. "Brother Lawrence" was Nicholas Herman of Lorraine, who became a lay brother among the barefooted Carmelites in Paris in 1666.

13. This includes a clear revelation of what is important to God. When a minister's wife was frustrated by her inability to perform her duties during a period of illness, she prayed, "Lord, I should be helping others, instead of being helped all the time. I should be out there working for You." The Lord whispered, "My child, your love and devotion are more important to Me than your service." Paul Tournier

3. *Coping with Psychological Problems*

The Christian mind, or thoroughly renewed mind, desires always to please Christ as the underlying and controlling motivation of life. It therefore values holiness more than happiness and obedience more than freedom. But this is seeing mind as an attitude, or "frame of mind" (cf. Phil. 2:5), a *phronēma*. It is the way one habitually thinks in relation to God and life.

But one may have a Christian mind in this sense, yet at the same time have a troubled mind, or confused mind, or some degree of mental illness. We are now thinking of the organ of cognition and reason by which we utilize our nervous systems in relating ourselves to life. The sanctification of "spirit, soul, and body" certainly implies cleansing the whole man from all sin; but not all which is in need of repair is sin. Many memories and traumas are buried in the mind and affect the way it functions as a personal organism. There are phobias—perhaps fear of dogs or enclosed places. There may be complexes—inordinate sensitivity to certain subjects or people or situations.

Beyond these minor problems can develop clinically pathological conditions of disorientation caused by arteriosclerosis, perhaps, or other ailments, or inherited traits that progressively develop. As a consequence holy people may have undesirable quirks of personality, and in cases of extreme degenerative diseases there may be behavior that is far from Christian. But the real spiritual state before God must be credited back to what such persons were before they became mentally ill.[14]

Meanwhile, in the area of lesser problems, we must learn to understand ourselves if we are to be able to cope. This underscores the need for a more detailed analysis of the carnal and the human.

---

warns us against a "theology of success" that is not a "theology of the Cross." Speaking of the utilitarian mood of the day, he says, "The idea of inner harmony has since been replaced by the idea of achieving records" (*The Whole Person in a Broken World* [New York: Harper and Row, Publishers, 1964], 128-29).

14. Books that may prove useful in acquiring an understanding of oneself and of others within a psychological frame of reference (though often falling short of a holiness perspective) are: C. J. Adcock, *Fundamentals of Psychology* (Baltimore: Penguin Books, 1964); Tournier, *The Whole Person in a Broken World*; Nelson, *Why Christians Crack Up*; C. B. Eavey, *Principles of Mental Health for Christian Living* (Chicago: Moody Press, 1956); W. Curry Mavis, *The Psychology of Christian Experience* (Grand Rapids: Zondervan Publishing House, 1964).

C. The Carnal and the Human

An approach that is sometimes helpful is to use the model of *symptoms*. While a symptom may suggest a specific disease, it may not in itself be sufficient evidence for a sure diagnosis, since it may also be associated with other diseases. A wise doctor therefore reserves judgment until either enough symptoms converge or his suspicions are confirmed by laboratory analysis, X ray, or other tests.

Similarly, in diagnosing the spiritual state of ourselves or others it is well to keep in mind that while certain undesirable traits may point to a carnal condition, they are not necessarily proofs, for their nature is such that their source may be infirmity rather than sin.

First one should be well aware of biblically identifiable manifestations of the carnal mind. The following is a working list, though not exhaustive:
> Unbelief (Rom. 11:20; Heb. 4:6, 11)
> Envy and strife (1 Cor. 3:1-4)
> Worldly-mindedness (Rom. 8:6; James 4:4; 1 John 2:15)
> Lukewarmness (Rev. 3:15)
> Covetousness (Luke 12:15; Eph. 5:5; Col. 3:5; Heb. 13:5)
> Bitterness (Eph. 4:31; Heb. 12:15)
> Quarrelsomeness (2 Cor. 12:20)
> Rebelliousness (Jer. 5:23; Heb. 3:7-19)

Over against these clear evidences are the following symptoms:

1. *Obstinacy*

Habitual stubbornness over trivialities, just because one is constitutionally averse to yielding any point to anyone (God or man), is certainly an indicator of a sinful spirit. Some people have such a sick ego that they just "have to be right." But a refusal to yield a point of personal conviction as a matter of courageous faithfulness is qualitatively different. Sometimes such obstinacy may be foolish instead of wise, yet be innocent of a bad spirit.

Unfortunately the "fault" often appears to others like plain, carnal bullheadedness. An evangelist whose first name was William had a wife who would say, "When he dies I'm going to put on his tombstone, 'My stubborn Will at last hath yielded.'" Yet all who knew them both well, knew that he was one of the humblest and meekest of men, strong as Gibraltor only in matters that counted.

2. *Nervous Irritability*

By temperament some people are easily excitable. Just as there is a qualitative difference between laziness and weakness (though sometimes not easily discerned), so there is a qualitative difference between an ugly temper that is destructive and hateful, and a moderate emotional upset in a tight spot. Habitual irritability and grouchiness that springs out of general hostility, selfish touchiness, and smoldering resentments cannot be justified. But quick reactions due to sick nerves, or a very high-strung, racehorse nature, require patience and understanding, not necessarily condemnation. Emotional poise in the crisis of undue pressure is an acquirement of growth, not an instantaneous gift of grace.

3. *Fear and Anxiety*

Undoubtedly much fear and anxiety have their source in unbelief or in a troubled conscience. But not all. Just as some people have a lower pain tolerance than others, so some have a lower fear threshold. Perfect love casts out fear of the Judgment, but not necessarily all fear—such as fear of cancer, tornadoes, or whatever. Neither does it eliminate anxiety when the teenagers are out at night. Nor should it.

Paul said, "Without were fightings, within were fears" (2 Cor. 7:5, KJV). Care is the mother of some degree of anxiety if one takes his responsibilities seriously. The anxiety that can and should be avoided by divine grace is that which is disabling and crippling (2 Tim. 1:7). To be habitually fretful and anxious does not honor God.

4. *Depression*

Generally, Spirit-filled Christians should be able to avoid serious depression. A habit of praise is the best possible preventive medicine. So also is quickness to obey and alertness in maintaining a clear conscience. But periods of emotional ebb tide, of inner deadness and inertia, may come. From a spiritual standpoint these periods have sometimes been called "the black night of the soul." Such seasons of depression may sometimes be of satanic origin. In such cases, holding steady in faith will sooner or later bring one through. But at other times the depression may be due to excessive fatigue. One is emotionally exhausted. The cure is rest, not fasting and prayer. At other times, the depression may have a serious mental or physical cause, in which case medical attention will be required.

When, therefore, is depression a sign of spiritual illness? When it is brought on by neurotic self-pity and self-preoccupation. Sometimes, also, people allow themselves to be mastered by their natural timidity and refuse to avail themselves of divine grace to do what they know God is calling them to do. Failing to obey, they withdraw, and the withdrawal sooner or later isolates them from means of help. Ultimately it sucks them into a deep hole of depression. The condition has now become physical, but the original cause was spiritual.

5. *Restlessness*

If there is a deep undercurrent of spiritual hunger or dissatisfaction, it can easily manifest itself in restless discontent and perhaps roving feet. On the other hand the trait may be inbred; it may be a family characteristic. Or it may be prompted by an active, driving temperament that is always seeking new fields of conquest. It may even be created by the Holy Spirit himself, who is trying to prod this person into some sort of action. Therefore restlessness is a symptom but in itself is too ambiguous to accept as an evidence of a carnal condition.

6. *Impatience*

This is similar to nervous irritability, but perhaps more deeply temperamental. Impatience takes three forms: *(a)* Inability to wait quietly and calmly either for others or for divine providence. *(b)* Inability to stay under a load. This is the basic meaning of *humomonē* (James 1:3; Heb. 12:1). Some people have a lifetime pattern, developed in childhood and youth, of failing to see an undertaking through. When difficulties arise it is easier to walk off and begin again somewhere else. This is a great weakness of character, even though it may not in itself prove an unsanctified state. The Holy Spirit will in time zero in on this. *(c)* Then there is impatience in the form of failure to be gentle in annoying circumstances. It is hard for the perfectionist to bear with the blunders of others.

Impatience may spring from basic selfishness, which makes one self-willed, impetuous, imperious, demanding, inconsiderate, uncontrollable, and explosive. On the other hand, impatience may be the product of unwise zeal. Such people tend to be intolerant with what appears to them to be inexcusable dullness. They may speak rashly rather than cautiously, either because of ignorance, youthfulness, or quickness of temperament. They may feel it is their duty to act right now, when in acting they do more harm than good. It would be much more helpful to learn to "possess [their] souls . . . in . . . patience" (Luke 21:19, KJV), sit tight, and keep their mouths shut. Insofar as such impatience is prompted by a right spirit, it may not be sinful. But it may nevertheless do great harm and certainly needs disciplining. Patience is a most significant mark of maturity.

D. Landmarks of Growth

A healthy organism will naturally grow more normally and even in some cases more rapidly than a diseased organism. This is equally true of Christians. Holiness is soul health. A healthy Christian will not forever be checking his pulse or living within himself. The very nature of holiness is the turning of the soul outward and upward. One will be more aware of one's mission in relation to the Great Commission. His objective will not be a reputation for saintliness but the attainment of usefulness. He will not seek a certain personal image but the honor of Christ; not professional success for its own sake, but souls for their sakes. The aim of the holy man is not self-realization but Christ-realization. Certain marks, however, will be noticeable where real growth is occurring.

1. Relating to Authority

Recent studies in developmental psychology by Piaget, Kohlberg, Stewart, and others, have not only analyzed the normal stages of maturation but also stressed the importance, if maturity is to occur, of independent thinking and deciding. At the heart of sanctification is an emancipation from slavish dependence on the opinions of others and a confirmation of independent personhood. But such development will be arrested rather than accelerated if the legitimate autonomy of self-decision does not find its equilibrium in relating to biblically identified authorities. For the first time (in the case of the entirely sanctified) one has the courage to let God be God, with every other enslaving bond severed. But this does not cancel (for youth) a relative obligation to the authority of parents, or (for adults) acknowledgment of the relative authority of the state and of the church. One of the marks of Spirit fullness is the ability to submit one to another "out of reverence for Christ" (Eph. 5:21).[15]

2. *Acquiring Discrimination*

One rendering of Phil. 1:10 is that our love is to so grow in knowledge and judgment that we can "distinguish the things that differ" (ASV margin). Many seem unable to distinguish between the vital and the negotiable, things that really matter and those that only seem to (or only matter to some people). Because of this, they are forever elevating the secondary to the rank of the primary, and giving to one as much attention as the other. As a consequence, what should be frankly relegated to the category of opinion, preference, or custom is made a matter of *conviction*, with resultant needless divisiveness. There are sinful, sensible, and silly divisions. A mature Christian discerns the difference.

3. *Maintaining the Tension of Love*

Loving in a Christian way is costly, because it requires the subordination of personal rights to the welfare of others. It never forgets the principle of the stewardship of influence. It gladly sacrifices personal liberties if those liberties will clearly be a stumbling block to more sensitive persons.

But the tension also is the tug-of-war between our compassion for the sinner and our hatred of the sin. Love, to be Christian, must be love of *right* as well as love of *people*. How do we handle the delicate crisis that arises when standing for the right will alienate people?

It has been claimed that Jesus never let principle come before people; but such is not true. Though Jesus loved the rich young ruler, His love was governed by principle, not mere compassion. It was principle that dictated the moral terms of discipleship He laid down. And He refused to waver when the young man walked away sorrowfully. The higher love sees that the compromise of principle is never in the long run the kind thing to do but the cruel

---

15. Tournier says, "By trying to justify the law of the strongest in the name of nature we today have undermined the whole concept of harmony, of sacrifice, of order, and finally of community. I see many married people in conflict. . . . If a true spiritual revolution does not take place in the couple, our efforts will be in vain. For what stands in their way is this very idea—so widespread today—that one must be strong in order not to be pushed to the wall and that to give in is a proof of weakness. That there is true greatness in making concessions, that forgiveness is a real victory, and that to renounce one's own will is a true joy—these are ideas which have almost disappeared today" (*Whole Person,* 129).

thing. A landmark of maturity is the intelligence that discerns the needs of people in relation to the claims of principle, and the courage to love without compromising.

4. *A Growing Sensitivity*

This is dual—a growing sensitivity to the guidance of the Holy Spirit, and a growing awareness of the moods and needs and hungers of people around us. Any "growth" is suspect if it does not make us easier to live with and easier to work with. The husband becomes more alert to the emotional needs of his wife. Church members become more finely tuned to the silent cry for help in wobbling teenagers and adults. There is a deepening personal humility that makes it easier to say, "I am sorry." There is a quickness in mending fences, whether with God or with people.

This growing sensitivity also includes a developing appreciation of personal culture. We no longer despise the refinements of propriety but see them as part of the larger stewardship. Some things that used to matter, no longer do; other things that didn't *now do.* It is only very immature Christians who throw off as inconsequential such matters as correct speech, suitable dress, and good manners.

5. *A Healthy Self-image*

The necessity of self-esteem, if we are to function well, is universally recognized today. The mature person has learned to evaluate himself *(a)* in terms of God's love (which makes him very important indeed), and *(b)* in terms of an honest and realistic inventory of his assets and liabilities as a person (which will be an effective antidote to pride). There must be a healthy equilibrium between humility and self-respect. It is not thinking of ourselves "more highly than [we] ought to think" (Rom. 12:3, KJV), but at the same time being healthily aware of our abilities. The ballast is in the even deeper awareness of our weakness apart from God, and the knowledge that no matter what our skills may be, our final and ultimate value to the Kingdom will be no greater than the Spirit's anointing upon us. Therefore, we neither depreciate ourselves nor exalt ourselves. We accept ourselves as God's instruments. We are content with His placement of us high or low on the totem pole of life.

6. *Becoming a Communicator*

Not all are called to stand behind a pulpit, and not all who are equally holy will be equally articulate. However, every Christian is called to be a Christ communicator, not only by example but also by word. For we cannot evade the purpose of Pentecostal power— *to witness* (Acts 1:8). This should be demonstrated in a growing ability to speak of holy things, if not often in public, at least in private, to loved ones, friends, and neighbors. It should be demonstrated also in increased wisdom in the style and form of our public testimony to God's justifying and sanctifying grace.

Sanctified Christians, taught Wesley, cannot "with a clear conscience" avoid the cost of open testimony. Undoubtedly, he says, such persons "ought to speak." He explains—

> Men do not light a candle to put under a bushel; much less does the all-wise God. He does not raise such a moment of his power and love, to hide it from all mankind. Rather he intends it as a general blessing to those who are simple of heart. He designs thereby, not barely the happiness of that individual person, but the animating and encouraging others to follow after the same blessing. . . . Nor does anything under heaven more quicken the desires of those who are justified, than to converse with those whom they believe to have experienced a still higher salvation. This places that salvation full in their view, and increases their hunger and thirst after it; an advantage which must have been entirely lost, had the person so saved buried himself in silence.[16]

7. The Deepening of Devotion

And here we strike the one indispensable key to both the life of holiness and the holy warfare, whether it be the maintenance of personal victory or the advancement of Christ's kingdom. All the lines of doctrine, testimony, life-style, and inner vitality intersect at the point of one-to-one contact with God. This is the "I-Thou" that will prevent our human relationships from ever becoming mere "I-It."

Prayer and the Word are together the appointed means of receiving and transmitting power. Our religion is no deeper or more authentic than the reality of our prayer life. Our work for God will be mere clutter and clatter unless energized by the Holy Spirit in answer to prayer. Holiness is *knowing God* or it is an empty

---

16. *Plain Account,* 56. For excellent advice on both the importance and proper manner of testifying to entire sanctification see J. A. Wood, *Perfect Love,* 133-54. He insists that the clear witness to the grace cannot be retained without humble, clear acknowledgment of it "on suitable occasions" (138-39). A lack of positive, joyous testimony reflects uncertainty in the heart (and often vagueness in the pulpit).

charade. The one controlling and continuous passion must always be to know God better.

It is as we pray that the Holy Spirit is able to teach, rebuke, correct, mold, refine, strengthen, galvanize, and reinforce us.

It is the praying person who is being transformed into the image of Christ "from one degree of glory to another" (2 Cor. 3:18, NBV).

It is the man or woman of prayer who will know fully what this means: "The path of the just is as the shining light, that shineth more and more unto the perfect day" (Prov. 4:18, KJV).

Selected Bibliography[1]

Agnew, Milton S. *More than Conquerors: The Message of Romans—Chapters 1—8*. Chicago: Salvation Army, 1959.

————. *The Holy Spirit: Friend and Counselor.* Kansas City: Beacon Hill Press of Kansas City, 1980.

Aikens, Alden. "Wesleyan Theology and the Use of Models," *Wesleyan Theological Journal*, Fall 1979.

Aldrich, Joseph C. *Life-Style Evangelism*. Portland: Multnomah Press, 1981.

Anderson, T. M., comp. and ed. *Our Holy Faith*. Kansas City: printed for Asbury College by Beacon Hill Press of Kansas City, 1965.

Arndt, William F., and F. Wilbur Gingrich. *A Greek-English Lexicon of the New Testament and Other Early Christian Literature*. Chicago: University of Chicago Press, 1957.

Arthur, William. *Tongue of Fire*. London: Epworth Press, J. Alfred Sharp, n.d.

Augsburger, Myron S. *Quench Not the Spirit*. Scottsdale, Pa.: Herald Press, 1961.

Baldwin, Harmon A. *Holiness and the Human Element*. Kansas City: Beacon Hill Press, 1919.

Bangs, Carl. *Arminius: A Study in the Dutch Reformation*. Nashville: Abingdon Press, 1971.

Barker, John H. J. *This Is the Will of God: A Study in the Doctrine of Entire Sanctification as a Definite Experience*. Rev. ed. London: Epworth Press, 1956.

Bassett, Paul, and William M. Greathouse. *Exploring Christian Holiness*. Vol. 2, *The Historical Foundations*. Kansas City: Beacon Hill Press of Kansas City, 1985.

Bonhoeffer, Dietrich. *The Cost of Discipleship*. New York: Macmillan Company, 1963.

Bonner, Harold, comp. *Proclaiming the Spirit*. Kansas City: Beacon Hill Press of Kansas City, 1975.

Boyd, Myron F., and Merne A. Harris, comps. *Projecting Our Heritage*. Kansas City: Beacon Hill Press of Kansas City, 1969.

Brengle, Samuel L. *Heart Talks on Holiness*. New York: Salvation Army Publishing House, 1900.

————. *The Way of Holiness*. New York: Salvation Army Printing and Publishing House, 1920.

Brice, Joe. *Pentecost*. Salem, Ohio: Convention Book Store, 1973.

Bridges, Jerry. *The Pursuit of Holiness*. Colorado Springs, Colo.: Navpress, 1978.

---

1. Wesleyan, Keswickian, and Unclassified.

Brockett, Henry E. *Scriptural Freedom from Sin.* Kansas City: Nazarene Publishing House, 1941.

―――. *The Christian and Romans 7: Bondage to Sin versus Freedom in Christ.* Kansas City: Beacon Hill Press of Kansas City, 1972.

Brokke, Harold J. *Saved by His Life: An Exposition of Paul's Epistle to the Romans.* Minneapolis: Bethany Fellowship, Inc., 1964.

Brown, Charles Ewing. *The Meaning of Sanctification.* Anderson, Ind.: Warner Press, 1945.

Burtner, Robert W., and Robert E. Chiles. *John Wesley's Theology: A Collection from His Works.* Nashville: Abingdon Press, 1983.

Byrum, R. R. *Christian Theology.* Rev. ed. Edited by Arlo F. Newell. Anderson, Ind.: Warner Press, Inc., 1982 (orig. 1925).

Carter, Charles Webb. *The Person and Ministry of the Holy Spirit.* Grand Rapids: Baker Book House, 1974.

―――, ed. *A Contemporary Wesleyan Theology.* 2 vols. Grand Rapids: Francis Asbury Press of Zondervan Publishing House, 1983.

―――, ed. *The Wesleyan Bible Commentary.* 7 vols. Grand Rapids: William B. Eerdmans Publishing Company, 1967.

Cattell, Everett Lewis. *The Spirit of Holiness.* Grand Rapids: William B. Eerdmans Publishing Company, 1963.

Cell, John Croft. *The Rediscovery of John Wesley.* New York: Henry Holt and Company, 1935.

Chadwick, Samuel. *The Call to Christian Perfection.* Kansas City: Beacon Hill Press, 1943.

―――. *The Way to Pentecost.* New York: Fleming H. Revell Company, n.d.

Chamberlain, William Douglas. *An Exegetical Grammar of the Greek New Testament.* New York: Macmillan Company, 1960.

Chambers, Leon and Mildred. *Holiness and Human Nature.* Kansas City: Beacon Hill Press of Kansas City, 1975.

Chambers, Oswald. *Biblical Ethics.* Fort Washington, Pa.: Christian Literature Crusade, 1947.

―――. *If Thou Wilt Be Perfect.* London: Simpkin Marshall, Ltd., 1939.

―――. *My Utmost for His Highest.* New York: Dodd, Mead and Company, 1935.

Chapman, James B. *Holiness, the Heart of Christian Experience.* Kansas City: Beacon Hill Press, 1941.

―――. *The Terminology of Holiness.* Kansas City: Beacon Hill Press, 1947.

Christensen, Bernhard. *The Inward Pilgrimage.* Minneapolis: Augsburg Publishing House, 1976.

Church, John R. *Earthen Vessels.* Louisville: Pentecostal Publishing Company, 1942.

Clark, Dougan. *The Inner and Outer Life of Holiness.* Edited by Anna Louise Spann. Portland: Evangel Publishers, 1945.

―――. *The Offices of the Holy Spirit.* Philadelphia: National Association for the Promotion of Holiness, 1879.

―――. *The Theology of Holiness.* Chicago: Christian Witness Company, 1893.

Clarke, Adam. *Christian Theology.* Salem, Ohio: Convention Book Store, originally published in 1835.

————. *The Holy Bible with a Commentary and Critical Notes.* 6 vols. New York: Abingdon Press, n.d.

Coleman, Robert E. *The Mind of the Master.* Old Tappan, N.J.: Fleming H. Revell Company, 1977.

Colson, Charles W. *Loving God.* Grand Rapids: Zondervan Publishing House, 1983.

Cook, Thomas. *New Testament Holiness.* London: Epworth Press, 1948.

Cookman, Alfred. *The Higher Christian Life.* Boston: Christian Witness Company, 1900.

Corlett, D. Shelby. *God in the Present Tense: The Person and Work of the Holy Spirit.* Kansas City: Beacon Hill Press of Kansas City, 1974.

Corlett, Lewis T. *Holiness, the Harmonizing Experience.* Kansas City: Beacon Hill Press, 1948.

Cox, Leo G. *John Wesley's Concept of Perfection.* Kansas City: Beacon Hill Press, 1964.

Curtis, Olin Alfred. *The Christian Faith.* Grand Rapids: Kregel Publications, 1956.

Dawson, Grace. *Set Among Princes: The Royal Road to Spiritual Riches.* Kansas City: Beacon Hill Press of Kansas City, 1979.

Dayton, Wilber T. "Entire Sanctification," *A Contemporary Wesleyan Theology,* Vol. 1 ed. by Charles W. Carter. Grand Rapids: Francis Asbury Press of Zondervan Publishing House, 1983.

DeWolf, L. Harold. *Responsible Freedom: Guidelines to Christian Action.* New York: Harper & Row, Publishers, 1971.

Dieter, Melvin Easterday. *The Holiness Revival of the Nineteenth Century.* Metuchen, N.J.: Scarecrow Press, 1980.

Doty, Thomas K. *The Two-fold Gift of the Holy Spirit.* Chicago: T. B. Arnold, 1891.

Duewel, Wesley L. *The Holy Spirit and Tongues.* Winona Lake, Ind.: Light and Life Press, 1974.

Dunning, H. Ray, and William M. Greathouse. *An Introduction to Wesleyan Theology.* Kansas City: Beacon Hill Press of Kansas City, 1982.

Earle, Ralph. *The Quest of the Spirit.* Norwood, Mass.: Norwood Press, 1940.

Edman, V. Raymond. *They Found the Secret.* Grand Rapids: Zondervan Publishing House, 1968.

Ellyson, E. P. *Bible Holiness.* Kansas City: Beacon Hill Press of Kansas City, 1952.

Field, Benjamin. *Handbook of Christian Theology.* New York: Methodist Book Concern, n.d.

Fletcher, John. *Works.* Salem, Ohio: Schmul Publishers, 1974 (reprint).

Ford, Jack. *What the Holiness People Believe.* Birkenhead, Cheshire: Emmanuel Bible College and Missions, 1954.

Foster, Randolph S. *Christian Purity: Or the Heritage of Faith.* New York: Eaton and Mains, 1869.

Forsyth, Peter T. *Positive Preaching and Modern Mind.* New York: George H. Doran Company, 1907.

Friberg, Barbara, and Timothy Friberg. *Analytical Greek New Testament.* Grand Rapids: Baker Book House, 1981.

Friedrich, Gerard, ed. *Theological Dictionary of the New Testament.* Translated by Geoffrey W. Bromiley. Grand Rapids: William B. Eerdmans Publishing Company, 1972.

Gamertsfelder, S. J. *Systematic Theology.* Harrisburg, Pa.: Evangelical Publishing House, 1921.

Gardner, John E. *Personal Religious Disciplines.* Grand Rapids: William B. Eerdmans Publishing Company, 1966.

Geiger, Kenneth, ed. *Further Insights into Holiness.* Kansas City: Beacon Hill Press, 1963.

————, ed. *Insights into Holiness.* Kansas City: Beacon Hill Press, 1962.

————, ed. *The Word and the Doctrine.* Kansas City: Beacon Hill Press of Kansas City, 1965.

Gordon, A. J. *The Ministry of the Spirit.* New York: Fleming H. Revell Company, 1894.

Gould, J. Glenn. *The Whole Counsel of God.* Kansas City: Beacon Hill Press, 1945.

Gray, Frederick Albert. *Christian Theology.* 2 vols. Anderson, Ind.: Warner Press, 1946.

Greathouse, W. M. *From the Apostles to Wesley.* Kansas City: Beacon Hill Press of Kansas City, 1979.

————. *The Fullness of the Spirit.* Kansas City: Nazarene Publishing House, 1958.

————. *Romans,* vol. 8 of *Beacon Bible Commentary.* 10 vols. Kansas City: Beacon Hill Press of Kansas City, 1964-69.

Grider, Kenneth, assoc. ed., *Beacon Dictionary of Theology.* Kansas City: Beacon Hill Press of Kansas City, 1983.

————. *Entire Sanctification: The Distinctive Doctrine of Wesleyanism.* Kansas City: Beacon Hill Press of Kansas City, 1980.

————. *Repentance unto Life.* Kansas City: Beacon Hill Press of Kansas City, 1965.

Hadley, Norval. *Sin and the Sanctified.* Kansas City: Beacon Hill Press of Kansas City, 1980.

Hall, Clarence W. *Samuel Logan Brengle: Portrait of a Prophet.* New York: Salvation Army, Inc., 1935.

Harper, Albert F., ed. *Beacon Bible Commentary.* 10 vols. Kansas City: Beacon Hill Press of Kansas City, 1964-69.

————. *Holiness and High Country.* Kansas City: Beacon Hill Press, 1964.

Harrison, Everett F., ed. *Baker's Dictionary of Theology.* Grand Rapids: Baker Book House, 1968.

Hartley, John E., and R. Larry Shelton, eds. *An Inquiry into Soteriology from a Biblical Theological Perspective.* Vol. 1 of *Wesleyan Theological Perspectives,* Arlo F. Newell, editor in chief. Anderson, Ind.: Warner Press, Inc., 1981.

Hegre, T. E. *The Cross and Sanctification.* Minneapolis: Bethany Fellowship, Inc., 1960.

Henry, Carl F. H., ed. *Baker's Dictionary of Christian Ethics.* Grand Rapids: Baker Book House, 1973.

————. *The Christian Mindset in a Secular Society: Promoting Evangelical Renewal and National Righteousness.* Portland: Multnomah Press, 1984.

Hills, A. M. *Fundamental Christian Theology.* 2 vols. Pasadena, Calif.: C. J. Kinne, 1931.

————. *Holiness and Power.* Jamestown, N.C.: Newby Book Room, 1983.

Hogue, Wilson T. *The Holy Spirit.* Chicago: W. B. Rose, 1916.

Hopkins, Evan Henry. *The Law of Liberty in the Spiritual Life.* London: Marshall Brothers, 1905.

Hopkinson, Arthur W., ed. *The Pocket William Law.* London: Latimer House Limited, 1950.

Hordern, William E. *New Directions in Theology Today.* Vol. 1. Philadelphia: Westminster Press, 1966.

Howard, Richard. *Newness of Life.* Kansas City: Beacon Hill Press of Kansas City, 1975.

Huffman, J. A. *The Holy Spirit.* Marion, Ind.: Standard Press, 1944.

————. *The Meaning of Pentecost.* Marion, Ind.: Standard Press, 1940.

Jessop, Harry E. *Foundations of Doctrine in Scripture and Experience.* Chicago: Chicago Evangelistic Institute, 1938.

————. *We, the Holiness People.* Chicago: Chicago Evangelistic Institute, 1948.

Jones, E. Stanley. *Victory Through Surrender.* Nashville: Abingdon Press, 1966.

Jones, Charles Edwin. *The Holiness Movement* (a bibliography). Metuchen, N.Y.: Scarecrow Press, 1974. Published jointly with The American Theological Library Association.

Joy, Donald M. *The Holy Spirit and You.* New York: Abingdon, 1965.

Keller, W. Phillip. *A Laymen Looks at the Love of God: A Devotional Study of First Corinthians 13.* Minneapolis: Bethany House Publishers, 1984.

Kempis, Thomas à. *The Imitation of Christ.* New York: E. P. Dutton, n.d.

Knight, John A. *The Holiness Pilgrimage.* Kansas City: Beacon Hill Press of Kansas City, 1973.

————. *In His Likeness.* Kansas City: Beacon Hill Press of Kansas City, 1976.

Koberle, Adolf. *The Quest for Holiness: A Biblical, Historical and Systematic Investigation.* Translated from the third German edition by John C. Mattes. Minneapolis: Augsburg Publishing House, 1936.

Kuhn, Harold B. *God: His Names and Nature.* Monograph published by *Christianity Today,* n.d.

Kuyper, Abraham. *The Work of the Holy Spirit.* New York: Funk and Wagnalls Company, 1900.

Law, William. *A Serious Call to a Devout and Holy Life.* Philadelphia: Westminster Press, 1958.

Lawrence, Brother (Nicholas Herman of Lorraine, Carmelite lay brother in Paris 1666). *The Practice of the Presence of God.* Mount Vernon, N.Y.: Peter Pauper Press, 1963.

Lightfoot, J. B., translator and editor. *The Apostolic Fathers.* Edited and completed by J. R. Harmer. Grand Rapids: Baker Book House, 1962.

Lindstrom, Harald. *Wesley and Sanctification.* London: Epworth Press, 1946.

Lowrey, Asbury. *Possibilities of Grace.* Chicago: Christian Witness Company, 1884.

MacKay, Donald M. *Brains, Machines, and Persons.* Grand Rapids: William B. Eerdmans Publishing Company, 1980.

Mahan, Asa. *The Baptism of the Holy Ghost.* New York: George Hughes and Company, 1870.

———. *Scripture Doctrine of Christian Perfection.* Boston: Waite, Pierce and Company, 1844.

Malony, H. Newton. *Humbleness and Holiness: Readings in the Psychology/ Theology of Mental Health.* Grand Rapids: Baker Book House, 1983.

Mavis, W. Curry. *The Holy Spirit in the Christian Life.* Grand Rapids: Baker Book House, 1977.

———. *The Psychology of Christian Experience.* Grand Rapids: Zondervan Publishing House, 1964.

McCumber, W. E. *Holiness in the Prayers of St. Paul.* Kansas City: Beacon Hill Press, 1955.

———. *Holy God—Holy People.* Kansas City: Beacon Hill Press of Kansas City, 1983.

McLaughlin, George A. *Inbred Sin.* Chicago: Christian Witness Company, 1902.

Meadley, T. D. *Top Level Talks: The Christian Summit Meeting; Studies in Scriptural Holiness or the Doctrine of Entire Sanctification.* London: Epworth Press, 1969.

Merritt, Timothy. *The Guide to Christian Perfection.* Boston: T. Merritt and S. D. S. King, 1839.

Metz, Donald S. *Studies in Biblical Holiness.* Kansas City: Beacon Hill Press of Kansas City, 1971.

Miller, H. V. *His Will for Us.* Kansas City: Beacon Hill Press, 1949.

———. *The Sin Problem.* Kansas City: Nazarene Publishing House, n.d.

Mitchell, T. Crichton. *Great Holiness Classics.* Vol. 2, *The Wesley Century.* Kansas City: Beacon Hill Press of Kansas City, 1984.

Morris, Leon. *Testaments of Love: A Study of Love in the Bible.* Grand Rapids: William B. Eerdmans Publishing Company, 1981.

Murray, Andrew. *The Believer's Holiness: The Full Blessing of Pentecost.* Minneapolis: Bethany House Publishers, 1984.

———. *The Believer's Secret of Holiness,* rev. (formerly *Holy in Christ*). Minneapolis: Bethany House Publishers, 1984.

Neely, Thomas B. *Doctrinal Standards of Methodism.* New York: Fleming H. Revell Company, 1918.

Nelson, Marion H. *Why Christians Crack Up.* Rev. ed. Chicago: Moody Press, 1967.

Nelson, Wilbur E. *Believe and Behave.* Nashville: A Sceptre Book, Division of Royal Publishers, 1979.

Newell, Arlo F. *Receive the Holy Spirit.* Anderson, Ind.: Warner Press, Inc., 1978.

Ockenga, Harold John. *Power Through Pentecost.* Grand Rapids: William B. Eerdmans Publishing Company, 1959.

Orr, J. Edwin. *Full Surrender.* London: Marshall, Morgan, and Scott, 1957.

Outler, Albert C. *Theology in the Wesleyan Spirit.* Nashville: Tidings, 1975.

Owen, John. *The Holy Spirit: His Gifts and Power.* Grand Rapids: Kregel Publications, 1954 (reprint).

Palmer, Phoebe. *Faith and Its Effects: Or Fragments from My Portfolio.* New York: Privately printed at 200 Mulberry St., 1854.

————. *The Way of Holiness.* Edited and abridged by Alathea Coleman Jones. Wilmore, Ky.: Asbury Theological Seminary, 1981.

Peck, Jessie T. *The Central Idea of Christianity.* Louisville, Ky.: Pentecostal Publishing Co., n.d.

Perkins, Hal. *Leadership Multiplication.* 8 vols. Kansas City: Beacon Hill Press of Kansas City, 1983.

Peters, John Leland. *Christian Perfection and American Methodism.* New York: Abingdon Press, 1956.

Peterson, Michael L. "Orthodox Christianity, Wesleyanism, and Process Theology," *Wesleyan Theological Journal,* Fall 1980.

Pope, William Burt. *A Compendium of Christian Theology.* 3 vols. London: Wesleyan Conference Office, 1880.

————. *A Higher Catechism of Theology.* New York: Phillips and Hunt, 1884.

Porter, James. *A Compendium of Methodism.* New York: Carlton and Porter, 1851.

Purkiser, W. T. *Beliefs That Matter Most.* Kansas City: Beacon Hill Press, 1959.

————. *Conflicting Concepts of Holiness.* Kansas City: Beacon Hill Press, 1953.

————. *Exploring Christian Holiness.* Vol. 1, *The Biblical Foundations.* Kansas City: Beacon Hill Press of Kansas City, 1983.

————, ed. *Exploring Our Christian Faith.* Kansas City: Beacon Hill Press, 1960.

————. *The Gifts of the Spirit.* Kansas City: Beacon Hill Press of Kansas City, 1975.

————, Richard S. Taylor, and Willard H. Taylor. *God, Man, and Salvation.* Kansas City: Beacon Hill Press of Kansas City, 1977.

————. *Sanctification and Its Synonyms.* Kansas City: Beacon Hill Press, 1961.

Ralston, Thomas Neely. *Elements of Divinity.* Edited by T. O. Summers. Nashville: Cokesbury Press, 1924.

Roberts, B. T. *Holiness Teachings.* Salem, Ohio: H. E. Schmul, 1964.

Rose, Delbert R. *A Theology of Christian Experience.* Minneapolis: Bethany Fellowship, 1965.

Rush, H. T. *The Way into Blessing.* London: Marshall, Morgan and Scott, Ltd., n.d.

Sangster, W. E. *The Path to Perfection.* New York: Abingdon-Cokesbury Press, 1943.

————. *The Pure in Heart.* New York: Abingdon Press, 1954.

Sanner, Elwood, and Albert F. Harper, eds. *Exploring Christian Education.* Kansas City: Beacon Hill Press of Kansas City, 1978.

Shaw, George. *The Spirit in Redemption.* Cincinnati: Press of Jennings and Graham, 1910.

Simpson, A. B. *Christ Our Sanctifier.* Harrisburg, Pa.: Christian Publications, 1947.

―――. *The Fullness of Jesus.* New York: Christian Alliance Publishing Company, 1890.

―――. *The Holy Spirit.* 2 vols. New York: Christian Alliance Publishing Company, 1924.

Smith, Allister. *The Ideal of Perfection.* London: Oliphants, Ltd., 1963.

Smith, Joseph H. *Pauline Perfection.* Chicago: Christian Witness Co., 1913.

Smith, Timothy L. *The Promise of the Spirit; Charles G. Finney on Christian Holiness.* Minneapolis: Bethany Fellowship, Inc., 1980.

―――. *Revivalism and Social Reform.* New York: Abingdon Press, 1957.

―――. "How John Fletcher Became the Theologian of Wesleyan Perfectionism," *Wesleyan Theological Journal,* vol. 10, no. 1 (Spring, 1980).

Starkey, Lycurgus M., Jr. *The Holy Spirit at Work in the Church.* New York: Abingdon Press, 1963.

Stauffer, Joshua. *"When He Is Come."* Berne, Ind.: Light and Hope Publications, 1948.

Steele, Daniel. *Gospel of the Comforter.* Boston: Christian Witness Company, 1897.

―――. *Love Enthroned.* Boston: Christian Witness Company, 1877.

―――. *Milestone Papers.* New York: Phillips and Hunt, 1878.

―――. *Mistakes Respecting Christian Holiness.* Chicago: Christian Witness Company, 1905.

―――. *A Substitute for Holiness, or Antinomianism Revived.* Chicago: Christian Witness Company, 1899.

Stewart, James S. *Winds of the Spirit.* Grand Rapids: Baker Book House, 1984.

Taylor, J. Paul. *Holiness, the Finished Foundation.* Winona Lake, Ind.: Light and Life Press, 1963.

Taylor, Jeremy. *The Rule and Exercises of Holy Living.* New York: E. P. Dutton and Co., 1876.

Taylor, Richard S., ed. *Beacon Dictionary of Theology.* Kansas City: Beacon Hill Press of Kansas City, 1983.

―――. *The Disciplined Life.* Kansas City: Beacon Hill Press, 1962.

―――, ed. *Great Holiness Classics.* Vol. 3, *Leading Wesleyan Thinkers.* Kansas City: Beacon Hill Press of Kansas City, 1985.

―――. *Life in the Spirit: Christian Holiness in Doctrine, Experience, and Life.* Kansas City: Beacon Hill Press of Kansas City, 1966.

―――. *A Right Conception of Sin.* Kansas City: Nazarene Publishing House, 1945.

―――. *Tongues: Their Purpose and Meaning.* Kansas City: Beacon Hill Press of Kansas City, 1973.

Taylor, Willard H., assoc. ed. *Beacon Dictionary of Theology.* Kansas City: Beacon Hill Press of Kansas City, 1983.

Tenney, Mary Alice. *Blueprint for a Christian World.* Winona Lake, Ind.: Light and Life Press, 1953.

Torrey, R. A. *The Baptism of the Holy Spirit.* New York: Fleming H. Revell, n.d.

————. *How to Obtain Fullness of Power in Christian Life and Service.* New York: Fleming H. Revell, 1897.

Tournier, Paul. *A Whole Person in a Broken World.* New York: Harper and Row, Publishers, 1964.

Tozer, A. W. *That Incredible Christian.* Harrisburg, Pa.: Christian Publications, 1964.

————. *Keys to the Deeper Life.* Grand Rapids: Zondervan Publishing House, 1957.

————. *The Knowledge of the Holy.* New York: Harper and Row, 1961.

————. *The Pursuit of God.* Harrisburg, Pa.: Christian Publications, 1948.

Turner, George Allen. *Christian Holiness: In Scripture, in History, and in Life.* Kansas City: Beacon Hill Press of Kansas City, 1977.

————. *The Vision Which Transforms.* Kansas City: Beacon Hill Press, 1964.

————. *Witnesses of the Way.* Kansas City: Beacon Hill Press of Kansas City, 1981.

Vine, W. E. *Expository Dictionary of New Testament Words.* Westwood, N.J.: Fleming H. Revell Company, 1966.

Walker, James B. *The Doctrine of the Holy Spirit.* Cincinnati: Walden and Stowe, n.d.

————. *Philosophy of the Plan of Salvation.* Cincinnati: Jennings and Pye, n.d.

Watson, Philip S. *The Message of the Wesleys.* New York: Macmillan Company, 1964.

Watson, Richard. *Theological Institutes,* 2 vols. New York: T. Waugh and T. Mason, 1834.

Wesley, John. *Explanatory Notes upon the New Testament.* Naperville, Ill.: Alec R. Allenson, Inc., 1958.

————. *A Plain Account of Christian Perfection.* Kansas City: Beacon Hill Press of Kansas City, 1966. Reprinted from the complete original text as authorized by the Wesleyan Conference Office in London, England, in 1872.

————. *The Works of John Wesley.* 14 vols. Kansas City: Nazarene Publishing House, n.d. Reproduced from authorized edition published by the Wesleyan Conference Office in London, England, in 1872.

White, Jerry. *Honesty and Morality and Conscience.* Colorado Springs, Colo.: Navpress, 1979.

Wilcox, Leslie D. *Be Ye Holy.* Cincinnati: Revivalist Press, 1965.

————. *Profiles in Wesleyan Theology.* Vol. 1. Salem, Ohio: Schmul Publishing Company, Inc., 1983.

Wiley, H. Orton. *Christian Theology.* 3 vols. Kansas City: Nazarene Publishing House, 1940.

————. *The Epistle to the Hebrews.* Revised by Morris A. Weigelt. Kansas City: Beacon Hill Press of Kansas City, 1984.

Williams, Colin W. *John Wesley's Theology Today.* London: Epworth Press, 1960.

Williams, Roy T. *Sanctification, the Experience and the Ethics.* Kansas City: Nazarene Publishing House, 1928.

Wirt, Sherwood E. *Afterglow: The Excitement of Being Filled with the Spirit.* Grand Rapids: Zondervan Publishing House, 1975.

—————, ed. *Spiritual Disciplines.* Westchester, Ill.: Crossway Books, 1983.

Wood, J. A. *Christian Perfection as Taught by John Wesley.* Boston: McDonald and Gill, Publishers, 1885.

—————. *Perfect Love.* Chicago: Christian Witness Company, 1880.

—————. *Purity and Maturity.* Boston: Christian Witness Company, 1899.

Wood, Laurence W. *Pentecostal Grace.* Wilmore, Ky.: Francis Asbury Publishing Co., 1980.

Wynkoop, Mildred Bangs. *Foundations of Wesleyan-Arminian Theology.* Kansas City: Beacon Hill Press of Kansas City, 1967.

—————. *A Theology of Love.* Kansas City: Beacon Hill Press of Kansas City, 1972.

Subject Index[1]

1. Page references provide leads but are not exhaustive (e.g., "Holiness").

Persons Cited

Index of Scripture References